ME

ME

THE AUTHORISED BIOGRAPHY

BY

BYRON ROGERS

Aurum

First published in Great Britain
2009 by Aurum Press Ltd
7 Greenland Street
London NW1 0ND
www.aurumpress.co.uk

A catalogue record for this book is available from the British Library.

ISBN 978 1 84513 431 0

1 3 5 7 9 10 8 6 4 2
2009 2011 2013 2012 2010

Text design by Peter Ward
Typeset in Vendetta with flourishes in Dalliance by SX Composing DTP, Rayleigh, Essex
Printed by MPG Books, Bodmin, Cornwall

To my wife Jo, at her request in the margins of this book,
and to the late Tom O'Shea, landlord of the Old Red Lion at
Litchborough, a good man

CONTENTS

A Warning to the Curious

AUTOBIOGRAPHIES are misleading. They present a life as linear narrative, written with what Henry James called 'the terrible fluidity of self-revelation'. Only a life isn't like this. When a man looks back what he remembers are moments, people, incidents; these bob to the surface like the floating debris watched by Jack Hawkins and John Gregson in 1950s British war films after yet another successful depth charging of a German U-boat. Such things are jagged, vivid, most of them having no connection with each other; but through them, with no order imposed, you get a sense of who, or what, once gave them meaning.

What follows is an attempt to write an autobiography in these terms. I was startled into writing it because of something which had the effect of a depth charge.

Ego autem coacervavi omne quod inveni.
(I have now made a heap of all I have found.)

NENNIUS, ninth-century *Historia Brittonum*

For reasons of self-preservation, certain names in the heap have been altered.

 1

Walking Away

THE LETTER CAME at just after eleven o'clock in the morning, which was the time the mail came round in the offices of the *Daily Telegraph* Magazine, then just off Fleet Street. When you write for a newspaper or a magazine letters come in various categories: crowing letters ('The capital city of the Treens was Mekonta, I am surprised you didn't know that'), pained letters ('I could see you were scribbling in a notebook, but I did not expect to find myself quoted in a national newspaper'), cross letters ('I take great exception to your references to Carmarthenshire County Council. I assume that at some time you failed to achieve employment by that body'), even the odd fan letter. The last I tended to keep, though in time I usually lost them. But one letter I have not lost.

Immaculately typed on four sheets of A4 paper, and addressed to me at the Magazine, it has, however, no home address, just a date: 3 May 1981.

> Sorry about the lack of tears. I do regret their absence as much as the lack of some emotions which may make me less of a woman. However, I had just undergone the most profoundly moving experience in my recollection. I had been looking forward to twelve hours (was it?) of you, and was utterly relaxed into the safety of this eternity of bliss. You are so thoroughly addictive, and you and your hands and your eyes and your mouth and your

1

tongue and your body had transported me to such realms of ecstasy that I had hitherto neither known nor even believed possible ...

What?

Until then it had been just another office morning. That is to say, at my desk I had been smoking my pipe, reading with some enjoyment the profile of a Welsh tramp I had spent six weeks writing for the Magazine (and hoped to spin out for another two), and, with even more enjoyment, watching the strong bare legs of the secretaries as they swore in their precise English upper middle-class voices, chewed their long hair, and lied to their boyfriends on the telephone ('What a bore, I can't make tonight, I have to go for drinks at my godmother's'). As far as I was concerned I hoped things might go on like this forever.

My years on a provincial paper and on *The Times* were over, and as the one staff writer on the Magazine I had found myself among more beautiful young women than I had ever known existed, let alone seen in one place. The office I was in was next door to the fashion department, into which, breezing one day for a light, I came on a model standing very naked and very lovely, trying on a new range of swimwear. She grinned, then laughed out loud as I bolted.

Here the scruffy young photographers came and were dispatched, once to Outer Mongolia, where, watched by blank-faced herdsmen, they photographed their even more blank-faced models against a vast sky. And then photographers and women were gone, to rainforests, mountains, polar landscapes, and, had this been possible, to the moon.

For this was a colour magazine in the time of its last hurrah, spendthrift, mad and confident, before the advertising revenues faltered, and the accountants came like the barbarians. It was a time of fantasy. And then at eleven o'clock on a May morning the letter came. I read on, as I am reading it now. The letter is yellowing and creased, but then I have been reading it over and over for twenty-eight years.

On Thursday came the pain, and no hangover to cover it with. I got up and dressed and people came to sit with me like you give your company to the bereaved to alleviate their grief or perhaps to hear something awful that may brighten by comparison your own life. I don't know because I could not talk and I could not cry, and I was left locked in my own personal Hell.

When I found myself alone I climbed the stairs to our bed. I had not washed and I would not change the sheets I had lain on with you. Besides, rising at all had taken all the resolve of which I was capable. I sank onto the bed, taking care to land where your body had been, and froze into a paralysed state, lamely thinking, if this is death, what has broken since it could not have been my heart?

I was so cold and could not move to switch on the electric blanket. Then I was suddenly hot as in a fever, and the centre of my body ached as if the emptiness were growing to fill me to the outer limits of my skin, and, ever growing, was about to tear me apart. Every muscle ached for you, and all of me was burning for your touch. Then those rich juices of love that were longing to mingle with yours came pouring out of my cunt.

At that I held the letter up to the window, but no, I hadn't made a mistake. Bloody hell.

I wasn't dreaming and only too aware of your absence, but those little muscles that you love so much when they are masturbating

3

and sucking your cock inside me started to move, yearning to feel you but feeling only a closing and opening on themselves and a seemingly endless flood of love-juice which soaked the bed and drained me so that I wondered if maybe it was blood. This went on for a long time and the realisation that without you there is no orgasm, no relief, and no end to the agony, became too painful to bear. At last I turned and twisted and found myself breathing into the pillow that still held a faint scent of you ...

At that point I put it down, for despite its wordiness the prose had an intensity you tended not to get on colour magazines. Was the writer a lunatic? After ten years on the *Telegraph* I thought I knew all that was to be known about lunatics.

The Magazine appeared inside the main paper, but was in, not of, it, rather like Montenegro, the independent little mountain kingdom that somehow survived inside the ramshackle Ottoman Empire, a place where the central authorities never came. It, the Magazine that is, had its own offices away from the main building, rooms here and there, the centre of its power seven floors up from the department where I lurked.

There, in a brown felt-lined room, dark even at midday, a thin ray of intense light illuminating a few inches of his desk, the editor John Anstey ruled absolute and withdrawn, a Grand Turk among the women. The editor of the main paper, which appeared six days of the week, had one secretary. Anstey, who edited a give-away weekly magazine, had four.

But then he needed them, for he communicated only by letter, even with his own staff, and then usually to sack them, in particular the few men he employed as feature writers and office managers. Men were a threatened species on the Magazine, and

4

had Anstey been able to recruit eunuchs he would have done so. As it was, men appeared and abruptly disappeared, some into other trades, one to become a carpenter, another to open his own restaurant, men who had spent their lives in journalism but who, as the result of life under Anstey, were prepared to take up any career so long as it had nothing to do with papers or magazines in this world again. Once there was a hiccup, and two features editors found themselves on each side of a desk, at first neither daring to ask the other what he was doing there, or even who he was. A few days later one was gone.

Anstey was a mystery. To meet, this large, impeccably groomed man was charm itself, and there seemed nothing the two of you could not do together. When he interviewed me for the job he talked of his plans to produce the Magazine from the capitals of the world in turn, which later made me think of that other interviewee, in another high place, being shown the cities of the earth.

I did not see Anstey for six months after that. And when I did it was because he had demoted his deputy features editor, an American woman journalist, telling her he was making her an office secretary. That was too much even for his little staff, and we walked out, the dozen of us, and I spent a busy morning phoning *Private Eye*, the Press Association and Reuters.

In the uproar which followed his shadowy bosses intervened, and Anstey was instructed to make peace with his staff, something which involved talking to them. We all crowded into his office and, in the course of an uneasy meeting, I heard him say, 'Byron Rogers has been going round telling everyone that he hasn't seen me for six months, though from what he's been saying about me, I wouldn't have thought he'd want to.' That was the moment I stopped disliking him.

For, like him, I was living out my fantasies. The few people I knew in journalism were rushing about all over the place, reporting on politics, writing leaders, while I was becalmed. What magazine editor today would commission a profile of a tramp, and a Welsh tramp at that? Or one of Jean Straker, the photographer who was then forever in and out of court because of his refusal on ideological grounds to airbrush his nude studies, something that allowed me to write the sentence 'He took a stand on pubic hair like other men took a stand on the Rhine' (though Anstey himself airbrushed this).

I had tea with Straker and one of his models on the lawns of the stately home he had bought when he sold his Soho studio. The model and Straker were naked, I was in a three-piece suit like a curate who had got in with the wrong set, and it was *Le dejeuner sur l'Herbe*, except that the model, a good-looking woman in her forties, had forgotten to put her teeth in.

On the *Telegraph* Magazine, if you were in favour, you could go anywhere you wanted; in my case Greenland, where a slipstream of farts from dog teams, fed on fish, hung in the thin Arctic air, ten straining rumps pointed at the sleigh. Or like the world's one nudist city, where the dress shops were a scrum of naked women, the bank a queue of creased buttocks waiting to change its Deutschmarks, and from which, emerging into the outside world after three days, I felt my heart pound at the sight of a woman in a dress. Anyone you wanted to meet you could, which for me meant Helen Mirren, a retired hangman and the men who had written the comics and the radio serials of my childhood.

It had its drawbacks, meeting your heroes. I asked the great Charles Chilton, who wrote the 1950s BBC serial *Journey into Space*, why he had made the last Martian a towering armadillo, something that had fascinated me since childhood. Chilton said the only reason he could remember was that he had taken his children to the zoo the week before. It was a time of startling explanations ...

By the historian A.L. Rowse, scuttling by to kneel behind me on the floor when I entered his rooms in All Souls. Not turning, he asked, still on his knees, 'You a hetero?' I said I supposed I was, but that I had never really thought about it. 'Knew it, knew it,' he said triumphantly. 'Knew you were heterosexual as soon as you scuffed my mat, and didn't straighten it.'

By Margaret, Duchess of Argyll, talking about her ten-foot portrait by James Gunn, which, because of its sheer size, had to be exhibited in a public art gallery. 'Not many people get hung in their lifetime,' said the Duchess, although when she read what I wrote about her she must have wished this might still be possible. Still, she managed to get an injunction on the whole Magazine which would have cost the *Telegraph* hundreds of thousands of pounds, had it not got lifted at the very last minute. Anstey among the lawyers was something I had never seen before: with everything closing in on him, his back to the wall, he was happy as the day was long. And this is how I shall remember him. After ten years on the Magazine I hadn't thought anything could surprise me again.

But by God it did.

Like a tank, the relentless eroticism was trundling on.

Nothing that I had hitherto decreed I would or wouldn't do was under consideration. I stripped my clothes off, still laying (*sic*) on my belly. When I got to my panties I could nearly hear you and feel your hands that are as soft and gentle as mine. My fingers had to find the hard and throbbing point. The touch that could have been yours released new floods and a torrent of ecstasy and pain. When I turned to lay (*sic*) on my back I was empty and so alone.

I began to hope that everything would go away: the emptiness, the need for you, the longing and the memory. If I were to go crazy, how would any alternative matter? If you had telephoned me then, I would have asked what I could do just to hear the sound of your voice, and I would have done anything.

As you said I would, I MISSED YOU. At that moment my body had nothing to cling to but the memory of you: the electrifying feel of your skin against mine, the ardent desire to touch as much that is you with as much of me as possible to set all the nerve ends tingling, to hear your voice in my ear, breathing words that no one has ever said to me before, to feel and to smell your hair and your skin and to have the glorious freedom to kiss and to lick every part of you. My breasts remembered your hands and your tongue, and my nipples stood erect and expectant. My legs opened as if they had a will of their own, and my cunt was as ready for fucking as ever. The burning need arose; again and again I fingered my clitoris in the centre of that humid swamp that seemed to lay (*sic*) in the eye of a hurricane. I don't know how many times I came, but in the end there was a kind of peace. I don't know whether I have told you that I sometimes pray, not very often, to ask for something. This seemed to be a suitable occasion. I prayed for my sanity and fell asleep.

As if I hadn't had my share of miracles in the last six weeks, another one occurred on Friday morning. I woke to find myself in a crystal-clear new landscape. Easter after Lent, or the newly-washed face of nature after a storm that has broken dams, washed away broken trees or dreams and the rubble of ignorance?

A new life has started. You cannot help being part of it because I owe it to you. You can partake of it on any scale because I am yours even if I never see you again. I know you to be like no-one else and regret the mistake of trying to make you fit one of the patterns I recognise. You are so many things. I admire most of them and now understand those that put you in another dimension and frightened me so much before.

I always knew that accepted standards never fitted me, but I did so long to conform and to be safe. Just now I remembered something else you said. You do have that effect on people. My anxieties seem to have shrunk away as to be barely visible. I have

grown and from you or God or somewhere I have got the
strength to handle an entirely new order of priorities. Also I love
you.

It was signed 'Gina'. At first I thought it a hoax, but it was too
elaborate for that. Hoaxes, like ransom notes, are to the point.

So whoever Gina was, some experience had hurt her into stately
wordiness. Reading it again now, I wonder if English may not have
been her first language, for there was the odd spelling mistake and
the confusion over 'lay' and 'lie'. Someone had clearly rung all the
bells for a very intense woman, religious, lonely, not too cursed
with humour, and probably not young. Only I hadn't rung them.

A fortnight later the second letter came, addressed to 'Byron
Rogers, The Daily Telegraph Magazine'. It was clear that the writer,
like Gina, had no home address for the recipient, and did not give
one for herself. It too was neatly typed, though this time just a
note. But in other respects it was very different. No mention of
feelings this time, or at least none on the surface: whoever she was,
the writer was remembering a romp, with three people involved,
also a dog in some obscure supporting role.

You never told me you wrote for *The Guardian* as well, you cheeky
devil . . .

I had written a short feature the paper had headlined 'Here's to You,
Mrs Robinson'. This had been prompted by a court case involving a
rather good-looking woman in her thirties, living somewhere in the
Home Counties, who for some years had housed French teenage
boys on school visits, then seduced them. Most had welcomed the
experience (according to one of their teachers the essays they wrote
about their holidays were effusive, though vague), but it all ended
abruptly when the latest two rejected her advances, running into the

street and bawling in their best English for, of all things, an ambulance. The judge gave her eighteen months. He also called her 'an evil woman', which I thought dreadful, considering that I, possibly he, and just about every other man had spent our teenage years waiting for something like that to happen to us. My feature brought down the wrath of the paper's feminist readers upon me, and I had a whole indignant section of the letters page to myself. But this letter writer hadn't seen it like that. At all.

> You have got a lot of strings to your bow – as we all know!
> Sandra said the article should have been titled ROGERS ON
> FUCKS AND HOW TO GET THEM. And what about Helen
> Mirren last week? I bet you charmed the pants off her too –
> coming off all bashful and on the edge of your seat.

That had been a feature interview, after which Miss Mirren had seen me off into the night, wobbling on my bicycle, with the remains of a bottle of whisky, most of which I and her then boyfriend Liam Neeson had consumed between us. I fell off the bike in Grosvenor Square and, unhurt, finished off the whisky at the kerbside. There followed two lost hours, during which my girlfriend, later my wife, went to the police, who thought it no end of a joke, and suggested I might have gone to some nightclub with Miss Mirren. Which set her mind at rest no end.

> I'm sorry I have got in touch with you again after 'that night'. I
> know I promised not to but I just keep thinking about it all the
> time and deep down Angie feels the same. She hasn't mentioned
> a thing but I look at her across the pool and she's got a funny
> smirk on her face. She was very upset about Steve coming back,
> she promised that he never comes back from the Scottish trips
> earlier than three days. Honest! Anyway he's such an idle sod he

didn't think there was anything funny about me and her starkers and playing with her daft dog! Not so daft if you ask me. I think he was pissed anyway – Steve, that is. You got back alright I hope, round the back. I know you were upset but we promise it won't happen again, so if you want to see teeny-weeny me and Angie again you'll know where to find us on Thursdays. Please, please...

Gilly. X X X.

So a typist this time (Gina had not mentioned jobs, and no locations apart from bed), and a good-time girl who every Thursday went on the town with a married friend from her office. But again she was writing to a sexual athlete who had appeared in her life like Spring-heeled Jack, then disappeared, though, again, Gilly had been told this would happen. Everyone I talked to about it (which was just about everyone I met) thought it hilarious, but I began to get worried. What would Jack do next?

The next thing was a postcard addressed 'To the town's Handsomest, Sexiest, most sought after Lover Boy'. On it this was written in a large, wild hand, 'S.O.B.'s presence is requested at a private dinner to be held at a venue yet to be arranged in aid of the "Misfits of the World". Dress optional. RSVP. E.B.'

So another disappearance, more bells having been rung, which clearly now hung idle. I went to see the police at this stage, who also thought it no end of a joke. 'Try to see our point of view, say we got him, what could we charge him with?' asked a detective sergeant at West End Central. 'I mean, all he's ever done is go to bed with women. And their only regret is that he's stopped doing it. The only complainant is you.'

As I was leaving he said idly, 'Just one question, sir, have you any idea why he should want to pretend he was you?' I said I hadn't, but as I went through the door I realised I hadn't quite liked the way he had asked that.

Still, his question was partly answered when the first phone call came. It was from a woman who wanted to know why I hadn't turned up at the weekend. She wasn't cross, she said she quite understood if I'd been sent abroad at short notice or something; she just wished I could have let her know.

I explained things to her, and there was this long silence. I asked where she'd met him, and she said at an afternoon dance at the Leicester Square ballroom, when he'd told her he was an international correspondent who was abroad most of the time, living out of a suitcase when he was in this country. She then started to cry, and there was a click as the phone went dead.

So that was it. It was quite smart then to say you worked for a colour magazine, and of course it was the perfect cover, particularly if whoever you told knew little about journalism. And I don't suppose anyone who turned up at an afternoon dance was going to ask too many questions. No address, no phone number, just Captain America coming and going, and out of reach of these vulnerable women, as I had now come to assume they were. Suddenly it had become sad.

There were other phone calls which I managed to avoid ('It's a Mrs Rowlands, says it's urgent'). But then one got through, and this time there were no tears. I went round to see a divorcee in her late fifties, living alone in a council flat twelve storeys up in a tower block above Hampstead, who was more annoyed than upset ('Ooh, the bugger'). She too had met him at a tea dance, for there was one thing about such places, she said, they did allow one to meet people, and she coloured slightly at this, implying the word covered a great deal. Her children having left home, she had begun to find life lonely.

Of course, I thought, tea dances, afternoon ballrooms: the perfect hunting ground for a sexual predator, the women would be of a certain age, and lonely. 'And they're that surprised,' a sergeant in the Scotch Guards who had stalked them in such places told a friend of mine, 'they put their hearts and their airses into it.'

My hostess made tea. She was a rather nice, well made-up woman with little lady-like ways (after the 'bugger' she had said, 'I don't know what made me say that'), but there was a toughness there. She said that if he got in touch again she would ask him round, and, if she could get him off guard, would take a photograph of him, which she would send me.

She showed me a poem he had sent, addressed to her. It was, and is (for I still have this too), written in sloping capitals.

> Lately my life has lacked the light
> Until you came, a star so bright
> Your very nearness warms my heart,
> Once more my life begins to start,
> Your happy bubbling ~~ever~~ effervesence (*sic*)
> Warms – draws me to your prescence (*sic*).

She gave this to me, saying she didn't want to see it again. Seduction is one thing; poetry, however bad, hurts.

A fortnight later she phoned to say she had the photograph. I have this too. Caught in flashlight, a man, leaning on a door frame, is grinning at the camera. He is thin, pale, not bad looking, but with the sort of eye-teeth for which Christopher Lee needed a make-up artist: they are the very long, very white teeth of a vampire. But what had made her cross, she said, was how perfectly at ease 'the creature' had been.

'I know who asked you to do this.'

'Yes, and he's getting a print.'

'Poor old Byron, I knew he was after me, but there's nothing at all he can do about it.'

Still it must have worried him, for the letters and the phone calls stopped.

———◆◆◆———

But the strangest development of all has just taken place. When I started on what you have been reading I got in touch with a friend of mine to check some of the details; now living in retirement in Cornwall, she was on the Magazine with me. A fortnight later she rang me.

'I can hardly believe this, it's the most extraordinary thing. I was telling a lady who's just moved down here from London about that chap who used to pretend he was you, and we were both roaring with laughter when I must have mentioned the name Byron Rogers, for suddenly she stopped laughing. She said, "Omigod, not him."

'If it's the same man, in the 1980s her mother had an affair with him. I gather they were all a bit worried at the time. But her mother's coming down at the weekend, I'll ask her.'

A few days later she rang again. 'It *was* him. I told the mother your story, and she was startled for everything checked out. Everything. Her daughter even teased her about whether he'd been a bit of a mover and shaker in the bedroom department, but all the old lady said was, "Yes." Perhaps you'd better not bring that up. Oh yes, I forgot, she's agreed to talk to you.'

This is her story.

In the 1980s I was in my fifties, separated from my husband and working as a housekeeper/caretaker in this block of flats in Mayfair. And every Monday night I and some friends used to go dancing at the Café de Paris. Monday night was Ladies' Night. And that's where I met him. He was tall and dark, had prominent teeth, I remember that, and was very likeable. He told me he worked for newspapers. In fact he had a whole briefcase full of his articles, sorry, *your* articles, for whatever you say about him, he was your number one fan. He must have cut out everything you wrote.

And even at the beginning that struck me as a bit odd. I didn't know any writers, but I didn't think they carried old articles around with them. Not to dances anyway. God, this makes me sound such a twit. Of course later you wrote columns, and your photograph began to appear, which would have put a stop to everything. All this is very sad, don't you think?

He had this wonderful knowledge of London. We used to go for long walks together. And suddenly there was all this sex. I'm not sure how it started, I mean I'm a bit of a prude and I'd sworn when my marriage broke up that would be it as far as I was concerned, so I was more startled than anything. It wasn't as though he was physically attractive, and I always used to put him in the bath beforehand. But the sex was ... amazing. Not that he did anything out of the ordinary, it was just that it was ... that's the only word for it ... amazing.

The only thing was that at no time did he mention anything to do with writing, and that's when I started to get suspicious. Then he asked me to his flat, which was in Harrow and very small. And there were no books in it, just paintings of animals on black velvet, and the only furniture a crumbling old sofa. That's when I confronted him, and he admitted it. Said he was a misfit, that he'd been sexually abused by an aunt when he was a boy. So he said. And then he told me that what he really did was manage a bookshop in the Charing Cross Road. Only there were no books in his flat. That's when I told him to piss off. I mean, even booksellers must read books sometime. It was so sad. And silly. I don't think there was any harm in him, but there are people like that, they can't bear to be ordinary.

I thought it was all over, and then years later I saw this drawing of a man's face in the *Evening Standard*. A man's body had been fished out of the Thames, and the police were trying to identify him. And it was him, I'm sure it was him, it was an uncanny likeness. I know I should have gone to a police station, but I couldn't face it somehow. It sounds daft, but I couldn't face getting involved again, even with him dead.

Suddenly it wasn't a matter of women wailing for their demon lover. To have invited her home would have been a major departure for him, so he must have fallen for her in a way he hadn't for any of the others, not one of whom even had his address. It must have been the one time he had stepped out of character, and he, who had stepped in and out of so many lives and disappeared, was himself made to disappear.

Her description of the flat was so vivid, the emptiness of the room, those awful paintings on black velvet, the tigers and elephants you saw for sale in street markets at the time, to which, his briefcase bulging with cuttings (I was churning the stuff out in those days), he came home each night. Well, most nights. And the effect on me was complex.

Shock had long ago given way to irritation, largely at not finding myself centre stage in my own life, but then this too had given way to awe. I suppose I had come to revel in the adventures of my secret sharer, this Mr Hyde of the Tea-dances. For I had never received such letters, I had never had that effect on anyone, and with me partings had always been messy affairs, mostly on station platforms and, once, in the Romano-British section of a research library. And these were partings which were usually reversed a fortnight or so later, which meant there were other station platforms, other libraries.

We had shared so much, he and I, except he got the ecstasy, I got the recriminations. As to the rest, I knew nothing about him, what he did, where he came from (though one of the ladies had mentioned South Africa). To me he was this long peep-show of Gina, of Gilly and Angie (and why had the husband not been surprised to come on the two of them naked with the dog?), and the others, only they disappeared as I approached the glass, and there was just me peering in.

When someone steals your credit card, and you need to check your statements, you are confronted by the patterns of your spending. But when someone steals your identity you are confronted by that identity as you find yourself staring at it, and in this case not alone but in company.

Just one thing, sir, have you any idea why he should want to pretend he was you? And then something I have forgotten to mention. The evening I went round to collect the photograph from the lady in the Hampstead tower block, I found myself staring at it and then at her. 'What's he like? Is he anything like me at all?'

She hesitated for a moment. 'No, he's nothing like you at all, dear. I'm not sure how to put this. Well … he's sophisticated.'

--------◆-◆--------

I don't know who he was – or where he is, if in fact he is alive – but if anyone is responsible for this book it is a man with long white teeth grinning in a doorway. Because of him I had found myself in a film in the production of which I had played no part. And the biggest shock of appearing on screen for the first time, the director Bryan Forbes once told me, is seeing yourself walk away. It makes you think about yourself in a way you never have before.

Goodbye

'You are the third generation of your race to read books. You are the second to live without the fear of poverty and old age. You are the first to choose the work you wish to do ...'

GLYN JONES, *The Valley, the City, the Village*

''STRAORDINARY ...' Sir Hereward Wake, fourteenth baronet, sitting in his library with the long windows ('so the dogs can see out in winter'), looked genuinely puzzled. ''Straordinary how few people know their eight great-grandparents.' He knew all his, and, beyond them, the ancestor who married a barmaid and whom death, intervening at the very last minute like the cavalry in Western films, prevented from cutting down every tree in the park for ready cash. He also knew the one, for we are accelerating in time now, who chose the wrong side at Bosworth, and, beyond even him, the chap who insisted on going on the Third Crusade. A man tends to know his family when property has accompanied it through twenty-nine unbroken legitimate generations in the male line. Property means records.

'We started in Normandy,' said the fourteenth baronet.

The Rogers family started in north-west Carmarthenshire, in Blaenwaun on the foothills of the Preseli mountain, a hamlet so windswept that, according to my cousin Brenda, no bird can stand on a branch, let alone sing there. A pub, a chapel, a line of houses, and the wind. We started there all of three unbroken legitimate male generations ago, which by our standards was going it some. Until my father briefly owned a house in the 1940s no one in the family had property of any kind, not even a pigsty. We had no records.

I know about the three unbroken generations in the male line only because the Mormons, using records they have buried under a mountain in Utah to give us all some chance in the afterlife, put the 1881 census on the Internet. So people who once believed in polygamy (a practice which prompted my mother, hearing of it for the first time, to comment, 'Well, they must have had very tidy houses then'), 7,000 miles away, whom I have never met, nor ever will meet, introduced me to my ancestors.

To Thomas Rogers, forty-nine, of Pilbach cottage, farm labourer, of whom no photograph survives, no line of writing in his own hand, no scrap of recorded conversation, which means that three generations back I am confronted by someone in my own family as mysterious as a man fleeing the glaciers of the Ice Age.

To Esther Rogers, forty-three, Thomas's wife. Then a line of children, six of them, from a young woman of twenty to a baby three months old, which are then followed, mysteriously, by two more, one aged two, the other five months old, probably a daughter's illegitimate children being brought up in the old way by her parents. The Rogers family was noted for two things, my father said once: one was illegitimacy, the other was farting. And while they might have been ashamed of the one, they exulted in their flatulence. My father claimed proudly that it had been possible to hear, a whole field away, and even over the winds from the Preseli, his grandfather Thomas under the thatch at Pilbach. 'My family might have been rough, but nobody ever accused us of that,' sniffed my mother. As to the illegitimacy, it is still possible to read the tight-lipped inscription, with no accompanying Biblical text, to the two generations of unmarried mothers in my family buried in the same grave in the local chapel.

And these are the only things I know about the people caught in that bureaucratic trawl of 128 years ago. My grandfather, Philip Rogers, then seventeen, had already left home and was a farm labourer in a farm 600 yards away. We were not adventurous men.

And where is this Pilbach? A bank manager in Leicester thought he knew once, having been entrusted with map references by my cousin David Rogers, then planning his own funeral with the care of a pharaoh. There were to be horses, and a scattering of ashes in the ruins of our family's cottage, for David, born in Manchester and speaking with an English accent, was a card-carrying member of the Welsh Nationalist Party who compared his life in England to time spent on an oil rig, and had announced that when it was over he would come home tidied away in a small box to rejoin his ancestors.

Until, that is, using these same map references I splashed up a lane to where the hedge became an earth bank, the only indication that people had once lived here. Ten years, my father told me, that was all it took for one of these little places to fall down, another ten and they were bumps in the ground. I walked among the bumps. What had they been like, my people, what had troubled them here, what dreams?

Under an ash tree I found some broken pottery, part of a plate my grandfather might have used as a boy. And then, my foot knocking against something, I found the remains of a cast-iron cooking pot. The bottom had gone, but as I scraped the earth away I felt as excited as an archaeologist in an opened tomb. Carefully I carried the pot back to the car.

And that might have been that, except, before leaving, I called at the pub to ask after the oldest inhabitant. Oh yes, said the ancient, he could just remember my great-grandfather (who had died in 1917). Neat little man. And the house in the lane? What house in the lane? Pilbach, our old home. He took off his spectacles. 'No, your family never lived there. They had a house in a field, they did. At least it's a field now. Your house was bulldozed years ago.'

I rang my cousin to tell him, but got his wife who, for some reason, could not stop laughing. And that was my one venture into genealogy.

--------◆◆◆--------

Anything and anyone before our grandparents is for most of us a haze, only it is not quite a haze. In my mind's eye I see small, lime-washed cottages at the edge of common-land, back and back in time, stone giving way to cob, cob to mud and straw, and, amongst them, farm labourer after anonymous farm labourer, back to the first clearing of the land. Not one of these owned anything or perhaps wanted to. My paternal grandfather Philip Rogers, refusing to buy his rented smallholding on terms even he could have afforded, said smugly, '*Mae Duw wedi dweud ta dyn bach 'r wy fod.*' God has said I am to be a little man.

They did not move far, my people, a few miles here, a few miles there; our world, said my father, was the size of a basin. Until now. I have moved away, I have English as my first language, but for a little while, until the age of five, I lived in the countryside and was a monoglot Welsh speaker, like all my ancestors.

So this account thus starts where most autobiographies end, with a goodbye.

The American writer Paul Theroux, in the course of researching *The Kingdom by the Sea*, his account of a journey round Britain, found himself one day staring out of a train window a few miles west of Carmarthen, he who for weeks had done little but stare out of train windows. Only this time, the more he stared, the stranger this landscape seemed.

> The hills were green and lumpish, and the valleys tangled with short leafy trees, some standing as hedges and boundaries and others in jumbled woods ... The land pattern and the foliage was new to me and I liked its wildness. It looked wild from neglect, like a place that had once been neat but was now overgrown. It had an untrimmed charm – the grass too long, the boughs drooping, like the shaggy imagery in a Dylan Thomas poem.

This was real country, he wrote, the first he had seen in South Wales, though his description of it seems to be out of the horror stories of H.P. Lovecraft, and all that is missing is Spanish Moss in the trees and the Undead waving politely as the train goes by. Which is what my family usually did, once to such effect that an army officer, leaning out of the window in wartime to wave back, had his uniform cap blown from his head. We kept it in the house for years.

For the landscape through which Mr Theroux passed so briefly was one both my grandfathers tried to farm. Philip Rogers had moved his family all of ten miles east, to the village of Llangynog, as had my mother's father Caleb Davies, a roaring boy, who managed to drink his farm away here before being obliged, like all ruined men in this community, to seek his fortunes, aged sixty, in the coal mines to the east. So both my parents were born here, as was I, in the low wet acres of a river valley. Except there is no river.

There should be, for, if you look at a map, the valley is the natural progression of the Towy from east to west, only the river has turned sharp left at Carmarthen. What happened was the result of that strange process known as a river capture, a high tide coming up a smaller, more vigorous river which then broke through, diverting the Towy and eventually sealing off its old route to the sea.

It is not known when this happened, but a few miles to the west a line of large processional stones leads from what once would have been river banks, suggesting one of the highways of the old world, which were its sea-ways, had its landfall here. This was long before men even built the two little churches nearby which face each other in ruin across the marsh. One of these, Llandeilo Abercywyn, is in the yard of a house still lived in, itself so old it is a dead ringer for King Harold's hall at Bosham in the Bayeux Tapestry. The other, Llanfihangel Abercywyn, has three thirteenth-century graves under a yew, the only medieval graves I have ever seen in a churchyard. They are said to be those of pilgrims overtaken by the Black Death. 'I saw them go by, but I never saw them come back,' said my maternal grandmother, a bit shaky on history. This is the old, old place.

For before these churches, before even the hill fort was built on the plateau above the valley, paths already led to Llangynog and the great megalith, three stones with a capstone eight feet by seven by two feet thick. Who built that, what their language was, and what harsh gods they appeased, will never be known. Thousands of years later, the men of the Middle Ages, marvelling at its dimensions and nervous of the possibility that there could have been a faith before theirs, called it Twlc y Filiast, the kennel of the greyhound bitch, grounding the mystery in the homely detail of the farmyard.

But all this is from a time out of time. Or names.

For us names are a beginning. Our own are the first sounds we recognise and quite possibly will be the last, yet in between they come under constant attack: from those who mispronounce them (my friend Geraint Morgan, after a lifetime in England of being addressed as Grunt and Gerund, finally got his university colleagues to call him G), from schoolmasters who in our beginnings deliberately mislay our first names, and at the end by breezy nurses who, just as deliberately, mislay our surnames. There is a power, assumed or withheld, in names.

And it is touching we should think of them as ours and ours alone, these things shared among so many. The past is in names, these fossils scraped from old religions, myths, forgotten battles (I once worked with a boy called Verdun), from long-gone headlines (I know of two graves where Alsace Lorraines are buried), some from other languages so we have forgotten what they ever meant. When the politician William Hague married a Welsh woman called Ffion, he became the first leader of the Conservative party to marry a Foxglove. So names are wished on us by fashion, families and the registrar.

'My mother liked sounds,' said Mrs Glenda Thomas of Meidrim, near where I was born. 'She called my sister Dardanella, after the landings in the First World War, and when my own second boy was born it was she who registered the birth, so we didn't know until later that she'd added Timoshenko, after the Russian general or whatever he was. Of course we never called him that, and when the local doctor came round to immunise the children we didn't know what he was talking about when he asked to see Timoshenko Thomas. We'd forgotten this was our Randal.'

And then there was me.

My parents had intended calling me Alan, but then found that of my two grandfathers, neither fluent in English, one had taken to calling me Allen, the other Alun, so to avoid rows I was called Byron. Or so I was told. God alone knows where that came from, but it probably dates from the early twentieth century, when the Welsh became enthusiastic about education; I have known Handels and Haydns, and one Holbein. There was even a man called Arthur Pendragon Jones whom my father once saw waiting for a bus: Arthur Pendragon Jones was wearing a green suit, a green tie, a green shirt and a green felt hat, and would have had no trouble popping back into the medieval myth from which he had emerged, apart from the fact that he was carrying a green umbrella. A few months later my father saw him again, and he was all in blue.

I have never liked my name; it embarrassed me in playgrounds, and laid me open to the sneers of gym-masters ('You there, the poet, let's see if you can do a handstand as well'). Even so I was irritated, after writing an article for the *Sunday Mirror*, to see it appear under the byline 'by Ron Rogers', for, whatever my feelings about it, my name like an old dog had padded behind me through the decades. The possibility that it may have padded behind others had never occurred to me until I met the first and only other Byron I have ever met, a West Indian Pentecostal minister.

'Glory be,' he said. 'Us Byrons must drink to this.' Only the drink when it came was in pint glasses, and it was Ribena. We had one each, then a second, though I made my excuses when I heard this iron man call for a third, for there is a thing you may not know about Ribena. Drunk in volume, it is the most potent wind-inducing agent known to man, so, buses and taxis being out of the question, I had to walk three miles home through rain in a slipstream of blackcurrant, cursing my one meeting with a namesake.

Still it never occurred to me that there might be anyone out there with whom I shared that *and* a surname, until three years ago I first typed Byron Rogers into the Internet, which is what freelance writers do when there are no good afternoon films on television. There were pages and pages of Byron Rogerses. First, the Stud. This Byron Rogers, a star of gay porn films in the United States, has his appearances posted by an organisation called Men Matter Most. He is now relegated to page ninety or thereabouts on Google, probably on account of the fact that in the photographs you are invited to summon up ('Click for dick'), he appears naked, sporting his main qualification for his chosen career.

Then there is the American politician, a man so revered in death people want to share their memories of him: 'The late Byron Rogers, a longtime Congressman from Denver, Colorado, once faced a much younger opponent who had written an open letter to God, appealing for His support in a very tough election. "If he gets an answer, Byron," a Democratic colleague advised, "I guess you should withdraw."' God clearly didn't reply, for there are references to a Byron Rogers Federal Courthouse, named after the passing of our boy.

Byron Rogers, knife dealer of San Angelo, Texas, and thinker ('Before the dawn of civilisation, fire and the knife were man's first steps towards a better life'). Byron Rogers, of New South Wales, horse-breeder. We band of brothers, the Breeder, the Knifeman, the Congressman and me, are a resident repertory group, though other

Byron Rogerses, an acrobat, a parson (from something called the Powerhouse Church of God), and a pest-control king, make the odd appearance.

But we four share a simplicity. I write books, the Congressman gets praised for his good deeds (once by President Kennedy), the Horse-breeder presides over perfect equine genes, the Knifeman is on a quest ('He travels over 10,000 miles a year, going to over 20 knife-shows'). And it seems we have always been doing this.

Still there was one birth.

I came into the world, I am told, on 5 April 1942, politely at teatime on a Sunday, which, with the young and the old packed off to Sunday School, was a time for conception, not birth, in Welsh-speaking Wales. Sunday School started at half-past two and ended at four, so, allowing for half an hour's pleading, which in Wales passes for foreplay, and for an hour's post-coital snooze, most of my generation was conceived in lawful wedlock at around three. Our parents, met again at teatime, usually looked bemused, as though they had just returned from a whirlwind tour of another country.

I was born into a house called Cowin Villa which stood in a country lane about a mile from the village of Bancyfelin, the sort of place that, like a halt on the Great Plains, was somewhere on the way to somewhere else. Buses stopped here, but most people just passed through on the A40 on their way to the sea, which they had recently discovered. As a boy my father saw an open-decked charabanc of coal-miners from industrial South Wales, all in bowler hats, all with gold watches, which, as one man, they drew out and consulted whenever they passed their country cousins. Two years later, after the General Strike, the charabanc came through again, and this time the miners, now in cloth caps, stared stonily ahead of them, and there were no gold watches. There is a bypass now, and if anyone notices Bancyfelin, or has time to notice it, it is a straggle of houses seen from a four-lane carriageway.

Quite why there was a village there is anyone's guess. It probably started with a mill at a crossroads, to which, in quick succession, there were added two pubs, a Methodist chapel, then a school, and houses. Here I watched American tanks trundle through to France, and once, which was far more interesting, a woman without a nose. Aged four, being held up, I also stared through a blue pane in the chapel door and, as in a trance, moved into the cold clarity of a blue world. It was not a vision, it was as though I was elsewhere, and time had stopped. This has never happened elsewhere, though I have peered through many blue panes; yet when I again looked through the one in Bancyfelin chapel, this time with sixty-year-old eyes, I was back in the blue world.

In the house called Cowin Villa there lived five adults: my father, my mother, her parents, whom my father had more or less rescued from poverty, and an elderly road-mender, whom they had been persuaded to take in as a lodger. Added to these from time to time were various aunts and cousins fleeing the bombing of the cities in the Second World War.

My years in the house were the happiest I have known. To my mother, who as a child had never had a toy of any kind, I was a living doll, and also the centre of attention for all five, my outings as supervised as those of an ailing solitary heir to a royal house. 'Far too cold for the little boy,' said my maternal grandfather Caleb Davies one cloudless day in June, he who had been a bare-fist fighter in the Rhondda, when his usual grim greeting on entering a pub was 'Anybody here been talking about me?' He and I, when temperatures reached eighty, would walk in the lane, gravely discussing the harvest, so that when we later moved to the town our neighbours were puzzled to be informed by a small boy that things looked good for the hay.

I had just one friend of my own age, a boy called Spencer who lived about a quarter of a mile away; unable to pronounce his name I called him Bempy, and he called me Beimo. But apart from him there were no other children, no contending egos: my power was boundless, my days through flowers.

Except of course that we were in the middle of a world war. Not that I knew anything about that, for it did not affect my family much, apart from the refugee relatives. We lived in the country, and, as most of our relatives were farmers, butter, eggs, chickens, bacon, meat were all delivered, some of these in suitcases forever after stained by blood, so it is as well that my family never got caught up in a murder investigation. Sugar came by post, my uncle Brinley being a London pharmacist.

Nobody went away, or, if they did, did not go far. My father spent most of the War building a research establishment in New Quay, Cardiganshire, where a top-secret navigational aid for planes was being developed. Its inventor, a Major Reid, gave him a Hornby electric train for me, a Mallard which came with a single rail, which, together with the fact that we had no electricity, so infuriated me that in the end I wrecked it.

As for the rest of the family, of my ten uncles only two saw military service. One, my father's brother Trevor, a schoolmaster, became a major, but it is the career of my uncle Billy Morgan, married to my mother's sister, which fascinates me. A professional soldier, he started the war as a private and, at a time when professional soldiers were given swift promotion, ended it a private, which must have required great qualities of mind on his part. When he chose to he could quote poetry by the yard, but I can see him in hose and hood taking his longbow to France, his musket to the Peninsula, all the time keeping himself to himself, invisible to the enemy, and, far more important, invisible to his officers. His attitude to his military career is best illustrated by the fact that he gave me one of his campaign medals for a toy, so that for years whenever I went out to play I had the Africa Star pinned like a sheriff's badge on my chest.

Two of my mother's brothers, too young for active service in the First World War, had served with the Army of Occupation in the Rhineland, in the course of which they met just once, in a brothel, one hissing at the other on the stairs, 'Don't tell Father.' Twenty years later in a Swansea pub, this man, with the bombs falling outside, was heard to say, 'Shouldn't worry, boys, it's only Herr von Davies looking for his daddy.' He was then a dock policeman, being a large man like his brothers. I have inherited their genes.

'You're tall, you in the police?' an old lady once asked.

'No, I work for newspapers, on *The Times*.'

'The *Carmarthen Times*?'

'No, the London *Times*.'

'Good God, man, have they got a *Times* in London?'

You may have gathered that I was brought up amongst people who heard a different drum from most of the inhabitants of these islands. Hitler was one of the few politicians my mother knew by name, and that was because he had frightened her. Later she was to be frightened by Gaddafi, but she fancied Edward Heath because she felt he needed looking after, always a shortcut to her emotions. In old age she declared proudly, 'Passion, that's something no one's ever been able to accuse me of.' She was interested in two things: other people's medical symptoms, which she would discuss endlessly with her friends (my wife once heard one of them say of a man that his head had been drained), and tidiness.

'A word of advice, Jo,' she told my wife just before we got married. My wife waited nervously, fearing it might be a pronouncement on what my mother called married things, something she once saw a couple engaged in, in a Ford Cortina, in the car-park of the Fox and Hounds in Bancyfelin. The advice was this: 'Dust is the enemy, you must never forget that.' And my wife never did, or could. A public-school-educated Englishwoman, she had never met anyone like my mother, and kept notes on her, as when, years later, she phoned to ask how our daughter had done in some school exam. 'Not that I can talk, I never passed anything in my life. And I've got no Brasso in the house either.'

But then my mother was a specialist. Like Jowett, the Master of Balliol in the limerick, she believed that what she didn't know just wasn't knowledge. In her case, beyond the symptoms and the dust, what she didn't know was all history, all literature, all science, all geography and all foreign languages with the exception of the Latin verbs in which she had tested me at grammar school ('Am-O, Am-AS, Am-AT'). But she could startle us. She once told me quite seriously that a cousin who had planned a holiday in Florence had been obliged to change this for one in Florida, 'on account of the statues'.

'What do you mean, statues?'

'You know, those naked statues.'

Another time she said, 'You mustn't look down on people just because they've never heard of Joan of Arc,' the name surfacing in her talk like a nuclear sub through an icecap. God only knows where she had heard it, for I did not once see her read a book and she read newspapers only if I had written in them, in case of what her neighbours might say. Mrs Waldo's cry in *Under Milk Wood*, 'What'll the neighbours say, oh what'll the neighbours say?', is not a joke; Dylan Thomas knew the Welsh inside out. 'How am I? What do you care? I haven't been out for a week because of what you said about the town clerk,' said my mother.

The tragedy for her, and for her friends, was that the education they were so keen on for their children would inevitably make strangers of them, so in adult life when they came home they were like men returning from a war. The mothers never realised this would happen, and it is so easy to make fun of them.

But my mother was a woman who laid out her own husband, my father, when he died in 1968. Few of you now even know what this involves, and I won't spell it out. But who among the high-minded, well-read women I have known would have been capable of doing that?

———— ✦✦✦ ————

My parents, grandparents and I were part of a monoglot Welsh community. Nobody spoke English by choice, and my father's view of the world was that if you rose in it at some point or other you met the Englishman lurking in its upper reaches like a Martian. The English ran things, with the exception of the Western Welsh bus company, which, according to him, was run by the Jews. He had never met a Jew, but the English were easy to spot on account of their big feet; we were a colonised people, which of course we were, and had small feet.

For my family the possibility that within a generation someone like me might make a living from the English language would have been as inconceivable as the possibility that I might make it from the Black Arts, more so in fact. One of our closest neighbours supported a family on the Black Arts, being consulted by rich farmers and their wives, though, alas, she looked in vain in her crystal ball for news of her son, missing at Dunkirk. His name is the only one from the Second World War to be listed on the village war memorial.

My cousin Felicity, at eight fleeing the V-bombs in London, found herself in a society where her own grandparents could not understand anything she said, and where, on her first unaccompanied walk, she wandered into a shed where chickens were being slaughtered, far from the eyes of Government inspectors. Amongst the screeching and the blood, she later said, she thought she had materialised in Southern Spain.

<hr />

My father was a carpenter and, on occasion, undertaker, the entries laconic in his one surviving diary, a black Stockfeeders Diary for 1940. Just the nature of the job, the time taken, and the names of farms or the dead. 'Door for Danyfforest.' 'Coffin for Davies, Llanybri.' Everything in English, which he never spoke well, for English was the language of bills. His year started as if there was no war. 'January 1, Monday. After the Hounds.' And then the long round of gates and coffins began.

It must have been a cold winter, 1940, for on 20 January he was making a sleigh for a Captain Evans. He could make anything, my father – wheels, gates, toys, furniture – and at the end was the last man in the area able to turn a stair, in a world (as he put it) where no bugger wanted his stairs turned anymore. Like most craftsmen he had a bitter streak in him. He was thirty years old, a shy, good-looking man who, a few years earlier, had locked himself all day in his room when his brother, the more confident Trefor on whom he had relied, left home to teach in Manchester.

The first time the War intrudes in the diary is at the end of August, when my father, like builders all over Britain, is making pill boxes, the concrete hide-outs the authorities thought would hold up a German invasion. He makes them on and off for the next two months, but by October there is the entry 'Beds', day after day, to which a week later he adds that these are being made for the local council, clearly expecting evacuation on a large scale.

On our last Christmas in Cowin Villa I woke up clutching the starting pistol we had got from somewhere and which, with the exception of my father's Home Guard bayonet, was my favourite plaything. Few toys got made here during the War (unlike Nazi Germany, where toy factories were still operating in 1944), yet now, as my mother opened the curtains, I saw an American tank transporter, a gypsy caravan with a horse and gypsy, a train with a tender, a horse on which I could ride, and a car big enough to take me, with pedals that worked. All were of wood, and, with the exception of the car which was bigger, each was two or three feet long. My father, contracted to make toys for a shop in Carmarthen, had kept one of each, and it was the most amazing sight I ever saw. I was so stunned I stood amongst them, clutching the starting pistol to me like a holy relic.

Had he been born at a different time, or had access to patrons, there is no telling what my father might have been – a cabinet-maker, model-maker, engineer. As a young man he had attended classes at the Carmarthen School of Art, where the accomplished watercolourist Morse Brown, recognising his potential, had encouraged him, but Morse Brown had then run off to the Riviera with a local grocer's wife, leaving my father amongst people who did not value, because they could not understand, his craft.

Before his marriage he had built a scale model of the Atlantic liner *Queen Mary*, fitting it with propellers attached to a large clockwork motor he had taken from a gramophone. I have only heard stories of this and of its stately progress through the waves at Llansteffan, for it was so big, and steady, it could take me as a baby. But when I was two my baby-sitting grandparents, who had never come on anything like it, gave it to me to play with, and watched as I spent a happy evening smashing the wireless masts and the funnels.

The one break in my father's diary occurs in July when another hand, equally laconic, has written 'The day.' This, his marriage, was a three-day job, the writer my mother, born some three miles from the smallholding in which he had been born. Six years her senior, he had sold raffle-tickets at the 1918 Bancyfelin baby show in which she, ten pounds at birth, won first prize, which, I suppose, brought her to his notice.

I did not once see my parents kiss, I never even saw them hold hands, but then this was not the fashion of a generation for whom the one public gesture of intimacy was the woman's hand slipped through the man's arm at elbow level, something you never see now. But they were as close as any two people can be, except in their forms of worship; my father was a Methodist, my mother a Baptist. Apart from the business of adult immersion, neither of them would have known what differences of observance or belief separated them, yet, with the exception of family funerals, neither was ever seen in the other's chapel. The Welsh Nonconformity of my childhood was about to enter its long sunset, but we did not recognise this at the time, for its prejudices cast a long shadow.

My father could remember the outrage among the elders in Bancyfelin chapel when news came that soldiers in the trenches of the Great War were being issued with rum before they went over the top. One man in particular, Davies bach Llwynon, little Davies of Ashtree Farm, a rich farmer notorious for the starvation diet on which he expected his servants to survive, was particularly incensed, repeating in his thin high voice, which my father imitated, 'Rum in the Trenches, Rum in the Trenches.' Had Davies bach, or you, or I, been in the trenches we should have required distilleries to get us over the top, but telegrams – not letters, telegrams – were duly sent to all the young Bancyfelin men still alive on the Western Front: 'ON NO ACCOUNT TOUCH RUM.'

My mother did not like my father repeating such stories, for, like the men in the trenches, she preferred to keep her head down. But the two rarely fell out, and when they did it was over the housekeeping. My father was a careful man who had saved up enough to buy the house where they started married life, but my mother was not good with money, and, as she often said defiantly, believed in buying the best. There was one big row in particular, which ended with her storming out into the night. 'She's gone, she's gone,' I cried, aged ten. 'Where can she go?' said my father mildly.

I remembered that when I read Gibbon later and came on the passage where he considers the impossibility for a man of fleeing the Empire. 'Beyond the frontiers, his anxious view could discover nothing, except the ocean, inhospitable deserts, hostile tribes of barbarians, of fierce manners and unknown language . . .' These might just as well have lain beyond the world of my parents. When she died, my mother's funeral cortege passed in less than three minutes the houses where she and my father were born, also the one she entered as a bride and in which she gave birth. I am now watching this house die.

For most people the houses they were born in died long ago, having been pulled down, or so changed or extended they no longer recognise them. To see a house die by degrees is usually the fate of someone living in a stately home who can no longer afford its upkeep. One old lady, living in one of these, a house that in 700 years had never once been sold or rented, told me, 'We'd hear a crash in the night as another ceiling fell in, and in the morning we'd turn the key on another room. And every time this happened we went on holiday for longer.'

Only my house, Cowin Villa, is like the one where Rupert Bear lived in the stories: it is small and once stood by itself in a lane which led to roads down which adventures lay. And it is just as it was when we left in 1946; at least it would be if you could see it. The retired farmer and his sister who bought it from my father changed nothing, and when they died it was sold at auction to someone who has never moved in. The result is that two years ago on one of my visits the garden met me at the gate, a wall of undergrowth seven feet high. Last summer the house itself began to disappear, and this summer it will be gone.

Nobody in the area knows who bought it, which tells you a great deal about twenty-first-century life in Wales (sixty years ago they would have known his father, and his grandfather, and what his aunt had got up to in the Austin 7 with the insurance man); some neighbours do not even know there is a house behind the leaves. But it is there, with the door my father built and the windows he installed, only it is like a house in fairy tale awaiting the horn blast that will bring it back to life, which in its case will never come. It has been a strange experience, seeing this take place.

For what it has meant is that time has stopped in a house I still think of as mine. When I go back, which I do obsessively ('Not again, not that blooming house where you were born,' my daughter used to groan in her teenage years), I am genuinely confused at how near everything is, but then I am looking through four year-old eyes. With the house as centre my childhood was perfectly contained in a 400-yard square.

Behind the brambles is a world I can conjure up, where the long tapeworm I passed and my mother retrieved is bobbing in the preserving jar above the water butt (we were a bit odd, I suppose, but then it was a talking point for visitors, whom I saw discussing it earnestly with my mother; I was proud of my tapeworm); my father's bayonet is rusting under the potatoes where I buried it to stop him disappearing with it for his Home Guard duties; a pig, a knife in its throat, leaps from a bench, scattering blood and its stealthy wartime slaughterers.

In front of the house, where there was a hedge then, there is now a line of enormous bungalows, with latticed windows and drives, of the sort my mother always coveted. 'They had a *beautiful* bungalow, but she left him,' she would pronounce in a puzzled way, the fact of the marriage break-up being less confusing to her than the leaving of such a house.

'Why don't you get married?' she said to me when I was in my thirties. 'You could have such fun.'

I was startled. 'Like what?'

'Well, wallpapering for a start.'

'I think there's more to marriage than that, don't you?'

'Not much,' she said.

The one house which survives from my time is sixty yards away, but unrecognisable. Then it was a whitewashed cottage in which an old lady lived, Mari Plaspant, a canny butter and egg merchant, who each night put a saucer of milk out to keep in with the fairies. Now it has solar panels on its roof, to keep in with the sun. And whereas then every man would have been a farm labourer or smallholder, a retired jet-fighter pilot now lives in my grandfather's old smallholding at Blaenffynon. Like the American pioneers, the English are pushing west in great numbers.

I know nobody living in these lanes, but I can fill them with the dead. With Arwyn Danybanc (for it was the Welsh habit to couple Christian and farm names), Arwyn Thomas, who at ten was so convinced he had been called to a chapel ministry that he honed his skills by praying and giving readings from the Bible over dead pullets which he buried in rabbit-holes, with my cousin Brenda, some years younger, conscripted as congregation.

With Twm Tynewydd, Tom Davies, jockey, village drunk (a position much contested), poacher, who every Sunday morning, hungover and dressed only in a nightshirt, would walk up the garden in his bare feet and thoughtfully kick the nanny-goat, turn, and walk in again. The nanny-goat never looked up from her grazing, but Tom, seeing my aunt Elsie, a Manchester girl, staring at him over the hedge as he went about this ritual, nodded and told her it was going to be a nice day. His wife was the fortune-teller.

With the Old Woman of the Crag of Night, Craig y Nos, that being the name of her house, a terrifying woman who, dressed all in black, stalked the lanes to escape her even more terrifying husband, whom no one ever saw. Once she hid all night from him under a bridge. Her name was Mrs Colegate.

I was frightened of her, as was my friend Spencer, but then we were frightened of everything, of shadows and wells and tree roots on the bank above the road which writhed (and still writhe) out of the earth like pythons. Spencer lived in the one cottage which had an English name, Umberton, but how it came by that we shall never know for now not a stone remains. Together we would check on the sick pony Jim, who, as he got older and weaker, came more and more slowly to our call, until there was the morning when we found his field empty. Years later I would stop my car and look over the gate, and would still be doing so except yet another bungalow stands in Jim's field.

The roll-call of the past continues. Here is my grandfather Philip Rogers, a neat, small-boned man, a horse whisperer who, mounted on a little pony, led the terrible cob stallions to their matings in farm after farm. 'And what sort of job was that for a man?' said my father. But the stallion man, or the Stallion Follower as D. J. Williams called him in his memoir *Yr Hen Dy Ffarm*, The Old Welsh Farmhouse, was a traditional, even notorious, figure in the Welsh countryside, when watching the matings was a spectator sport among the racier farmers' wives. An oil painting of one of these stallions survives; the horse, my uncle Trefor used to say, had the biggest balls he had ever seen on any living thing. My grandfather was a link with a long country past.

There was little else in the way of work he could have done, a chaff-cutter having taken off the thumb and first two fingers of his right hand when he was a boy. When the doctor came three days later all he could do was tidy up the stumps, but, balancing a pencil in these, Philip Rogers could still write.

He wrote englynion, intricate four-line poems with internal rhyme and assonance, a form dating back to medieval times, and described in the *Princeton Encyclopaedia of Poetry and Poetics* as 'the most sophisticated system of sound-patterning produced in any poetry in the world'. This is one of his: *Y Llafurwr*. The Farm Labourer.

> *Llafurwr yw'r dyn sy'n gaeth – i welliant*
> *Diwilliol ei arfaeth.*
> *Dyn o foes yn dwyn ei faeth*
> *Dan urdd Eden hardd eu odiaeth.*

What follows is not a direct translation, but it is as close as I can get to the sense and the form. Here, faintly, you may get some idea of the complexity and the miniaturisation.

> A workman yoked to the land – its care
> his in a great order.
> A man of honour, drawing succour
> In Eden from his expertise.

I showed his work to Professor Bobi Jones of Aberystwyth University, probably the best living Welsh poet, who said, 'These poems are very, very interesting, first because of what they represent in the history of Welsh verse. In the 200 years up to 1536 you had a tradition of classical poetry in Wales as good as anything in Europe, for you had a professional class of poets writing for their patrons, the gentry. Then in 1536, with the Act of Union, this came to an end, just like that. The gentry went to England, to seek their fortunes in London, and the poets were out of work. And then something amazing happened in Welsh poetry: the peasantry took over. People like your grandfather.

'This was a man, born in the second half of the nineteenth century, who, given the fact that his education would have been in the English language, would not have heard a word of Welsh spoken in school. So he would have known nothing of Welsh verse before the Methodist hymn-writers, yet he could write poems like these, which are much better than anything I expected. This is a working man inheriting a huge tradition solely by word of mouth. And here he is, exploring theological themes, writing two or three drafts of the same poem, a working man who was part of a great social culture.

'I should like to have met this man.'

In other words, this was no hedge poet. My cousin Brenda, who looked after my grandfather in his old age, came in one night to find him sitting in a chair by the fire, one arm crooked above his head and stabbing the air. For a moment she thought he had gone off his head until she realised what he was doing: he was counting syllables.

A cultured man in the Welsh language, my grandfather's English was a mystery as he was never heard to speak it, though it did allow him to read the deaths column in the *Western Mail*, something he studied with more and more interest the older he got. He died at ninety-four, which just showed, according to my father, the benefits of complete idleness.

My grandmother Margaret Rogers did most of the work on their smallholding. Her English was terrible, but, unlike her husband, she unleashed it every chance she got, telling one startled English visitor, 'You're nothing but a laughing jagged arse.' She had intended to say jackass. Most of her intellectual efforts went into outwitting her husband, selling eggs and butter on Carmarthen market (and pocketing some of the proceeds), also chickens, still warm, which she had killed (and plucked) before leaving the house when he wasn't looking. She was wily and kind, and there was no harm in her, apart from a weakness for country-house sales. They lived in a small house full of things that had once belonged to ruined squires, and death was everywhere: above the leatherette sofas, unblinking stuffed owls descended on rabbits, Landseer Highland prints showed cornered stags, and, where there was space, walls bristled with antelope horns and skulls. Only one oil painting struck a jarring note in this hecatomb. Life intruded, monstrous and gleaming, as the black stallion with the big balls trotted, and will trot forever, up a long white road.

Quite how my grandparents managed to survive, and bring up a family, I don't know, but then the same would have been true of all their neighbours, not that they would have noticed their own poverty or that of others. When everyone in a rural society is poor, with a few animals and a garden, poverty becomes invisible. Nobody owned anything, and mysterious landlords from the towns, usually shopkeepers, turned up once a year for the rent, in my grandfather's case a Mr Hodges from Swansea, of whom nothing is known, or will be known.

But there was one exception to the poverty. The lane led to a plateau on which lived a man so rich he was known as the Lord of the Seven Seas. Lord Kylsant, controller of the White Star Line, also the shipyard Harland and Wolff (until in 1930 he was sentenced to twelve months for issuing a false prospectus), towered over his tenants not only financially but physically, being six foot six inches in height. When his daughter married the heir to the earl of Coventry in 1919, Pallas Athene walked the streets of

Carmarthen, a head taller than her bridesmaids, and beautiful, and still walks them in the film that was made of her wedding. After her father's release from his gaol sentence forty men met the train at Sarnau Halt and, with ropes, pulled his car through the lanes and up the hill to his home at Coombe. It is a Cheshire Home now, to which in 1998, a very old lady, Pallas Athene returned to die in the house from which she was married.

I have often wondered what my life would have been like, had we not moved. Welsh would have been my first language for a start, and that would have changed everything. When I was growing up in the 1950s it would have been hard to over-estimate the sense of inferiority felt by Welsh-speakers. From 1895 on there had been departments of Welsh in the universities, but in these, as late as the 1930s, was the bizarre spectacle of Welsh lecturers, even a great poet like Williams Parry at Aberystwyth, addressing their Welsh students on Welsh literature – *in the English language*. What made it even more bizarre was that such men had written some of this literature themselves. Even in the 1950s, when I was at Carmarthen Grammar School, the Welsh-speaking boys from the country were a quiet species of their own, less sure of themselves than the English-speaking town boys.

'Who were absolutely cocky and confident,' said Fred Bevan, one of the former. 'I played rugby, and that did help, but I never got the captaincy of the school First XV. That went to a town boy.' Fred went on to play first-class rugby for Llanelly and Cardiff. The town boy did not.

A girl, also from the country, a chapel minister's daughter who was at the grammar school the same time as Fred and myself, remembered, 'When I look back there were so many hang-ups, hang-ups over the language, hang-ups over religion, hang-ups about sex, and especially hang-ups about the English. My father was always very disappointed if he found he liked an Englishman. That was why it was such a shock for me when I married my husband, a Londoner. He had no hang-ups at all.'

A popular Welsh pop-song of the 1960s had as refrain '*Dwy'i eisiau bod yn Sais*', 'I want to be an Englishman': it was meant as mockery, but it conveyed what many felt, who couldn't wait to get away and lose themselves in the anonymity of the larger English-speaking world. There was then a very real sense of the medieval German saying, '*Stadtluft macht frei*', 'a town's air makes a man free', in our case free of the chapels, particularly of the Methodists, the Stalinists of Nonconformity, which had closed the door on Welsh history and an intellectual past which had once been part of the European past, substituting for this the varnished pine and the pursed lips and the geography of the Middle East, its place names borrowed for our chapels. And free of the mothers whom these chapels had shaped, with their cult of respectability.

Of course it has all changed now, the Welsh themselves have seen to that, perhaps too late, but these were the certainties of the community in which I would have grown up. Yet even then, underneath it, the old, unkillable rout of a people who had survived conquest, poverty and the chapels, surged on.

My father was a remarkable story-teller, and, sixty years on, I can fill a field with the folk he conjured up for me, not figures of fiction but real men whom he had known. Listen, here he comes, the Perjurer, whose main delight was to display in pubs the bribe he had received for his evidence in a trial. 'Anybody here want to know the time? Hurr, hurr.' He had this dry cough. 'A gold watch, boys, for telling the *truth*. Hurr, hurr.'

But it was the old liars my father loved. Each village had what the writer D.J. Williams called its own Transparent Liar, a man who reigned in pubs and farmhouse kitchens. 'What was the Boer War like?' said a man in the Fox and Hounds at Bancyfelin. 'Let me tell you. Squish, squash, up to your knees in blood. Squish, squash, your friend's head under you, and you treading on it.' The joy was that he knew, and knew that his audience knew, that the fighting had been over long before he got to South Africa.

Men who boasted about their farmer employers. 'I tell you, that man is so strong, I've seen him uproot a whole tree, and stick it in a fire where it burned for a week.' A small pause. 'Or two.' Or about their own work experiences. 'Don't talk to me about digging the road. Me and Jo Bach, we went so deep down, near Whitland, the earth started going away under us, and there was this huge hole widening. Boys, I looked in and there was Australia, with people looking up at us. What did I do? I tapped the earth down fast because they were beginning to fall in.' The outside world was always a bit unreal.

Dan Saer, Dan the Carpenter, went to Vladivostok with the Allied Expeditionary Force, and brought a belt back to show he had been, but lost it. Ben the Blacksmith was filled up with beer by some Tory supporters, who then taught him one English phrase, 'Have a care', and planted him in the front row of the audience for Sir Alfred Mond, then Liberal MP for Carmarthen. Ben's villainous appearance (he was a gaunt man with black sidewhiskers) and his thundering 'Have a care' interjections so unnerved Mond that the MP cut short his speech and his electioneering. The blacksmith was known as 'Ben Have a Care' for the rest of his life.

Ah, so the quiet was. Before television, before radio, before all the things which pushed us to the side of our own lives, and in the process severed the generations, there was, as there had always been, just the one voice of the storyteller in firelight, in candlelight, in lamplight, the shadow of his gesturing arm moving on the wall.

I will never forget those Sunday nights when, with the other adults in chapel, there was just my father and me, my father unlocking his word-hoard, with the spoons and cutlery in front of us which my parents had been given as wedding presents and which each Sunday night I insisted he unpack from the white silk in their wooden presentation boxes. For some reason these fascinated me almost as much as the stories, his own and those he had heard.

From Joe Bach, who had survived the Dardanelles: 'I came round a bush and there he was, Johnny Turk. What did I do? What could I do? I gave him the bayonet. I can see him now as his false teeth fell out.' A little dried leaf of a man, Joe Bach could himself have been blown over by a spring breeze. And then the guarantee of truth: 'I think we've still got the teeth somewhere.' Stories like that, endlessly told so in time they became a corpus as complete as Homeric myth, only this was a Homeric myth centred on a few square miles of countryside. And all of it now blown away as though it had never been.

> *Yr hen wr llwyd o'r cornel*
> *Gan ei dad a glywodd chwedel*
> *A chan ei dad fe glywodd yntau,*
> *Ac ar ei ol mi gofiais innau.*

> The grey old man in the corner
> Of his father heard a story
> Which from his father he had heard,
> And after them I have remembered.

But there is another reason why all this is so vivid for me. My childhood amongst these people did not fade as other childhoods fade. It stopped dead when we moved away, so its outline is precise, not made hazy by growing up. I have only to walk through the Wardrobe to be in Narnia again, and I do it again and again. The only thing is I am alone there, all those who shared it being either dead or dispersed.

But then this happened.

Someone I had never met wrote to my publisher to say that my old friend Spencer Evans, after a lifetime travelling the world as a professional soldier, had come home, and wanted to get in touch. Promoted from the ranks, he had been a regimental sergeant major before being commissioned, and was a major before his career was cut short by multiple sclerosis. We hadn't met in sixty years.

I rang the number I had been given.

'Yes?'

'Major Spencer Evans?'

'Speaking.'

It was a clipped voice, one used to parade grounds. I said who I was, and there was a pause. When the voice spoke again it was soft.

'Hello, Beimo.'

After which two old-age pensioners found it impossible to speak.

When they could, and met, they talked, as you might expect, as though they couldn't stop. About what? About tree roots which writhed like pythons, and old ladies in black who stalked the roads, and wells, for the two had last met in a world of wells. 'Old Mari Plaspant she said to me, "Spencer, you bring me water, and I'll remember you in my will when I go." But when she did she hadn't.' And then, bemused English wives circling with cups of tea, Spencer remembered his manners and began to make small-talk about what it had been like to hide for five days with surveillance equipment in Crossmaglen.

But all that was a long way into the future, when, aged five, I moved with my parents and grandparents, and my life was changed forever. Did we go abroad? No. Did we go to another country? Well yes, in a way we did. We moved four miles up the road to the town of Carmarthen.

3

The Boy in the Striped Blazer

LAST YEAR I went back. The father of the young Polish family now renting our old house showed me round, and it was a puzzling experience, as such a return always is. Everything was so familiar yet at the same time so overwhelmingly different, it was as though I had once read about this place in a book I only half-remembered.

'You live here?'

'Yes,' I said.

'No.' He took a step back, as though I had said I had survived a gulag. 'Is terrible house.'

I stared at him crossly. A terrible house it might be, but for twenty-five years it was my terrible house. I was happy there.

I have lived in two houses in streets, each, by a freak, for a period of twenty-five years. One was in a street in Islington, where, across the gardens between us, one of my neighbours, a tall blonde woman, stood naked in the window every morning applying her make-up, and one hot summer afternoon copulating so noisily that, across two gardens, a Chinaman inspecting his hydrangeas ran in, arms over his head, as though the sky might fall on him at any moment; and I never even knew her name. The other house was in Union Street, Carmarthen, where none of my neighbours

ever stood naked in a window or sent anyone running indoors. But I knew all their names.

We, that is, my parents, my maternal grandparents and I, moved from the country in the cold early spring of 1947. Both my grandparents, and my father, would die in this house, and we were not to move until 1972, when my mother married again. In all that time, though I had gone to university in England, then worked in London, I thought of the house as my home, in fact I still do, and for twenty-five years, in varying hands and various coloured inks, wrote in the flyleaf of every book I bought, from *Five Go To Smugglers' Top* to *The Reader's Digest Repair Manual*, 'Byron Rogers, 6 Union Street'; 'Byron D. Rogers'; 'B.D. Rogers'. Proudly I brought girls home here.

It did not occur to me not to ask them, though it must have been a bit of a shock to some of them as they, one from a Tudor stately home, another from a mews cottage in Belgravia, found themselves being ushered into a house of a sort they had never seen outside the gritty film documentaries of the 1930s, let alone entered. No. 6 Union Street did not have an indoor lavatory, and as late as the 1970s a chamber-pot, washed daily, sat under every bed. Such details would have been too incredible to figure in the worried inventories of their mamas. 'Was there a drive?' asked one, she really did. 'Darling, you must never forget that when you marry you are marrying for all of us.' An earl's daughter, whose ancestors had introduced the thumbscrew to Scotland, her concerns were still those of an edgy aristocracy in the late Middle Ages.

6 Union Street was my home. It did not even occur to me to ask any of them what they made of it, and it is only now in my sixties that I see it as those long-ago girls must have seen it, as a small terraced house in a small terraced street.

The street had been built in the early nineteenth century to house the less well-off officers in the nearby garrison, whose richer colleagues occupied the rather grand tree-lined terrace at its foot. Carmarthen in its time had known many garrisons.

First there were the Romans in the red-brick fort which they had built, as they usually did, in full view of the tribe, the Demetae, nervously occupying the hill fort on Merlin's Hill, to the east of the present town; in Carmarthen the overlords have always relied on geographical features to awe the locals. Long after the Romans, the town gibbet stood on a hill where it could be seen from all sides until in 1804, after the hanging of an old man who had stolen a horse, a splendid individual (described as 'a wretch' in the town history) cut it down and made it into a bed. The holding of two fingers up to authority is the old Carmarthen way of those with nothing to lose.

But there is another old Carmarthen way, energetically pursued by those with a great deal to lose. This is the town recorder welcoming the Duke of Beaufort, Lord President of Wales, in 1684, the Duke having turned up with his son:

> But our joys must not be wholly laid out for your Grace. Part is due to the additional satisfaction we conceive at the presence of your noble son, who is heir even in your life of your incomparable virtues. As that may seem a paradox in law, so 'twill appear as high a contradiction in reason, that though your Grace had entirely unto his Lordship your excellent endowments, yet notwithstanding that bounty, your own original stock and abundance is not in the least impaired or diminished.

Were the chief executive of Tesco to turn up today, he would be similarly greeted by the chairman of a county council which has allowed the company to build three supermarkets in the town in twenty-five years, one in the centre, one on the site of a medieval friary, and the third so big it needed a whole rugby pitch to accommodate it. It is just that the overlords have changed.

There was the English castle built on a bluff above the bridge to dominate the approaches to Carmarthen, the garrison of which during the great Welsh rebellion of Owain Glyndwr included the poet Chaucer's two sons. That site became the county gaol, then the offices of the county council, from which the town is now under a state of permanent siege as it gets torn down to accommodate the sheds of Debenhams. And Boots. And Marks & Spencer. And all the others in the rollcall of urban corporate despair.

All the Welsh past was here, its earliest manuscripts collected in the town priory, its artefacts, including the gravestone of a king for whom Arthur might have been a living memory, all cared for by local antiquarians. For men once loved this place, its alleys and its views, which is now a trading post of sheds and pedestrian precincts, a nowhere town, one just like a hundred others, successive councils having, like the Khmer Rouge, tried to erase that past.

To remind people of how awful that past was they have set up pictorial reconstructions, in one of which a soldier in some long-demolished alley is about to ravish a woman. Ravish is perhaps too strong a word, as she is pulling up her dress to be of some help, and the soldier is clearly an exponent of safe sex. 'It makes you proud to come from this town,' said a local builder. 'That man is in full chain mail.'

But one thing has not been pulled down. The early Victorian

barracks, built in the shadow of a Peninsular war hero's column (which at one stage the council cut in half, saying it was taking the stones into care, but, in the outcry, was obliged to restore), is still there, for not even Carmarthenshire County Council can prise the hands of the English military from anything it has ever owned. But the officers have long gone from Union Street.

I was five, watching as the children crowded round to watch my toys being unloaded, what remained of the five-foot-long *Queen Mary*, and the wooden toys my father had made for me. But I was even more fascinated than they, for until then I had no idea the world had so many children in it. The only thing was, I couldn't understand a word they said. They spoke in English, so we stared at each other like two alien but perfectly friendly life forms.

This experience was not unique in Wales as the drift to the towns gathered momentum after the War. On his first afternoon in Carmarthen my friend Martin Walters was directed by his father to go out and play with the boy next door. A few minutes later he was back, genuinely worried. *'Hey, mae rhywbeth yn bod ar y boi na.'* Hey, there's something wrong with that boy. Martin, also five, had, like me, encountered the English language. But, again like me, he was up and swarming all over it within weeks; small children can do that.

Only in the process we disinherited ourselves.

We both became Carmarthen boys. That is to say, we came to believe that Welsh speakers were an inferior people, a belief underwritten by our time at the Queen Elizabeth Grammar School. There English was the language of education and they called the Welsh-speaking Welsh of the countryside 'boskins', a word you will not find in any dictionary. It survives only in such

eighteenth-century archaisms as 'bosky wood', and they were the people of the woods, *pobol y goedwig*. And we, whatever we were (we were a bit hazy on this), we were their superiors, as we had been since the foundation of the Norman town.

The first inhabitants of this were English, drawn by what would draw them to all outposts of the Empire, the prospect of lording it over the native population. Only they could live in towns (at one point it was a capital offence for any Welshman to be found overnight in Caernarvon). Only they could hold markets within fifteen miles. Seven hundred years on, my generation and I, we are, or were, the last colonials.

I never lost my Welsh, it was just that, to survive in the playgrounds, I didn't tell anyone. Now the new official bilingual employment policies have done away with the old colonial attitudes (56 per cent of Carmarthen is employed by the state in its various forms), and the ambitious parents of my time who brought their children up not to speak Welsh have given way to even more ambitious parents who have enrolled their children in Welsh-language schools. The tide has run out for us.

The house in the street we rented from two bachelor brothers who ran the carpentry firm for which my father worked; we were not to own it until after he died in 1968. It had a large cellar, one room of which was a bunker into which we could shovel the free coal to which, following a colliery accident, my grandfather was entitled, and which the Coal Board delivered in lorry loads, five tons at a time, tipping this onto the road and pavement. Today, in Cromwell's phrase, we would have been as chaff to the chariot wheels of the Environmental Health lot, but amazingly neither the authorities nor our neighbours complained. The other room was my father's workshop. Here he made curved Regency sideboards in mahogany, Bible chests in oak, and, for me, twelve model aircraft, three racing trolleys and a sledge.

Above in the terrible house there were two downstairs rooms, and a large kitchen extension which meant our middle room had no outside window, so, with the fire lit, I could sit there alone, read ghost stories and feel safe. Above were two bedrooms and, above these, two large attic rooms with skylights, from which, one moonlit night, my parents and I watched, entranced, as a local pharmacist went mad.

A huge, friendly man who had made throat pastilles for Caruso, he had already shown signs of what was to come by driving his wife to Tenby in their grand Humber Super Snipe in second gear all the way, with the heating full on and the windows shut, on the hottest day of the year. He had also in a speech at the local girls' grammar school prizegiving advised his teenaged listeners to marry a rugby player ('Girls, you will never regret it, you will be marrying a safe pair of hands'). That night he was smashing bottles and singing the Rose of Tralee. Next day it took six police-men to carry him away on a stretcher, strapped and snoring, to the great Gothic lunatic asylum on the hill, which served three counties and, with a population of close on 2,000, one-sixth the size of Carmarthen, was a town in its own right.

Number 6 Union Street, lacking an indoor lavatory, had a whitewashed privy at the end of the garden, in which, perched, I read by candlelight. There wasn't much room in our garden. It was small to start with, but it also contained the household furniture my father had allowed his in-laws to bring when they moved in with us. Why it wasn't thrown away I don't know; perhaps my father was salvaging their pride, perhaps he hoped wistfully that one day they might move out again. But it meant there were tables and cupboards piled on top of each other, peeling and rotten, into which I could climb and play at castles and pirates with my friends. When I got older I thought them an eyesore, and, at fifteen, when the grown-ups were out, I took an axe to the lot. And nobody said a word, that was the odd thing. But I couldn't destroy our air-raid shelter.

This, the only one in the street, and, I gather, one of only two in all Carmarthen, was the only private air-raid shelter I have ever seen. It had been built of brick and reinforced concrete by the two brothers, only they, who made coffins, doors, windows with ruler and tape, had forgotten to run either around the hips of the sister who kept house for them. The result was that on a trial run she got stuck in the entrance. They then knocked a large hole from the pantry into the shelter, but she could never be persuaded to use this again, so it was as well that Carmarthen, like Aberystwyth, was never bombed. The writer Caradoc Evans recorded in his wartime diary, 'Mary Tycanol tells me that Hitler was in college in Aberystwyth. That much is certain. Miss Arnold corroborates. O yes, everyone knows that Hitler was in college in Aberystwyth. He gave special orders that, though London be razed, Aberystwyth must be saved . . .' The Welsh have an unshakable sense of their own importance. Carmarthen, I was told, was not bombed on account of the mist which rose out of the river, so the Luftwaffe couldn't find it, though they were searching all the time.

<hr />

There were twenty-seven houses in our street, which would have given it a population of close on a hundred, perhaps more, for some lived in rented rooms, a Victorian touch, the householders having retreated to the dampness of their cellars and their airless attics. This was a bit of a shock to anyone encountering it for the first time.

Martin Walters, he who had reeled from his first contact with English-speakers, remembers being asked home by a boy who lived in Union Street. 'We went in and he opened this door, and all I could see was steps leading down into darkness. He went first, it didn't seem to bother him, and I groped my way behind him. When we got to the bottom the only light I could see came from a grating. Good God, we were in a bloody dungeon. And then this mass of shadow moved. "Do you take sugar and milk, Martin?" It was his mother. There were people living in Union Street then who must have had eyes like cats.'

There must again have been poverty, not that I noticed, but I noticed everything else. Never before had I known so much about

so many, and I never would again; this was the only time in my life
when I was part of a community.

It was a very strange little community. I am looking at a group
photograph taken in a graveyard at the time of the street party for
the Coronation of 1953. I am in one of the front rows, my mother
at the back looking grim, so I must have done something wrong.
But you wouldn't notice that; your attention would be drawn to a
line of boys, teenagers, all in women's dresses, bang in the centre of
the group, and to one of these in particular. Most of them look
embarrassed, but one of them, rouged and mascaraed, in a white
wedding dress with a tiara on his head, looks like the Queen of the
May. In fact he looks quite beautiful. He would have been about
fifteen then, and had dragooned his brother and their friends into
the cross-dressing which was his main interest, then somehow got
the Mayor of Carmarthen to judge the line-up, which of course he
won. And nobody thought it in the least odd.

I was eleven and I knew the names of everyone in the photograph (and, which was far more important, those of their dogs). I
knew what the men did for a living; they were mechanics, clerks (a

job description as antique as shepherd now), a tin-man (who repaired, and made, saucepans, also a drum for me), a bus driver whose wife was a bus-conductress, a butcher, a grocer and, a moment of social history, in those twenty-seven households there were four men who worked on the railway, where now I doubt four in the whole town do.

I knew who owned cars (there were three, where now they are parked bumper to bumper); I knew the causes of death: three from TB, and one, tragic, suicide. There were no divorces. I knew all this because, before the coming of television, I listened to the talk in our kitchen, and my mother, like all the other mothers gossiping on doorsteps and over the garden walls for periods of up to an hour at a time, was part of a clearing house of information more efficient than GCHQ at Cheltenham. In West Wales men feared the mothers (even the supernatural hounds of terror were called *Cwn Bendith y Mamau*, Dogs of the Blessing of the Mothers), for nothing happened without the knowledge of these women. But now they are dispersed into jobs, the garden walls untenanted, and adulterers can writhe easy in their Ford Mondeos, knowing the gossip, which in my time could name them and the laybys in which they parked, is stilled forever. Ah, but once ...

'Have you heard ... isn't it awful ... it's the children I feel sorry for ... how she has the face ... how he has the face ... and the doctor said ...' But I never heard what the doctor said. 'What's that boy doing there? Why don't you go out to play? I didn't realise he was there. Honestly.'

Only one thing to my knowledge stunned the mothers, and that was when a tramp, having sought, and presumably been refused, alms, showed his feelings by walking the length of the street with his 'you know what, his ...' hanging out, or, if I interpreted the intakes of breath aright, sticking out. This was a talking point for weeks. 'Did you see . . . I couldn't believe my eyes . . . Where were you, I'd just come back from town . . . Mrs Jones told me . . . Ooh, those Catholics. Catholics. Catholics.'

————◆◆————

For Union Street ended in a Catholic church built in the middle of the nineteenth century, the first in the town since the Reformation, with a presbytery, a school and a convent, the full set, apart from the Inquisition. What made this even more extraordinary was that its immediate neighbour, like an opposing guard at a frontier crossing, was the chapel of Cromwell's old sect, the Independents. Together they made the top of the street into a religious Checkpoint Charlie, through which we children breezed.

Not into the school playground; we were too terrified of the nuns, one of whom, a short scrubbed woman in rimless glasses, was said to own, and use, a metal cane. Our playground was the church itself. We took tea with the merry little brother who cooked for the priests, knocked conkers from the great chestnut tree among the graves, crossed ourselves with holy water, for the Catholic church, unlike the grim Independent chapel, was never locked. We felt able to do this because the church, with its little painted statues (the Virgin Mary always in sky blue) and its strange smells, seemed a stage production in itself, added to which was the fact that its congregation included nobody our parents knew, so there could be no retribution. In Carmarthen the Catholics were the children of Irish immigrants, also the last recusants among the old county families, and some European refugees, so their church was an alien place. We did not realise then that we were playing in our own past.

I didn't notice until this year that the stoup at the foot of its steps came from a thirteenth-century chapel, the site of which, out

63

in the fields, has been long lost. When Tesco tore into the foundations of the friary, where Tudur Aled, one of the great Welsh poets, was buried, along with the father of Henry VII, king of England, the broken bones turned up by the bulldozers, 'monks (miscellaneous)', came namelessly home to be interred in the Catholic graveyard at the top of the street, though no gravestone records this, just a block of green grass. There was so much we didn't know.

Still, we knew all about our neighbours. I knew what their houses were like inside, for, having spent so much time in my grandfather's company, as a small boy I called on the old. Some I didn't call on, like those who never came out at all, the only evidence of their existence a white hand raising and lowering a cloth blind.

But listen, here she comes, tip tap tippity tap on high heels, my particular favourite, the lady from No. 9, a small golden person whose smile lit up the street for me as she passed. Only she got pregnant, married a little limping man, almost as small as she, and they had to move in with her mother. Within a year or two my friend was dead of cancer, and, within another couple of years, the little limping widower had cut his wrists, drunk disinfectant, then hanged himself in his haste to get out of a world that contained his mother-in-law, who then brought up the little girl.

I came on their grave in St David's churchyard, a couple of streets away, the church, because of structural problems, kept locked, awaiting the day when the Church in Wales has managed to amass the money to pull it down. I know many names here ('You know how long you've been away,' someone told me, 'when you find you know more people in graveyards than outside them'). Here is Mrs Paige from No. 1, who had a red setter, Mrs Griffiths

from No. 3, who had a dalmatian which ignored me. And here is the little laughing boy I remember who is buried here, aged eight, having died by degrees of cancer, whose mother told me something I will never forget. 'At least we'll always know where he is.'

And Delme Davies, 'tradesman of this town, 1937–2000'. I never exchanged a greeting with him, but I remember him, for once this was a leader of men. When I was seven I saw him, aged twelve or thereabouts, leading his gang across Carmarthen Park. Only this wasn't a gang, this was a small army of boys, fifty or more of them with bows and catapults and sticks, and they had flags, all of them streaming across the rugby pitch with the terrible disorder of a medieval charge. For these, you must remember, were boys who had lived through the War and knew about organisation. Where they had come from, and where they were going, I have no idea, but I never forgot it: it was like that moment in Conan Doyle when a hermit, hiding behind a rock, sees the coming of the Huns. Attila, tradesman of this town.

And here too is 'Alan Raymond Jones, Worthy of Remembrance'. A Teddy Boy at school, when the headmaster, lacking Stalin's expertise in airbrushing out his enemies, sent him home whenever a photographer called, he was a Teddy Boy at the end when every hymn at his funeral was from his own rock 'n' roll collection. I wrote his memorial address, for I had known him for almost sixty years, using such Carmarthen slang as *mush*, pronounced 'moosh', the old Romany word for man, only the vicar who read it pronounced it as 'mush', an instruction to dog teams in the Arctic.

As I walk between the rows of black marble I am struck by how peaceful a place this is, though not to all. I remember the memo I once saw from an editor of the *Sunday Express* to his features editor about the column I was writing for the paper in the 1980s: 'Try to keep him out of graveyards in future. Given the age of our readership, these are a bit too close to home.'

----◆-◆----

I am walking in our street now. The gate pillar has gone at the foot of the drive to the Catholic church, against which my old friend Peter Davies and I used to play cricket on summer evenings. We used a tennis ball, knocking up scores well into the hundreds, hour after hour, evening after evening, until the shadows lengthened, and we could pretend it had gone into Miss Protheroe's garden, so we could steal the apples she never picked.

You could play anywhere in the street then, with a cardboard box as a wicket, and the grown-ups joined in. Once Jack Evans the grocer drove a ball through a window. 'Which of you ...?' the old gentleman, whose house it was, had burst out, but then he stopped, seeing the bat in the hands of his son-in-law, and it was a lovely moment, neither knowing what to say next. I loved our street. Where children now get driven to each others' houses to play, all I needed to do was step outside our front door.

At night I listened. Neighbours called, and the grown-ups sat round the fire telling stories as they had always done. There was Uncle Gwyn and the tomcat. My mother's brother, working as a farm servant, was starved by his employer's wife, as most Welsh servants were in the 1920s. Increasingly desperate, he broke into the larder one Sunday night, ate the cold family joint when they were in chapel, then, in a moment of inspiration, put the tomcat in and closed the door. Later, dozing in his bleak little bedroom, he heard shouts and screeches all over the house. There were other tomcats. I heard about my father's cousin being trained for the ministry who, also fed up by the fact that his landlady fed her huge tom better than her lodgers, applied some turps to the poor animal's backside as it sat in front of the fire. For a while nothing happened, then as the warmth got to it the tail began to move like a metronome, quicker and quicker, until *waaaark*. The landlady happened to be in the room as the cat rose vertically in the air, then raced around the flat surfaces, shattering vases and a figure of Garibaldi. There was a cruel, often macabre, edge to these tales.

I listened as they talked about the gentleman farmer who, obsessed by hanging, offered his services to all the hangmen of his day and had them to stay. Their portraits lined his front room, and, to make them feel even more at home, so did the nooses they had used. He lived in the farm called Fern Hill which Dylan Thomas celebrated in verse as a vision of childhood, not hanging. They talked about Dylan Thomas too, whose wife my father's apprentice, then aged twelve, saw walk along the foreshore, dropping her clothes, until, stark naked, she entered the tide. The boy, one of a group which had been smoking on the rocks, said at that point they all went nervously home, for this was West Wales in the early 1950s, with naked women thin on the ground.

And then the listening stopped. I can remember the first television set in the street, when I had only to knock to be allowed in to watch, which sounds extraordinary now. Imagine the kindness of a family which saw nothing odd in a teenager coming in out of the night, asking to see the Wednesday Play. The family included a daughter my age, who in her early teens looked like a sultry Italian starlet, so I would watch, one eye on her, the other on wobbly eyed Margaret Tyzack who specialised in middle-class hysterics, which was what Wednesday Plays were about. Margaret, who was usually shrieking, shrieked, the sultry one, who was usually grumbling, grumbled, and time passed agreeably.

It passed agreeably in our cricket marathons as well, except that Peter Davies now had an ambition to join the police force. The trouble was his height. When we were in our teens he would write to constabulary after constabulary, and back came forms he would read through until the portcullis crashed down. Five foot nine. Five foot eight. But there was the night he excitedly showed me the form from the Nottingham force, five foot seven and a half inches, I think it was. Peter was then five foot seven, and it was like that moment in the Polish film *Kanal* when the people escaping through the sewers see daylight, only to turn a corner and see the tunnel ending in a metal grille, for Peter never did grow that last half-inch. It was so sad. I grew taller and taller, and Peter became a grocery delivery boy for his uncle, the window smasher, then a male nurse.

And I am passing the field where one hot afternoon one of the older girls got Elfyn Thomas and myself, both aged seven, to play doctors. Elfyn later became the pop singer Elvin Leroy (and his sister one of the Brotherhood of Man), but that afternoon we were both patients, and the girl was the doctor. She got us to take our shirts off, then lie down and close our eyes, at which point the treatment started. This consisted, first Elfyn, then me, of having our nipples stroked with grass stalks, which was nice. She stroked, the sun beat down, and Elfyn and I passed into a sort of dream. I think I fell asleep at one point.

<hr />

Beyond the street there were other, riskier, playgrounds like the Park, and, beyond this, fields where we encountered adult imponderables like courting couples and farmers. We built dens inside hedges, weaving branches through each other until, once inside, we were almost invisible. Not that the courting couples would have noticed; once they had lain down among the reeds they would not have noticed anything. On one occasion, five yards from two small boys, there were big white legs and, though puzzled and bored, we stayed stock still for what might have been a week, though it was probably half an hour, before it started to rain and the white legs were put away like cricket stumps. The farmers, more observant than courting couples, were always a threat. 'Damn you, I'll have the police on you, d'you hear?'

Aged twelve, I was bought a bow with metal-tipped arrows, with one of which I almost transfixed a Mrs Branch. She was a bit strange, Mrs Branch, and wore so much make-up that a bulky geisha walked the streets of Carmarthen. She had a bull terrier, whose arse she wiped vigorously with tissues after it had shat, though she didn't bother to pick up the shit. She and the dog were about this curious ritual against a tree across the road from the Park when the wind caught the arrow I had shot into the air, and I suddenly realised it was moving out over the railings, out over the road. It slapped into the ground inches from the two of them. When I got there Mrs Branch was standing with the arrow in her hand, and I could see a world about to fill with policemen, teachers, parents. But no, she didn't say anything, she just handed the arrow over, smiled, in so far as she could smile, and she and the dog walked away. Like William Brown, I found in childhood that the strange were no trouble at all.

About this time my cousin David, who lived in Bath, passed on the plans for a model glider he had been given by his friend Flagg, who worked for the aircraft company English Electric. Only these were no ordinary plans. They were the plans for a top-secret jet fighter, the P1. Do you understand? In the early 1950s a small boy in Wales had in his possession the exact configuration of wing sweep and span, and the overall outline, of what would become the Lightning, then the plane with the fastest rate of climb in the world. Had I turned up at the Soviet Embassy with those, it would have been 'tovarich, tovarich' all the way.

I knew something about that rate of climb. For these gliders were not launched by hand, they hurtled into the sky, or at least sometimes they did. My father built them for me in solid balsa, with a nail fixed at a certain angle into the fuselage so a brass ring could be fitted to this. The ring was attached to six feet of thick elastic leading to a wooden stake hammered into the ground, so it was a brutal catapult launch. When you got the angle just right... whoosh. One moment it was in your hand, the next moment there was a white dot in a blue sky, for the gliders were so aerodynamically perfect they could go for a hundred yards or more, and I lost a few in the undergrowth of the vicarage garden next to the Park. But when you got the angle of launch wrong, given the power of the thing, it was splinters in the grass. Which was why, after making twelve, my father called it a day.

There were four lavatories in Carmarthen Park, every inch of which was covered in writing, or at least in the Gents they were. Above the urinal stalls was poetry ('There was a priest, the dirty beast/His name was Alexander . . .'). In the cubicles where scribes might sit at ease it was prose, lengthy reminiscence that wasted no time on exegesis, or on realism come to that ('I met this woman by a bus-stop. She asked me if I wanted a fuck. I said, "Well, I've got half an hour"'). Every now and again the council would paint over the chapters like Cromwellian troopers in a church, and when that didn't work they rough-cast the walls, so the scribes took to the sills where, because of the constraints of space, the writing acquired an urgency. 'What a town, 9 years I been here and no cock-fun.' In the end the council just turned the keys, and time stopped in the lavatories, just as it stopped in the tombs in the Valley of the Kings. They still stand locked, awaiting the archaeologists.

I learnt new words in Carmarthen Park. One afternoon I heard the big boys use the word fucking, and, this being new to me, asked what it meant, which made them fall about. But then one took pity on me and said it was what happened when a boy and girl wrestled on the ground. Ah . . . As it turned out, a little later I must have annoyed one of the older girls, for she pinned me to the ground and pulled my nose. When I got home my mother had a visitor, one of the ladies from her chapel. 'So this is your boy. And what have you been up to today, young man?'

You can see it coming, can't you?

They were sitting with cups of tea on their knees, though not for long. 'We played cricket, only we lost the ball,' I said politely. 'So this afternoon I have been fucking in Carmarthen Park.'

But there is another afternoon, one as golden now as it was then. 5 April 1949, was my birthday; I was seven. When I came in from play I found my mother had baked home-made buns, the big heavy ones. My aunt Mary had called, leaving me a copy of *Folk Tales of Wales* by Eirwen Jones, illustrated by Alfred Bestall, the Rupert man. Then a little later my father came home from work, bringing a flagon of farm buttermilk made that day. I can remember thinking, on my fourth bun and second folk tale, this is about as good as it gets. And it was.

But then, a few weeks earlier, I had fallen in love.

———◆———

It is 1967, and in a phone box on the outskirts of an industrial Welsh town a man is dialling a number. He is very nervous, for he thinks this is the most important call he will ever make. He is twenty-six, and is hoping that the phone will not be picked up. But it is.

'Hello.' It is a bright little voice.

'Hello, yes. Is that ...?' No matter what the name is, she will be a grandmother by now.

'Yes, that's me, or was. Who's that?'

'This is Byron Rogers.'

'Who?'

'We were in school together.'

'Which school was that?'

'The Model in Carmarthen, I just happened to be in the area.'

There is a pause, then, 'Were you a friend of Robert and Roger Thomas?'

And of Graham Jones. And Alan Jones. And Ynysbaddaden Penkawr Jones. I am not Prince Hamlet, nor was meant to be, am an attendant lord ...

'Yes, I suppose I was.'

'Yes, you had a striped blazer.'

--------◆◆◆--------

For sixteen years I was in love with her, totally, obsessively in love. From the age of six until I was eleven I had seen her every day at school, and every day the room we sat in, like Camelot at Pentecost, was bathed in light. In the years which followed I saw her three times. No matter.

I am sixty-seven now, yet when I walk past her house it still means something to me, even though this makes me smile for it is more than half a century since she lived in the little semi-detached built at the end of the War on a ridge above the road.

For it is not true what Donne wrote in his seducer's charter, *The Ecstasy.*

> So must pure lovers' souls descend
> T'affections, and to faculties
> Which sense may reach and apprehend,
> Else a great Prince in prison lies.

When none of this happens, when no intimacy of any kind is pursued and hands do not even touch, a vast ship gets assembled in space which, freed of the limits put on it by gravity, acquires a size and a speed that are without limit. For me the assembling began on a spring morning in 1949, in Standard One of the Model School. It was all because of something she did.

When I started school, being able to speak English only with difficulty, I found myself becalmed in the lower forms, puzzling as to what the goblins, not a Welsh-speaker amongst them, were saying in our reading books. But I then began to understand what the goblins said, and as a result was moved up a class in mid-term, into the Big School. Here there was more structure to the lessons and no goblins, but one morning, out of nowhere, there was gym.

Now for some reason the Model provided gym-shoes for its pupils, black shoes passed on from one year to the next. The first time these were produced I crowded round the big cardboard box with the others, picked a pair, hoping they would fit (for all shoes I had been given previously had of course fitted), and took them to the back of the class where I sat quietly, staring at them as though they might explode. For the gym-shoes had laces. I had never tied laces; if you were an only child in Wales at that time, and a pretty little boy, there was no need, it was done for you by your mother. A former professor of history at the University of York told me that, having taught him how to shoot and read maps and put up tents, the British Army progressed to the really important stuff, and taught him how to tie his shoelaces just in time for D-Day.

I put the gym-shoes on, I could do that, and sat there, moving my feet around in them, sunk in misery. Had I appealed for help, had I put my hand up, I should have been the laughing stock of the school for the rest of my time there, like the little girl my wife remembered who cried out as she came awake on her first morning in a dormitory at Malvern Girls' College, 'I'm awake now, ready for my tea', and was forever afterwards known as Ready for My Tea. When you are small, and in the ruthless company of children your own age, you do not draw attention to yourself.

And then she was there, clucking at my foolishness. Without a word she knelt and laced the gym-shoes fiercely, tugging at them, then smiling. She had little red hands with cracks in them; sixty years on I can see those hands now. And that was it. I was six years old, and I was in love.

There can be no doubt that she was a remarkable little girl, for she had noticed, at a time when small children do not notice a great deal, and had sensed what was happening. Think what she might have done. She could have ignored me, or she could have drawn the class's attention and advanced her popularity. Instead of which, and this was what was so startling, she quietly helped me. It would be impossible to forget such kindness, and such tact. From then on I was hers.

She tied my laces for something like a fortnight, and then said, bossily, 'Now you're going to have to do this yourself from now on.' Which I did, for by then I had learned how, though I hadn't told her.

I had not thought about her at first, she was just one of the girls, but afterwards I thought about little else, more than about toys or books or, my new interest, Heinz Scotch Broth. Her desk in class was under a poster of some real brown leaves gummed to a painted landscape, so for years I associated autumn with her. She wore a dark green jerkin that zipped up, and a skirt in Campbell tartan. I have a school photograph of her in front of me as I write this. She has fair hair which she wears in two short pigtails, and is grinning, but what makes the grin so mischievous is that she has a full lower lip that protrudes slightly: she looks like a young Julie Christie. She was beautiful.

She was also a tough little girl. She climbed trees and pushed the boys, and was naughty. Her friend Eirwen Thomas tells me that when a student came on teaching practice and gave us a geography lesson on fishing in Milford Haven, the only geography lesson we had in all our time in the Model, the two of them deliberately wrote nonsense in their exercise books just to get him into trouble with his supervisors. Mermaids combed their hair in Cardigan Bay, sharks cruised, penguins strutted, great whales held sports days.

And of course she was bright, which mattered intensely. In the end of term exams she came second, I was top, but I daydreamed that we might rule together like William and Mary over the spelling tests, soaring over the traditional ditches like *receive* and *licensed*, and over the arithmetic we called Problems, over baths which forever filled and were emptied of water, and cellars, and passing trains. I saw us concocting together short, unbeatable essays about holidays and pets and the views from our respective bedroom windows.

Why didn't I tell her? What could I have told her? When the hero kissed the heroine in films I groaned, for even had we wanted to there was absolutely nothing we could have done together; it was enough just being in the same room as her, when I could treasure her occasional request for a loan of my rubber or my Derwentwater purple pencil. The rest of the school was a backcloth, though an interesting one.

Towards the end of our time there the head boy, adolescent at the age of eleven, fell in love with one of the girls, and would stand outside her house at night like a dog in heat, though she never came out. If asked, for he was a generous boy, he would show you his pubic hair and his big new dick in the boys' lavatory. Sometimes there was a queue. 'No, you've seen it. Come on, I can't stand here all day.' One of the big girls acquired a bust, but we just thought her fat.

Some of us had only just emerged from a long battle against our bodily functions, one boy in particular still fighting a rearguard action so desperate that when we were drawn up in lines in the playground none of us would stand behind him. Once he peed on the floor in class, then, seeing my horrified face, said, 'Don't worry, watch me.' He poured his inkwell into the puddle and stuck up his hand. 'Please miss, can I get a mop? I've spilt some ink.'

She would have known nothing about any of this, boys to her and the other girls being little more than a nuisance. They ignored us most of the time, while they sent catty little notes to each other in class. 'Pam Phillips thinks you've got piggy eyes.' That was written in her hand, and, dear God, I kept it for years. There was just one night when we were thrown together. What follows is as close to what actually happened as I can make it.

It was a June evening, and with two twin brothers I was in an area of land we called the Gorse. In the 1950s the fields were very near in Carmarthen, which now have long been built over, but then, once beyond the houses, we were where the writ of the grown-ups did not run, something that was at once exhilarating and dangerous. So we had been crouching in the reeds, ever since we had heard voices in the next field. Both twins would end up working for NASA, but that evening we were in the Middle Ages, where someone was always laying claim to something.

The voices were on the gate now, girls' voices, and as I raised my head I could see one of them already in the field. Her dark hair in ringlets and tied in a great red bow, for she was the girl with whom the Head Boy fell in love, she looked out of place among mud and hedges. But the other was laughing and, standing on the gate, was rocking it, holding on with both hands. I knew those hands.

'I can see you ...'

'Where?'

'There, among the reeds.'

First I, then the twins, stood up. 'In their macks,' said the dark girl. 'In their new macks.'

The twins looked at each other and for a moment were overwhelmed. One pulled out a small and grubby handkerchief and began to rub at the mud, but all this did was rearrange it in wild, circular patterns.

'Don't do that,' said the fair girl. 'Wait until it dries, then you can brush it off. Have you done your homework?'

'Yes,' said the twin.

'What did you get for the one about the sacks of potatoes?'

'Six and two-thirds, him and me.' He nodded at his brother. 'Both.'

The dark girl said nothing, for school was not one of her interests. I too said nothing, for I hadn't been able to do that one. 'We heard some shouting before you came,' I said to change the subject. 'Who was that?'

'Two boys from the grammar school,' said the fair girl. 'You know, that boy from the garage and his friend. They've got a bow and arrows, they were making the arrows stick in trees.'

'They threw stones at him last week,' said Little Twin, so called because his head was slightly smaller than his brother's. That apart, they were remarkably similar, both big and clumsy as hippos, and both of them very bright, the worst possible combination in childhood. Everyone bullied them. 'They threw him in the gutter. My mother wanted to go round and see his father, but Dad said he might want to change his car this summer.'

'Let's play something,' said the fair girl.

'Touch.'

'No, it's too wet round here,' said the dark one.

'All right then, hide and seek.'

'So long as we get away from the pond.'

'Can we play?' asks Big Twin. In their short lives he and his brother had known much rejection; they will always remember the playgrounds, are probably remembering them now among the rockets.

'Oh yes,' said the fair girl. 'All three boys stand in a line. Eeny meeny miney mo, catch a nigger by his toe.' For all this was long ago. 'Eeny meeney miney mo.' The little finger was pointing at me. 'You're IT. Go on, close your eyes, and count to a hundred.'

'And no counting in your head. Count out loud so we can hear, and no going fast at the end,' said Little Twin.

'A'right,' I said, closing my eyes. 'One, two, three ...' I had got to twenty-one when an oddly familiar sound slapped into the darkness. FFFTHUTTT. I knew that sound. I had heard it in Western films, I had practised it, spitting breath through my front teeth. But this was ... here.

The arrow was standing out of the reeds, the two blue circles on its shaft very bright, and I was standing perfectly still, staring at it. It was just five feet from me, and I was more frightened than I had ever been in my life.

'Don't move.'

A big boy in specs on the other side of the gate was fitting another arrow into his bow. 'And you others, come out. We can see you. You go over first, Vernon, and I'll pass this to you,' he told the boy with him, who was smoking. Both were wearing the blazers of the grammar school and had long trousers.

The four children emerged from bushes, the dark girl sniffing. And suddenly I felt as though anything could happen.

'Right, let's have it back, Vern.'

I knew this boy. He was thin and pimply, and had big horn-rimmed glasses, the sort you couldn't get on the National Health. He was known to have a real steel sledge, which everyone thought a great joke as it hadn't snowed in years, but he had a red racing bike as well, which wasn't a joke at all.

He pulled the arrow out of the reeds near me, and I saw he had another four in his belt. Six arrows. Six arrows, each one costing two shillings and sixpence. Then the bow was lifting. For a moment it pointed at me, and I could see the small metal tip of the arrow, but then it was past me and pointing at the twins who were standing close together as they always did when something was wrong.

FFFFUTT. I didn't see the arrow until it was in the ground a foot in front of the twins, one of whom began to sniff. The smoking boy laughed. And suddenly I was cross. I wanted a bow like that (and three years later would get one), I had seen it in the local sports shop, a long white lancewood stave that cost ten pounds. But what was that to these two? They were too old to have bows, they should be at home growing up. The twin who had sniffed was crying openly now, and the bow had lifted until it was pointing directly at him. I started to run.

I was splashing through the puddles at the pond's edge and I could feel the wet in my shoes, but it didn't matter. Nothing mattered, I was running as I had never run before, bounding into the air. I could hear the big boys shouting, then something flicked over my head. As I passed I grabbed the arrow and then, aware of the enormity, snapped it in two. I heard a scream behind me.

But I was at the garden of the first house, and safe. A woman with pegs in her mouth as she hung out her washing looked at me but I ignored her. Looking back I could see the big boys pushing the twins around, the way drovers did at the cattle mart, and I heard the faint gleeful 'how, how, how'. And I knew what I had to do: I would break the strongest taboo of childhood, I would bring the grown-ups.

The fair girl's house was nearest, the semi-detached one with a bay, the sort thought posh in the 1950s. It had no bell and no knocker, so I banged on the front door with the flat of my hand. No response. I banged again and this time a window went up somewhere above me. 'All right, all right, what is it?'

A Dervish in a white turban was looking down. 'What's the matter?' The voice was sharp. 'Come on, I don't want to catch cold.' It was her big sister, who was in the sixth form at the girls' grammar school.

'It's some boys, they've got your sister.'

'Hold on, I'm coming down.'

When she opened the door she was in a long dressing-gown, and was barefoot, each of her toenails painted a bright red. 'Do come in,' she said, as though the vicar had called. 'Come in here, I'll put the fire on. I've been washing my hair. What is it?'

'They've got your sister and her friend and the twins, and they've got a bow with real arrows ...'

'Who has?' She had taken off her turban, which in fact was a towel, and was dabbing at her hair as she looked at herself in a mirror, sucking her cheeks in.

'That boy from the garage.'

'Oh that one.'

This annoyed me, for it was quite a different perspective on his villainy. 'Oh please come, please.'

She looked at me, then her face softened. 'All right,' she said. 'Just let me put a few things on.'

The electric fire had artificial logs, and artificial flames flickered. When I lifted the logs I could see a turning metal wheel above a red bulb, which, when I stopped it turning, meant there were no flickering flames.

'Come on then,' said the big girl in the doorway. She had put a blue headscarf on and a bright red lipstick that matched her toenails. 'What do you think?' she said as she saw me looking. But then it did look odd with her school blazer.

'Please come.'

We went out and I was startled at how dark it had become, but I dared not ask my companion to run. When we got to the corner of the street we could see some figures in the dusk coming towards us, and as they came under the street lamps I saw, first, the dark girl walking with the boy called Vernon. The other girl was with the boy with the bow, which he had unstrung. She showed no sign that she had seen me.

'I was coming home,' she told her sister.

'Cowardy custard,' the dark girl said to me, and the boy she was with laughed. The boy with the bow did not laugh. He just stared, the lamplight making sinister puddles in his specs. Then he nodded. Ominously.

The big girl looked down at me, then mussed my hair. 'I enjoyed our walk,' she said, and everyone laughed. And her sister laughed, looking at me as though she had seen me for the first time.

When they were gone I stood under the street lamp. Two boys in dirty mackintoshes were walking down the road towards me, one behind the other, each with one foot on the pavement, one in the gutter. But I didn't really notice them. Betrayal was something new in my world. Still I forgave her. I would have forgiven her anything.

I was fond of the Model School. I even liked the strange old headmaster whom we rarely saw except during the school sports and the carol service; when he wasn't brandishing a revolver during one or a baton for the other he spent most of his days in a self-imposed exile in the school shed, which, one of the women staff told me darkly much later, none of the female staff dared enter. What he got up to in there I don't know. But then there was so much about the school I didn't know, or notice.

'Remember the humiliation?' asked Eirwen Thomas. 'Twenty-five minutes in every lesson was taken up with humiliation.' No.

'Surely you remember the way the less bright children were ridiculed, the way they were always asked to read aloud so the whole class could laugh at them. That's why it took us twelve weeks to get through *Black Beauty*. And even then it was a condensed version.'

No.

Eirwen was in my class at school, a small, brown, darting girl, who, as far as this is possible, has total recall of the past, so for her it is something she can pop into at will, like a child sent on an errand. She noticed everything. She noticed how, unlike now, no mothers ever waited at the school gate; the children just walked home. She noticed the family of very quiet, very pale children, with their enormous tummies whom the big boys picked up by their ears and called the Stinkers; she remembers her pity, rare in a child, and the way the whole family disappeared overnight, being taken into care, which was even rarer. She remembers how the half-pints of free milk were always lukewarm. She remembers how much school dinners cost. And Clarks' sandals, bought new each year, shabby after a week. And sherbert. And comics, even the ones her mother did not allow her to have.

'Do you remember me?'

'Oh yes, you had a striped blazer.'

And then there was the 11-plus.

We had heard the sound of it whole classes away, like a weir on a summer river, and for two years had been in training for it. So there had been a new pace to the emptying baths and the filling cellars, and even the trains passing each other seemed to be going faster. And then it was on us.

'No point you even going,' the headmaster callously advised one girl. 'Still, I suppose the walk will do you good.' The exam was always taken in the town's two grammar schools, the one for boys, the other for girls.

I remember the day. I remember the creaking of the shoes worn by an invigilating master, I remember my feelings of growing terror as, however much I checked my answer to a sum, it still came to two-thirds of a man (I had done my calculation on the basis that there were fifty weeks to a year); I remember the jelly we had for lunch (in childhood you forget the main courses). What I do not remember is the way the results were announced.

'You must remember that,' said Eirwen Thomas. 'And the way some children cried, not hearing their names read out.'

No. All I remember is that I heard my own.

--------◆◆◆--------

The first act Hitler passed when he became chancellor banned the boiling of live lobsters. The first thing the novelist J.L. Carr did when he became headmaster of Highfields primary school in Kettering was to ban the reading aloud of 11-plus results in the school assembly. It was to him the cruellest feature of a state education. All right, all he did was mitigate the cruelty, for this was still there as a trapdoor opening under two-thirds of your generation.

And where did they go? Carmarthen was then a small town of 12,000 people; I had grown up there, I know where everything was, yet I did not know, and over half a century on I still do not know, where the secondary modern school is, or was. As far as the parents and the children were concerned, it was a wastepaper basket, and those who went there became to the rest of us the Disappeared Ones. When we meet in the streets now we do not greet each other, we are too embarrassed, so it seems kinder to pass by, and this is something that right-wing columnists wistful for the grammar schools ignore. What it meant was that in 1953 most of the children I had grown up with, played with, seen every day, had gone.

The love object had also gone, for, though she passed the 11-plus, her family had moved away to Swansea. I was to see her again just three times and talk to her just once.

———◆◆———

When I saw her next I was fifteen, lying on the grass in Carmarthen Park with my peers, boys my own age who a couple of years earlier would have been rushing about everywhere. But puberty brings languor and a chance to sneer at the personalities we were stealthily, and nervously, assembling for adult life; we spent a lot of time lying in grass. And sneering.

But then we fell silent for two girls were walking around the cycle track above us. Both were very good-looking and blonde, the elder especially, in high heels already a young woman. The other was younger, thin and coltish, walking with her eyes down as though unsure of who she was. But I knew who she was, I would have known her anywhere. I didn't move.

The two had moved on, then stopped as the elder talked to a university student she seemed to know. The younger just stood there. Why didn't I say something? Why didn't I, in front of my peers, get up and introduce myself and smile? Why didn't I? I was fifteen. Do you remember what it was like being fifteen? I was so self-conscious, so awkward, I had to be one of two or three just to walk into a coffee bar where a group my own age was already assembled. One cutting remark, that was all it needed, and I would crumple. I watched the two girls walk away.

Two years later I saw her again. With my cousin, I was on the sea-front at Swansea, a rundown beach beyond a rundown town, melancholy at the best of times, but the end of the world late on an October Saturday afternoon, the daylight going. I saw her near the sea's edge in the firm sand, throwing a beach ball around with a group of young people and making a lot of noise; they looked so happy, that was what really turned the knife. Again, all I needed to do was walk up to them, but I did nothing. And that was when I began to go barmy, for around this time the dreams started.

Always the same dream. She and I would meet by chance, on Swansea station or on a train moving out of it, and that would be it as far as we were concerned. I sometimes had this dream once or twice a week, and while it lasted knew a happiness that lasted well into the blank day. I really came to believe that she and I were made for each other, that it was only a matter of time.

At Aberystwyth University I met a girl who had known her at grammar school. She had been, she said, a very jolly girl (I didn't much like the sound of that), but she gave me her address. She wasn't sure what had become of her.

I tapped the number out on the rest of a public phone. You could do that with the old black phones, and not only did it mean you didn't have to pay, it also gave the impression that you were ringing from home or an office. I got through to her mother, as it turned out, and, with a handkerchief stuffed into my mouth, the following conversation took place.

'My name's Pugh, I'm the headmaster of the Model School in Carmarthen.'

'Oh yes, my daughters went there.'

'That's why I'm ringing.'

'Excuse me, have you got a cold, Mr Pugh?'

'Yes, I have. How did you know?'

'I'm having a bit of a problem hearing you.'

'This better? Good. Look, I'm forming an old girls' association and would just like to ask a few questions. What is your younger daughter doing now?'

'What's she doing? She's just started training college.'

That was a blow. I thought my future wife should have a degree at least. 'Didn't she want to go to university?'

'Well, it didn't turn out like that.'

'Too many boyfriends, I suppose.' My heart was turning over.

'What? No, nothing like that. Mr Pugh, forgive me, but what's this got to do with an old girls' association?'

'Just background detail. Facts. You know, we're going to kick off with a tea dance.'

'A tea dance?'

'Yes, they're the coming thing. Dancing to Maldwyn Stephens and his Rocketeers. Do you know Maldwyn?'

'I don't think I...'

'Oh, just look at the time. Must fly. The forms will be in the post. Everyone welcome.'

'Hello?'

In 1967 I decided it all had to end. I was leading a fairly normal life, I had girlfriends, but the dreams had gone on and on. Hitchhiking for a week round Ireland with an old friend, I had them every night. With one week of my holidays still to go, I drove from Carmarthen to Swansea. As I say, I knew the address; for years I had been dreamily looking it up in the Directory. It was half-past ten in the morning.

I rang the bell. No answer. I rang again, and this time there was the sound of feet on the stairs and a cheerful 'Hang on, hang on.' The door was opened by a good-looking young woman still in a dressing gown, her legs bare. I explained that I had come to see an old schoolfriend.

'Oh they've moved, love. She's married now, married a dentist, a friend of my husband's. They haven't gone far, mind. I've got her address here somewhere.'

Which was how, an hour later, I found myself sitting in a pub beside an arterial road at the edge of a small industrial town, drinking with some miners who had just come off the night shift, for they still had mines in Wales then. We had a couple of pints together, for I was nervous, and then I rang the number I had been given.

----◆◆◆----

Did he call on her, the boy in the striped blazer? Oh yes, he called. So what did he want of her, did he really think it would be as it was in dreams? I don't know. Forty years on, I can no more see into his mind than I can into the mind of a medieval man, except I think he was ever so slightly out of his.

It was a house surrounded by others just like it in a new development. A harrassed-looking young woman, a small child trying to attract her attention, stood in the garden in front of it.

'You found it then,' she said, her lower lip jutting in the old way. 'Come in, I'll make you a coffee. You've got time for a coffee, have you? By the way, I hope you don't mind the sight of a pregnant woman.'

'No, no.'

On reflection it was a strange thing to have asked, but what was stranger was that at the time he hadn't noticed.

'That your car?' He had come in a Volkswagen Beetle. 'They're reliable I'm told, how many miles do you get to the gallon?'

'I don't know.'

And that was just about it. Twenty years of fantasy, longing, dream, ended there, in a query about petrol consumption. There was half an hour, though it seemed longer, of slightly baffled small-talk, mostly about teachers, as he drank his coffee.

'Who's the headmaster now?' she said suddenly as he was getting into the car.

'I don't know.'

'It's not someone called Pugh, is it?'

'Why do you ask?'

'Oh nothing.'

<hr />

And I got on with the rest of my life.

4

Teenage

The Sacred

'Mind if we sit down?'

A sturdy man in his mid-thirties, he has one of those unfocused smiles that seem to be stitched on the face. He is in a dark suit, and the woman with him, also stitched and smiling, is in a grey two-piece and a white blouse. Had they been in wetsuits, or full evening dress, they could not have looked more out of place in the pub.

'Please,' I say, pointing to six empty chairs. It is half-past nine in 1983, and I am sitting at a table in the Kings Arms at Farthingstone in Northamptonshire, waiting for my wife who is somewhere out in the night lecturing on the Great Exhibition to the old-age pensioners of the W.E.A.

'Actually we'd like to talk to you.'

I must look alarmed, for he goes on, 'If you don't mind, that is.'

'What do you want to talk to me about?'

'We'd like to talk to you about God.'

'Oh no, no. Anything but that.'

They exchange glances, then the woman says, 'May we ask why?'

'I'm Welsh.' But, seeing the bewilderment, then the suspicion, I feel obliged to add, 'Me and God, we go back a long, long way.'

When I was ten, my parents took me to Barry in south-east Wales for our summer holidays. Barry would have been an extraordinary choice even for an afternoon, for, once a booming port, it was by then the biggest scrapyard in Britain. Sad terraces dropped to the sea, cranes stood idle against the sky, as on deserted wharf after deserted wharf they cut up old railway wagons, and finally, from the late 1950s on, the locomotives themselves, as British Rail scampered out of steam.

This was the elephants' graveyard for the Castles and the Kings and the Halls – only, and this is the amazing thing, the elephants were competed, and in some cases fought, over by steam preservation societies intent on their resurrection. Dai Woodham, whose yard it was and who saw the trains only in terms of scrap metal, was a baffled man among his canyons of rust. 'This woman rang me up, pleading with me not to sell her husband a train. She'd discovered he'd taken a mortgage out on their house.'

Nobody went on holiday to Barry, it would have been like going to the Klondyke after the gold ran out. An enormous funfair survived from the boom time between the wars, hanging on by its fingertips, the paint peeling, the attendants of its rides as expressionless in their booths as funerary statues in a necropolis. But as far as my parents were concerned Barry had one thing going for it. My father's cousin lived there.

My parents were great ones for cadging holidays off relatives, all my friends' parents in West Wales were, remembering long-lost cousins in Folkestone and aunts in Eastbourne. Nobody stayed in hotels, they could not have afforded it. I don't know what the financial arrangements were, but I remember we travelled with two suitcases, one full of clothes, the other full of dead chickens and fruit cakes.

In strange towns I got to see lawns, for some relatives had prospered, and not lawns like the ones we knew, which were the size of tablecloths, but long ones that glistened with dew. I also got to see tottering marriages at close range (nobody divorced in the 1950s), and the strain, particularly at mealtimes, could be sensed even by a very small boy, though the partners did their best to be polite to each other for the time of our visit. So perhaps we did some good, this little peace-keeping force of relatives parachuted in like the United Nations, summer after summer. But Barry was different. There I went through the first, and last, spiritual crisis of my life.

My father's cousin had two sons, one of whom was my age, the other a couple of years older. They were nice boys, and we mooched around and broke into deserted houses, of which there seemed to be no shortage in Barry. I had no idea how tough my new companions were until one afternoon we broke into a house and found another gang already there. What happened next took me aback, for the only rows I had known had their rules like little eighteenth-century wars, a trading of insults followed by a perfunctory scuffle, after which one side or the other withdrew. Instead, the elder of my two new friends stepped forward and with all his force hit the gang-leader on the nose. There was a horrible click and, the next minute, blood. 'We're off now,' he told me, for I was still standing there.

But things went beyond that the afternoon the two of them suggested we go to the pictures. It was a Sunday.

I asked my mother, who looked flustered, for she clearly had no idea such a thing was possible; where we came from, only the chapels and the hospitals were open on Sunday. She told me to ask my father, which she did only when she felt something was beyond her own experience of life: in our family this was the equivalent of a referral to a supreme court.

We were sitting in some sort of park, one of those melancholy municipal places with geometric flower beds and deckchairs in which, from time to time, small children got their fingers caught. Being out of doors on a Sunday was unusual enough for us; at home, if we didn't go to chapel, we stayed in as though expecting an air raid at any moment, which of course was what a Welsh Sunday was all about.

It was the one day of the week when my father didn't hammer in a single nail, for that could be heard, and my mother didn't put clothes out on the washing line, for they could be seen: being heard, or seen, by our neighbours mattered, though some families took it further. A friend's mother never used a pair of scissors on a Sunday since, unlike neighbours, God could see indoors. 'Of course you can't go out,' said my mother as she, my father and I watched from behind net curtains in our front room the faithful processing to the chapel at the end of our street, my mother passing comments on the clothes and, in some cases, on the characters of the passers-by. 'Who does she think she is, just look at that hat.'

It was the only time, until my father died and was laid out in it for inspection by friends and relatives, that the front room was used. And of course if we went to chapel ourselves there would be others watching, as unseen as Apaches, from behind net curtains in their front rooms. Before television came, when they could watch murder and adultery, juries sat in the front rooms of Carmarthen. 'Look at that old man.' A man in a trilby was passing, the palms of his hands turned behind him like those of an ape. 'I don't know how he has the face to go to chapel.'

'What's he done?'

'Never you mind what he's done. Have you finished your homework? That boy's got ears on him like a bread van.'

But they had to endure me. Once I persuaded them to let me out to play on a Sunday with the children in our street, and I fell over. When I got in, my knees bleeding, my mother said, 'There you are, see', which was her usual reaction to tragedy, and from that moment, aged six, I knew I had been pushed. It wasn't a matter of belief; I *knew*, for God, like fractions, was always around somewhere in my childhood. I even knew what he looked like.

Mrs Rees Abergwili in our street had a picture of him in her passageway, seated somewhere in a space which wasn't dark or empty, but some kind of interstellar terminus crowded with angels and cherubs, with Jesus Christ next to him. I never believed in Michaelangelo's God, he just looked like a rugby coach attending to Adam, but Mrs Rees's God was the real thing. Her Jesus was a smiling young man in open-toed sandals, but you couldn't see God's feet, and you wouldn't want to; his face was enough. He was an old, unsmiling man with a long white beard, but not an old man like Father Christmas: this one seemed to be staring right through you from the stars. Once was enough. I didn't call on Mrs Rees again, and I didn't ask to be allowed out to play in the street on Sundays again either.

But Barry was industrial South Wales, where people were friendlier and tougher, and didn't seem to worry about their neighbours or about unleashing their children on Sundays. We in the West were another species. When in 1950 it was mooted in Water Street Methodist Chapel, Carmarthen, that the Sunday

School trip that year should go to the amusement fair at Porthcawl, the elders went into an agonised special session after Mr Dyer, the town park-keeper, said he had heard that on Sundays the cinemas were open in Porthcawl. We weren't even going on a Sunday. Still they did go to Porthcawl and, aged five, I went with them, being photographed in a studio at the wheel of a US Army jeep.

In the end I went to the pictures, for it would have been embarrassing for my father to have refused in front of his cousin when his own boys were going. As we left my mother, grim faced, whispered to me so no one else could hear, 'On your head be it.' My parents, startled into English, could use phrases out of the Old Testament, my father on one occasion describing one man as a whoremaster, though I can't remember why.

I was ten years old when, on a Sunday afternoon, I went to see Gene Kelly in the musical *Singin' in the Rain*, and was terrified.

———◆◆———

My mother was a kind woman, it was just that she had a mindset inherited from her mother, who had inherited it from hers. For, around the middle of the nineteenth century, the Welsh, hitherto a merry and light-hearted people, went underground, virtually as an entire nation, into the tunnels of Nonconformity, and into the darkest, deepest tunnels of all, those of Methodism. The Unitarians were too intelligent, the Baptists loved rollicking hymns, but the Methodists were the people of the Book, whose unique status underwrote their intolerance.

My father, a Methodist, remembered terrible scenes from his youth when unmarried girls who had become pregnant were publicly excommunicated. My cousin Brenda remembered this being done by a panel of elders in a vestry adjoining the chapel, but that was in the 1940s, when the Welsh, prompted by Hitler, had become a bit more broad-minded. My father, born in 1909, remembered it being done in full chapel: crying girls, teenagers some of them, being expelled from a community which was all they had ever known, a community which felt no pity, expressed no remorse. As for the men responsible, they were not named, or blamed, and they were not excommunicated.

Even now, over half a century on, *Singin' in the Rain* is to me the darkest film ever made. I have only to see Gene Kelly splashing in the puddles to remember an afternoon when I expected to see a trailer for the Day of Judgement amongst the Forthcoming Attractions. So it was all very well for the lights to change from green to red to blue, for the great rucked curtains to open and shut, and the women with ice creams to come and go, all marvels I had never seen before: they meant nothing.

When people write about the vision of the great Welsh Nonconformist hymn writers Williams Pantycelyn and Ann Griffiths you must remember one thing: what that vision led to was a small boy in the shilling seats, amongst the song and dance and the Technicolored joy, convinced that he was damned.

I blame the mothers. Fathers went out to work, but at that time women stayed at home, caught in a round of family, chapel and gossip, and my friend Geraint Morgan is of the opinion that most of them were half mad, hysteria bubbling away like the toffee which did get made on Sundays. A university lecturer, he used to tell his students that he knew all about the Taliban, having been brought up by one. His mother told him that if he inhaled the smoke from burning brown paper he would get brain cancer; needles, if they penetrated the skin, streaked straight to the heart like heat-seeking missiles; the white fluffy surrounds of oranges produced stomach cancer. Cancer was a back-up for the mothers of Wales, like one of those anonymous men in fedoras standing behind James Cagney.

Geraint's mother at eighteen had made an impassioned speech before the whole congregation of her Methodist chapel in Aberystwyth when the minister, an intellectual with a doctorate in divinity from Heidelberg, proposed putting a small silver crucifix above the keyboard of the organ. The proposal was shelved. She did not live to see, given the shortage of ministers, a Catholic priest preach from the pulpit of the Methodist chapel she and her family attended in Carmarthen, or the life-sized cutout of Vinnie Jones with the two shotguns from the film *Lock, Stock and Two Smoking Barrels* in a pulpit in Aberystwyth, the Calvinist Methodist chapel it stands in having been converted into a pub. Other chapels have been converted into mosques, gymnasiums, bingo halls, recording studios, squash clubs, a lingerie factory, a strip club. And mosques. All this within one man's lifetime. Mine.

'Come with me,' said the comedian Max Boyce. 'I want to show you social history.'

We were in the club-house of the Glynneath rugby club, of which he is President, and where, occupying most of a wall, is a roll-call of First XV captains dating back to 1889. 'See this, 1939–1945, with a black line drawn under it. No captain. Second World War, right? And here, 1914–1919. No captain. First World War.

'But this is what I want to show you. 1904–1906. No captain. 1904–1906? Just a black line, and one word. Revival. An old man in the club said he remembered him, said he was an outside half called Roger Revival. That is how much people have forgotten.

'Those are the only things that have ever interrupted Welsh rugby. Two world wars. And a national religious revival.'

It swept the land: men stopped playing rugby, they held prayer meetings underground, they saw the Holy Ghost in flames amid the pine pews (and Evan Roberts, the most charismatic figure in the Revival, saw the Devil in a hedge one Sunday afternoon at Newcastle Emlyn, and, what was worse, heard him *laugh*), as weekly they were reminded that they were the Elect, amongst whom there could be no impurity; or if there was, a minister in Llanelly declared, it had sneaked in from England.

Some, understandably, went mad, the state of ecstasy and of terror conjured up being such that, in the early months of 1905 alone, sixteen people suffering from religious delusion were confined in Carmarthen Lunatic Asylum. My old friend Professor P. Mansell Jones of Manchester University told me of the sermon he had heard in Lammas Street Chapel, Carmarthen, when the preacher described a damned soul flitting back to the gates of Hell after aeons in the outer darkness, only to see that on the great clock *the second hand had not moved*. Mansell Jones, who had heard that in 1904, was telling me about it sixty years later, for he had been unable to forget.

'And what came of it all in the end?' I heard my father ask the blacksmith of Llangynog.

'Nothing,' the blacksmith said. 'Nothing.'

We had not been the Elect of God.

The chapels, built at the rate of one a week, were still only too obvious in the Wales in which I grew up. For these were not the humble and beautiful chapels of early Nonconformity. These were vast barns in which architects had been encouraged to ape any building style they had ever read about, with the exceptions of the pagoda, the pyramid and the igloo. Just the frontages though.

> The Trellwyn Methodists have built a church.
> The front looks like an abbey.
> But thinking they could fool the Lord,
> They've built the back part shabby.

Frontages Gothic, frontages Byzantine, frontages Doric, frontages Corinthian, frontages Romanesque, frontages Doric and Corinthian and Romanesque. I passed them every day on my way to school, and did not find them in the least odd; I thought they, and Nonconformity, would be there forever as they had always been. I did not realise then that Nonconformity had only been a dominant factor in Welsh life for roughly a hundred years, from around 1850, say, to the 1950s, and that before it there had been a quite different Wales. It is only now that the erotic Welsh poetry of the Middle Ages, raucous and wonderful, is being published, its editor, the present Professor of Welsh at Swansea, an Englishman, having to form his own publishing house to do so.

Similarly the Sunday closure of pubs, that other part of the package, only dated from 1881, so that too lasted only a hundred years, but these were years of ingenuity, for clubs in Wales were allowed to stay open. Members of the newly formed Ammanford Conservative Club swore blind that their club was formed 'to promote the interests of the Conservative Party', and a courtroom collapsed with laughter, for everyone there knew it had been formed so its members could drink on Sundays. Bleakly a police inspector quoted from its accounts: seventeen shillings and sixpence spent on books and newspapers, £86 6s 10d at the bar.

Central Office in my time sent down hopeful MPs to address such clubs, for their membership was larger than in any of the Home Counties; politely but distantly they were received in constituencies where an orangutan stood as much chance of being elected as a Tory.

A new chairman at Caerphilly Conservative Club decided to take a hard line with would-be members. Was he, he enquired of the first applicant, a Conservative? 'No.' Did he perhaps have friends who were? 'Good God, no. What do you think I am?' The chairman leaned forward. So what was he doing, wasting their time? At the door the applicant turned. 'What about Sundays?'

When he had gone one of the committee said sadly, 'Bit of a mistake there, Mr Chairman. Think what it would have been like with one honest man about the place.'

I never knew the ecstasies of Nonconformity, though once, in Water Street Chapel, Carmarthen, after a sermon by what was called a Great Preacher, Dr Martin Lloyd-Jones, I saw a tall woman, her eyes shining, get to her feet and, to show a friend across the gallery what its effect had been, hold her left, large, breast in her hand, and raise it; I was sixteen, and transfixed. 'You should have said, "Like a hand, madam?",' said my friend Teifion.

My father never questioned his faith; he enjoyed its Nonconformist practice, and could, and did, quote sermons by the yard, as when the old preachers for emphasis translated phrases into English, a language in which some of them were not fluent. *Mae nhw'n codi eu trwynau at Dduw.* They cock their nose at God. For whatever else it was, Nonconformity was pure theatre to my father.

The Rev. James Thomas, minister of Tabernacle Chapel, Carmarthen, was not quite of this world but moved in it like an astronaut, encased in such simple wonder it awed, and amused, his congregation. For it meant no one, not even the palace guard of his deacons, could find fault in him, an activity which traditionally gave drama, and enjoyment, to chapel life. Ministers imperious, ministers intolerant, ministers inebrious, even ministers lascivious, their minds full of suspenders and guilt, looked down on their flocks, but here, in Tabernacle, there was pure innocence. On Sundays I used to stare at the round, pink face, ageless and untroubled, enthroned above us in the huge pulpit beneath the boards of which was the baptismal pool. The minister was still a figure of power when I was a boy.

When he stood up, the great pipes of the organ above him streamed from his head like the diadems of the later Roman emperors, and it didn't matter that you could hear the sweets being unwrapped from one end of the chapel to the other, Caesar stood in Tabernacle. And in Shiloh. And in Cana. And in the other great barns with names that suggested the Middle East was here amongst the lanes and terraces, which is why every flashpoint in the Middle East still has the puzzling suggestion of domestic incident to people like me. But this power was at odds with the character of the Rev. Thomas.

Of his earlier career in the poverty-stricken industrial Valleys, it was said that whenever he went for a walk he came back with fewer clothes than when he had set out, having given away overcoats, gloves, scarves, even umbrellas. He was unmarried. 'He's a good man,' said my mother, then, nervously, 'a real Christian.'

He was once persuaded to form a youth club, which met in the vestry, to which I went, or, rather, to which I was sent. It must have seemed a good idea to the elders, only there was one thing they hadn't thought out: what was youth to do when it got there? Cards were out of the question, we couldn't play table tennis for there was no table, so, amazingly, he accepted someone's suggestion that we play postman's knock. Every Tuesday night, week after week, a girl or boy would call out a secret number with which one of the opposite sex had also been given, and the couple would then retire to a small, dark side room, heavy with stained pine furniture and lined with engravings of whiskered ministers, where ...

Not pecks on cheeks, oh no. This was full-blooded snogging between teenagers who before this may not have exchanged a word. I remember going out with a girl a couple of years older, when a tongue, like a length of stair carpet, came out of nowhere. Couples would emerge after five, perhaps even ten, minutes, or however long it took for an erection to subside in adolescence. 'Sit down for a moment,' said my companion kindly. 'Then we'll go back in.'

Only one night a couple did not return. One of the bad boys of the town had turned up, a tattooed Teddy Boy, a teenager from Hell, and he and a girl went out together. Ten minutes passed, fifteen, twenty. 'Well, well, well,' said the Rev. Thomas softly, his usual response to anything untoward. We never saw either of them again in the youth club, which folded soon after.

The Rev. Thomas was a great caller on his flock, an event that in Welsh Nonconformity always caused consternation. Football pool coupons would be pushed behind the curtains, slippers kicked under chairs, and, worst of all on the rare occasion when there was such a thing, the Bristol Cream whisked into the pantry. Once he called when I was alone in our house.

It was a time when my mother had started work as a nurse in the lunatic asylum on the hill, and I, then sixteen, had been assigned certain household duties. Initially one of these was cooking, but I had been relieved of this after I roasted a small sewin in half a pound of butter, stuffing it with mustard cress, lettuce and radish, a mush so rich my mother was off work for two days. My other duties consisted of making the beds, emptying the chamberpots, and lighting a fire, the last of which I found difficult, so I would soak the paper and kindling in the surgical spirit my father, a diabetic, used when he injected himself. Unfortunately the day our minister called I had found some petrol as well.

'I'll light the fire for you,' he said, as I went out to the garden for something. Without thinking, I said, 'Right ho, Mr Thomas.' I couldn't have gone more than three steps when I remembered. 'No,' I shouted, but it was too late. WHOOOOMPH.

He was in a chair, arms trailing, like Jerry the cat after the dynamite concealed in his cigar has gone off, his blackened face broken by the white pools of his eyes. 'Well, well, well,' said the Rev. Thomas. Later that year he baptised me.

I had put this off as long as I could, but my mother's persistence had worn me down. 'Why can't you be like all the others?' In the 1950s ours was the most conventional society outside Tibet (where, according to my old friend Michael Wharton who wrote the Peter Simple column, there were only two political ideas: it *is* the custom, and it is *not* the custom).

I didn't see the point of baptism, having already been baptised at birth by the Methodists, but then I had started going to my mother's Baptist chapel, where the pool awaited one as inexorably as the 11-plus. I wish I could say that I had intellectual objections, but the truth is much simpler: I just didn't want to get wet. Anyway in the end I went.

There were eight of us, four girls and four boys, and we were all dressed in white. I had borrowed a pair of white flannels from a boy in the school First XI, and these, unfortunately, were tight. The chapel was crowded, and, above us in the pulpit, the minister was wearing, of all things in a chapel, a black cassock, and black thigh-length fishing waders. The organ boomed, and he descended into the white tiled pool where he awaited us. The girls went first, the organ boomed, and ...

The girls were wearing filmy white dresses, which, when wet, became diaphanous, and, knowing they were going to get wet, they were not wearing bras. Their breasts swayed as they climbed the pulpit steps, and that was just the beginning. When the first of them, a very pretty girl, came out of the water, her nipples were like organ stops. Then the next went up the steps.

Each time the congregation sang 'Hallelujah', apparently totally oblivious of the fact that in front of their eyes, in a chapel in Carmarthen, there was being enacted the most erotic tableau outside *And God Created Woman*, which had the young Brigitte Bardot coming out of the Mediterranean. Could no one else see this? I looked down the line at the other boys but they had their hands over their eyes as though they were praying, which most probably they were but for all the wrong reasons.

We were fifteen, an age at which it was possible to get erections even in trigonometry. My friend Lloyd Watkins used to get them when made to climb a rope in gym, which meant he had to cling there until the pain kicked in, when, propriety restored, he could fall.

From my seat in the second row I could see in my imagination the horror unfold, the gasps, the organ faltering, the sudden terrible silence, as I climbed the pulpit steps. Oh no, please ... if they excommunicated girls in living memory for being pregnant, what would they do to a priapic me? Drown me, all of them piling into the pool? I had a brainwave. I began to think, desperately, about the French Revolution, which was not difficult for the parallels were obvious: the crowd, the high place, the victims ascending one by one. I heard my name called. *It is a far, far better thing I do, than I have ever done; it is a far, far better rest I go to . . .*

I scuttled like a crab down the aisle, up into the pulpit, then, missing the last step, into the pool, so the minister had to grab me. I can remember it now, the waves of water, the cold, the wonderful anaesthetic cold. The idea was that you let yourself go backwards into the water and into the minister's arms, only I was tall even then which made things awkward as he staggered backwards. I was down for about thirty seconds more than I should have been and came up, gasping for breath, then ran down the stairs, and squelched along the aisle like the Beast from 10,000 Fathoms, the Hallelujahs in my clearing ears. All those open mouths, my mother's amongst them.

———◆▶———

So I became a Baptist. I ate the crumbs, I drank the communion wine from glasses so small they could have been made for elves, I attended Sunday School, and being at an age when I read three or four books a week, became a pain in the arse for Mr Davies, a jeweller, who was in charge of our class of young baptised men.

'Do you think Socrates went to Heaven, Mr Davies?'

'Socrates wasn't a Christian, I'm afraid he won't have gone to Heaven.'

'But he was a good man.'

'Yes, but . . . well, if he was a good man then he'll have gone to somewhere quite near.'

'You mean, like Abergwili?' Abergwili was a small village just outside Carmarthen.

'I think it's time for us to open our Bibles now, boys.'

I sat in the gallery, daydreaming about the young matrons in the main body of the chapel beneath, and holding quiet auditions for my private harem. When I went away, just seventeen, to Aberystwyth University at first I did go to chapel, dressed in my Sunday best, or rather the Sunday best chosen for me by my mother, a green check suit and a yellow waistcoat with brass buttons. 'You can't go to chapel like that,' said my landlady. 'You look like a bookie.'

Later at Oxford I had a black suit but there seemed to be no Welsh Baptist chapel to wear it to. If like me you were on a college scholarship you were expected to pronounce a Latin grace in Hall and to read in the college chapel. I wrote to the Chaplain, explaining I had lost my faith, when the truth was that I had a terror of doing anything in public. 'How refreshing that a young man these days should take such matters so seriously,' the Chaplain wrote back. And that was the end of my religious life.

My mother, like all mothers whose children had gone away, continued to make contributions on my behalf to the chapel, only these were not made as anonymous cash in a collection plate. In all Welsh chapels they were placed in sealed, and numbered, envelopes so that at the end of the year the published accounts revealed just how much each member of the congregation had given, how much the GP, the dentist, the schoolmaster, the pharmacist, and their wives. It was an unpleasant practice. 'That's how things have always been,' said my mother, poring like an accountant over the columns of figures. But after a few years she stopped making contributions on my behalf.

Thirty years later the pubs, followed by the supermarkets, opened on Sunday in Wales, and the chapels began to close. And if the Devil laughs, no one can hear him in space. Or in Tesco.

— The Profane —

We were burying Ray, the second of my friends to go. Or rather we were burying Ray's ashes, when, embarrassed by the perfunctory ritual that has been cobbled together for this new form of funeral, I found my attention wandering over the graves, over Hughes, the first to die, to the graveyard wall. And it was then I remembered *where* we were.

Flush against the graveyard wall there was a house. The wall hid the bottom storey, but above this a window looked out over the graves. As soon as I saw that my jaw dropped (for it is true, jaws do drop in life as well as in romantic fiction). I could feel Ray pulling my sleeve and pointing, which is what he would have done, and I saw the two of us collapsing in laughter at the wonderful irony of it.

For he and I were once part of a secret society. We met in the perfect place for a secret society to meet, where the living never went by choice and where we could see the approach of anyone who did. Near where I now live is the upper room above a gatehouse where Guy Fawkes and his fellow conspirators concocted the Gunpowder Plot. Our upper room was above a graveyard. *That* graveyard.

We were thirteen years old, and for a year we were part of the very exclusive, all-male club which in later years we called the Penbryn Boys, or at least Ray and I did, for we thought it funny; the others never mentioned it. The house above the graveyard is called Penbryn.

There are some forms of human activity you never find in novels, certainly not in autobiographies. One is sex in old age. Another is sex in early adolescence, that is, if this is uncon-summated; if it is consummated the writer will have gone to town on flower catalogues and detailed physical description. But full-blown affairs are rare in early adolescence, at least in Carmarthen they were. Which is how the Penbryn Boys came into being.

Tommy Thomas, Tom Twice as we called him, was an only child who lived in Penbryn with his parents. Everyone liked Tom, largely on account of two things. The first was that Mrs Thomas was the first of our mothers to go back to work, in her case as a nurse, which meant that during the holidays he, and we, had the run of the house. We could smoke the fags he had hidden behind his set of the *New Universal Encyclopaedia*, which his parents had bought for him, but which neither they nor he ever read, which meant the fags and the cold meat he had cut from the family roast and also hidden there were quite safe. Tom was very keen on cold meat.

So we would sit there, in the room above the dead, smoking and scoffing, and then at some point in the proceedings Tom would present what the author of *Fanny Hill* called 'the master member of our revels'. For the second reason for his popularity was that Tom, who had matured earlier than the rest of us, had the biggest knob any of us had ever seen.

I can see it now, for this was the first, and the last, time, apart from porn films, when I saw another erect human penis. Not that I liked the look of it much, though we pestered him for a sighting. I didn't like it because not only was it big, it was a perfect cylinder. The damn thing looked *industrial*.

In the beginnings of the Penbryn Boys nobody did anything to it, not even Tom. There was no need. Once up, that thing never went down, but reared over us benignly like a tribal ju-ju. In the 1950s, in its early days, there was briefly in Camarthen something out of prehistory, a society devoted to phallic worship.

It would have been of interest to that single-minded Victorian lunatic Dr Alfred Witt, the mayor of Bedford, who in the course of a long and industrious life collected what he called 'Symbols of the Early Worship of Mankind'. That is to say, he collected every sculpted representation of the erect penis he could get his hands on. Straightforward dicks. Dicks with eyes, with wings, with hawks' heads, dicks in the form of rings, brooches, lamps.

Ivory dicks, bronze dicks, wooden dicks, from Egypt, Assyria, Rome, even the South Seas. On his death the doctor left his entire collection to the British Museum, in his innocence expecting them to house it in its own public gallery, but the Museum put the lot in a cupboard and turned the key. I have seen it. Cupboard 77.

In Penbryn the awe fell away as, one by one, we caught up with our host, at which point an element of competition was introduced, a school ruler being passed around. There was a lot of argument at this stage. 'You don't measure it from there, you measure it from *here*. Hey, that hurt.' But wherever, or whatever, we measured, we never got close to Tom's dimensions, something we put down to the fact that, at thirteen, he was still eating Farley's Rusks (they too were behind the encyclopaedias).

Why nobody writes about any of this I don't know, for it has a vein of comedy, and is in its way rather touching. Of course if we'd been caught, had Tom's mother come home early, all Hell would have been let loose, it would have been a matter for the priest and the doctor. One of my friends was caught masturbating by his father, a hard-drinking plumber, and told, not unkindly, 'You're lucky it was me who caught you. If it had been your mother, she'd have been straight down the White Bridge.' This was the railway bridge over the river Towy at Carmarthen, from which would-be suicides jumped.

In later life he and I turned this incident into a racing commentary as we imagined the mothers stampeding through the reeds. 'And here's Mrs Jones, she's setting a steady pace. Yes, and here's a late entrant. Mrs Rogers has overtaken one, two, three, four. What *has* she seen?' I wrote about this fantasy in a book review in *The Spectator*, and a prisoner rang me from gaol to say it had made bearable a spell in solitary confinement.

For we also had Mr Thomas's soft-core porn collection to consult, which was considerable and hidden under his parents' bed. Mostly these were magazines like *Spick* and its sister publication *Span*, but there was also some harder American stuff he had got hold of from somewhere. The British magazines showed young women in skirts having problems with brambles, which resulted in the display of large white thighs and stocking tops.

There were only four of us in the Penbryn Boys. Potential recruits from time to time were invited to join, and, if they refused, were told to go home and play with their soldiers – in one case, with his dolls' house, for the more effeminate the boy the less likely he was to join in, which is curious when you think about it. But then none of us would have considered there was anything homosexual about what we were about.

--------◆◆◆--------

Years later I heard of one boy in the town who had gone a lot further than any of us would have thought possible. He too was about thirteen, and lived next door to a girl about four or five years older, being in the sixth form at the girls' grammar school. In the holidays, after both sets of parents had gone to work, she would come into his house in the morning when the two of them would go to bed. She was the prime mover in this and set the rules, so she was allowed to do anything she wanted to him but all he could do was look, and, if she was in a good mood, reverently touch her pubic hair.

All my adolescence, and much later, I dreamt, like all teenagers, of such a thing, and more, happening to me, in particular of the humorous, patient, older woman who would translate my fantasies into real life. The galling thing is that at university I heard stories of women who had actually done this.

There was the jaunty divorcee who, inviting her godson up to London, walked into his bedroom on his sixteenth birthday ('Andrew, I hope you won't mind, but you're going to have a slightly different present this year'); the girl who told me this said that with his newly acquired expertise he had on his return spread chaos through the lower sixth. Then there was the boy at Marlborough who, going to stay with a friend, found he had just gone down with 'flu. 'On the second day his mother came up with my breakfast on a tray, said she knew how bored I must be, and just got into bed. I mean, this was a flower arranger, a large twin-set and pearls woman. It was like finding myself in bed with St Paul's Cathedral. Only then it wasn't at all.'

The closest I got to that wonder was when a young woman, a friend of my mother's, called one winter's evening when I was alone in the house. She lived in the country but worked in town, and asked if she might have a bath before going on a date. I showed her to the bathroom, which was just off the kitchen, and then, when I heard splashing, applied one thirteen-year-old eye to the keyhole. She was sitting in the bath, I could just see her head which at one point she turned towards the door, and I was convinced she had heard my heart. BUDOING. BUDOING. BUD BUD BUD. And then she rose. It is more than fifty years ago but I remember that unairbrushed glory when for a minute at just before six o'clock a shop assistant, under a sixty-watt bulb in Union Street, Carmarthen, blazed like Botticelli's Venus in the waves. She must have suspected something, for when I made her a cup of tea later I found it impossible to phrase a single coherent sentence. 'Very quiet, isn't he?' she told my mother.

Apart from that it was all books, some of them very odd books, like *Love in the South Seas* by someone called Bengt Danielsson, a bestseller in the 1950s. This included a description of the sexual initiation of young men, when the man and an older woman would retire to a hut, the raffia curtains would be let down, and 'gravely' she would set to work. It was that word 'gravely' that did it: the adverb tolled through my adolescence. In case my mother found it I buried the book, along with Alberto Moravia's *Woman of Rome*, in a hedge in the field below Carmarthen Park, where Tesco is now, and where, from time to time, I would dig the two up and carry on reading, until one morning, after a thunderstorm, I found them pulped.

And then I came on a reference to the Oneida Community, a batty, if high-minded, group of around three hundred people who got together on forty acres of land in New York State in the 1850s. All property was held in common and there was group marriage throughout the community with, and this is what appealed to me, sexual initiation of all male teenagers just after puberty by older women. But the really batty thing was that this was rigorously and bureaucratically enforced. It reminded me of my piano lessons.

'Byron, it's seven o'clock.'

'Yes, I know.'

'Byron . . .'

'I just want to finish this chapter in Biggles.'

'Now you know we can't keep Mrs Thomas waiting. I don't want that fuss again which we had last week.'

'Do I have to?'

'Yes. And comb your hair. Have you done any practising this week?'

And so off he trudges to his weekly date with destiny. The truly amazing thing about Oneida is that it lasted thirty years, at which point social unity had so disintegrated that one of the survivors said it had become difficult to borrow a hammer.

The Penbryn Boys only lasted a year. I baled out when I discovered poetry, and felt superior. Tom and Ray went on a bit longer. Then each of them discovered pop music and girls; later they both discovered divorce. For a time I worried about the possibility that when we were grown up one or the other might blackmail me, but that passed. By then I had something else to worry about.

The Bully

'He was a shit,' said Garry Good News with all the venom of the actor Ed Begley heading a lynch mob, which, when he wasn't trying to start World War Three, was what Ed usually did in films.

'He was a *what?*' I said. I had just told him that Gwynfor Evans, formerly our saintly MP, had died.

And for a moment on a wet night in Lammas Street, Carmarthen, two men stepped out of time.

Garry runs a newsagents he has called Good News, an inspired piece of marketing, for when was the news ever good? We were once in the same form, and bump into each other from time to time, but that night we just stood there, oblivious to the rain drifting under the street lamps, neither with a clue as to what the other was on about.

Then Garry said, 'That tan, you must remember the tan.'

'Ah,' I said. '*That* Gwynfor.'

When two men meet, who were in the Queen Elizabeth Boys' Grammar school at Carmarthen in the 1950s, one topic of conversation comes up. Suddenly one or other of two old-age pensioners is howling his indignation into the night, or the snows, at the memory across half a century of one man.

'Wotabastard,' shouted Garry Good News.

'Those shorts,' I said.

He was not a serial killer, this man, he did not bring fire and sword into the Towy Valley. All he ever did was teach gym for ten years between 1947 and 1957 in a small Welsh grammar school. At least in theory he did, for a man has no time to teach anything when his main aim in life is to humiliate as many boys as possible in front of their fellows. The result is that, apart from a few rugby players, his praetorian guard, none of us remember anything about sport or gym, for he taught us nothing. But we remember him.

In their beginnings gym masters formed a sort of non-commissioned rank in teaching, a rank many of them had actually held in the Army, particularly the boxing sergeants of the public schools. During the last War to teach gym you had to be over sixty to avoid the call-up, so his gym master, said the Welsh poet Bobi Jones, died in the gym, 'of old age'. Then things changed. After the War, which had interrupted things, from their breeding grounds like Loughborough and Carnegie, both colleges founded in the late 1930s as places where 'physical education' was taught for the first time, these creatures came into their own, as convinced as the SS of their responsibility for a new order.

And their vision was just as narrow for they could not accept that in a class of thirty, only half a dozen, say, were going to be any good at gym. So what were they to do with the twenty-four? Unlike the SS, they couldn't shoot them. But one man in Carmarthen had no doubts. The twenty-four were there to be put on show, in particular the brightest amongst them, who were inevitably the worst at gym, boys more unsure of themselves, unfinished, as unsteady as young fawns.

Our school turned on the examinations of the Welsh Joint Education Council. Anything else was an irrelevance: the art master was an object of derision, the music master, who spent his days playing us classical records, was an object of distant curiosity like one of the last Romans, kept on as a diversion in the courts of his new barbarian masters. But at least these men wore gowns; the gym master alone had no gown.

He would have felt this keenly, for he was a vain man. So he made a feature of his difference, in the tan which somehow, even in West Wales, got topped up winter and summer, being daily and duly revealed by his very white, very brief shorts; I can see those awful bandy legs now. He was a balding man, and ugly, his lower lip jutting in a perpetual pout, for he never smiled, even when every morning, about half-past nine, with the tarpaulin rolled back and prayers over in the gymnasium which doubled as the school hall, he entered his kingdom. Unlike the art and music masters, he had no doubts about his place in the scheme of things: he was the school bully. Only, unlike all other school bullies, he never grew up or went away, and, as a member of staff, his position was unassailable.

Before each lesson, at the headmaster's desk on the stage, he would sit opening the sick notes those of us trying to avoid gym had persuaded our mothers to write, and then read each one through very slowly. He never made a comment; he would just put the letter down, smooth it out, then stare at the suppliant. It was like standing before a revolutionary tribunal, some grubby man of blood opening the requests for a stay of execution, as the maimed, the halt and the blind waited. Of course we weren't

really maimed, or halt, or blind, we just aspired to be so. Illness was the only sanctuary we had against him, for this was something at which even he dared not sneer, he who in his gym was the pack leader.

◆━━◆

I remember the cold first. There must have been some heating, but it is the cold I remember, and that pervasive musty smell which small boys generate when they sweat, the sort of smell you get in the snake house at London Zoo. And there was always the fear of some private humiliation. Small boys are nasty bits of work: they sneer at each others' underwear, at the boy who like an aspiring porn star wore sock suspenders; they forcibly debag each other. And if they didn't do it, the gym master would.

He took a great interest in underpants, especially when these were kept on under gym shorts because of the cold. I gather this is a preoccupation of the species, only he went further. If he caught you wearing underpants you were made to take these off, *and* your shorts. I remember the day he made a boy in my class do this, then carry on doing gym dressed only in his vest. I can see the boy now, he would have been about twelve, a despairing figure made to go over the wooden horse, over and over again, clutching his pubescent genitals, releasing them, then clutching again and falling. I have no idea what became of him but, if he is still alive, wherever he is, an old-age pensioner will remember every second, frame by frozen frame.

I never did work out what gym was *for*. I loved sport, I spent most of my time outside school playing cricket and soccer in our street or in Carmarthen Park; I didn't need exercise. None of us did, we exercised all the time, so all those bars and horses seemed to have no purpose apart from preparation for life in a prisoner of war camp. I am sixty-seven years old now. I cannot do a handstand, I cannot leap the horse, I still cannot climb a rope. I never could. But whereas any normal sixty-seven-year-old wouldn't give a strawberry fuck, the fact that I can do none of these things, *and* not find myself jeered at, is a matter of amazement to me.

Listen....

⸺◆◆◆⸺

'God, the Handstand Detentions,' said Billy Griffiths. There was a pause as he tried to stop laughing, but then Billy was the finest gymnast to come out of the school, and, when bored, did cartwheels the length of our street. To him the terror was something viewed from afar.

'Those boys who couldn't do handstands, he'd keep them behind after school. That meant all the fat boys and the awkward ones, night after night, week after week. And at the end they still couldn't do handstands. Was he still doing this in your time?' Billy is a few years older than I am.

'Oh yes, he kept me in,' I said. And if the bugger had had his way I should still be there, still trying to do handstands, my wife, dog and mortgage waiting politely outside the gym.

'But what I remember most is that if he'd really taken a dislike to a boy he would, at the end of the lesson, set the whole class on him. And this boy would disappear under this heap of bodies until eventually there'd be somebody waving the shorts they'd pulled off him. Then this white little face would emerge, trying not to cry. *How did he get away with it?*'

Billy is a retired gym master.

⸺◆◆◆⸺

'I remember the year he introduced boxing,' said Eddie Evans, landlord of The Drovers, who has died since our conversation. 'I was there the day the gloves actually came, and he called me out for this demonstration bout. With him. I was a big boy, I was sixteen and fat. He was a man in his thirties and in good shape. And he gave me no instructions, nothing resembling any kind of teaching. We just put the gloves on and he started cuffing me all round the ring. I mean, he was really hurting me, showing off to the boys. So I thought to myself, "Sod this." I threw this hay-maker, and it must have been a moment when he was too busy doing his Cassius Clay shuffle to see it coming. He went down as though I'd hit him with a hammer. Know what he did then?' Eddie shook his head in wonder. 'He had me up in front of the headmaster, who shrugged and told the two of us to go away. How *did* he get away with it?'

'When I was in my first year I developed a kidney infection,' said Geraint Morgan. 'What this meant was that there was to be no gym, not just for a week or a term, but no gym . . . ever. I had my leper's bell, if you like, and if you remember how he took illness personally, just think how he regarded long-term illness. Anyone else would have told us to get on with some schoolwork, but he had me and another boy, who was suffering from a heart condition, out on the rugby pitch picking up stones. Winter and summer, wind and rain, just the two of us and our buckets on that field.

'How *did* he get away with it, how was he allowed to wander round exuding conceit and malice?'

'I think it was because nobody knew,' says Margaret Jones, the school secretary, 'though once I did see something. He was in my office when a Chinese boy came in. I don't know what the boy had done but he got him to bend over there and then. He caned him in front of me. And him such a little boy, I just couldn't bear it, I walked out. I suppose I should have told somebody, but who could I tell?'

The headmaster was ailing, and would die in office within a few months, so the story has the elements of a fairy tale, with the king dying and evil loose in the land. But how had he got away with it until then?

Two reasons. The first is that our parents were almost all from the working class. They were Welsh and they were in awe of authority, especially that of a school which few of them had attended, and which for their sons was the one route to getting on, something very important to them. If only there had been one middle-class Englishman amongst them, one bloody-minded and bright man – but there wasn't.

The second reason is that the school, like many grammars of its time, saw itself as an imitation of a public school, so there was a certain tolerated brutality. It had prefects, whom some headmaster had given the power to beat, which they did, enthusiastically, every Friday afternoon.

'I slippered Rogers,' said Denzil Davies, then an MP, intro-ducing me to his colleague Merlyn Rees. We were at a book launch, and Davies was recalling when, as head prefect of Carmarthen gram, before the long years of Labour opposition, he had for the only time in his political career known real power.

'What had he done?' said Merlyn Rees.

'He walked through the wrong door.' This was a door reserved, for some tribal reason, for the staff and the Upper Sixth.

And when a grammar school aped the public schools it needed a rugby team, so anybody who could deliver this would

have been on a very long leash. And the gym master did deliver it.

'It was amazing, once a year the whole school closed down for three days so he could hold his seven-a-side tournament. Three days,' says Fred Bevan, a retired headmaster. 'You can hardly believe it, can you? But then a new head came and put an end to that.

'Still he was a good rugby coach, at least he was to those of us who were good at rugby, he didn't bother with the others.' Fred went on to play first-class rugby, so, like a former member of the KGB discussing his old boss Beria, he walks a delicate line when he talks about the gym master.

Before each rugby lesson, or what passed for a rugby lesson, the man would have us all lined up, and then two boys would pick their teams. This was a cruel experience, as he must have known it would be. The best were picked first, and then the next best, and so on down the line until only the timid, the fat, and those contemplating a career in women's hairdressing were left.

'What was it like being picked first?' I was genuinely curious.

'You felt a certain warmth,' said Gerald Davies, later of Wales and the British Lions, who hadn't forgotten it either.

<hr />

The reign of the gym masters lasted perhaps twenty years. Then the comprehensives came, and there was no more aping of the public schools, for with them came the parent-teacher associations, and the home finally had a foothold in the school. How he would have coped with this, I don't know, but by then he had long gone from Carmarthen Boys' Grammar.

In 1957 the school matron, who doubled as the head cook, was found gassed in one of her ovens. She was a nice woman, in her early fifties, who, if you reported sick, would let you lie on a day bed and read her son's comic-book annuals, which, because he had left the school long before, were old, so you could read about your heroes in their beginnings. It was her prescription for everything, comic annuals and rest. Sickness is my fondest memory of the school.

We were all very upset to hear of her death, for before we even got in that morning the rumour had gone round that she was suffering from cancer. I was then Attendance Monitor, which meant that during the first period I went round taking down the names of those boys who were off sick, also, as instructed, telling the masters which of them would have to take a class for an absent colleague. The gym master was amongst those whose names were on my roster that day.

When I got into the gym he was seated at the head's desk on the stage, not doing anything, which was odd. Below him a class was doing circuit training or just chatting, which was even more odd. But I gave him the list, which he initialled, and it was the last time I saw him in the school.

He had been having an affair with the matron, an affair which, perhaps having read all the annuals, he ended abruptly. Only she had left a note, which he wouldn't have known about when I saw him, and, shorts, tan and all, he was gone before the morning break.

The Lower Sixth was agog. 'Sir, isn't it awful?'

'What did you expect?' asked the English master, but wouldn't say more. 'Right, *Winter's Tale*, Act Two, Scene One. Rogers, you're Hermione.'

'But sir, I was Hermione last week.'

'Not afraid of being typecast, are we?'

I went back to the school about ten years after that. It was summer and one of the sixth forms was out on the rugby pitch. Some were practising archery, others were kicking a soccer ball around, and one group was just sitting, talking. They were as languid as Victorian curates.

The Road

In my teenage years I had grown increasingly solitary on account of a habit that came to obsess me, and which not only cut me off from my contemporaries but was one I dared not even mention to them. I had started writing poetry.

I was under the spell of someone I don't think anyone reads now, James Elroy Flecker, introducing a selection of whose verse, J.L. Carr noted beadily, 'He wrote two remarkable lines, "Their bosoms shame the roses. Their behinds/Impel the astonished nightingales to sing ..." then crossed them out.' But Flecker had also written *To a Poet a Thousand Years Hence*, a poem addressed to me.

> O friend unseen, unborn, unknown,
> Student of our sweet English tongue,
> Read out my words at night, alone:
> I was a poet, I was young.
>
> Since I can never see your face,
> And never shake you by the hand,
> I send my soul through time and space
> To greet you. You will understand.

This, in my grandfather's old room which my father had

redecorated, with the smell of new paint everywhere, I did read out at night alone, and under his influence began to write poems about places like Isfahan (Flecker was very keen on the Middle East), the brunt of which my English master bore. 'Expressed yourself lately?' he would inquire breezily at one stage, but he grew wary under the bombardment.

'Do you know where Isfahan is?'

'No.'

But poets were things of the syllabus, in particular that of the Welsh Joint Education Council, and, though I pored over their photographs, and cut out those of the poets of the First World War (curiously enough, the better looking they were the worse their poetry), all of that was from far away and long ago. I did not know anyone who in life had known them. And then I met someone who had.

He would get to his feet as I came in, even though I was just a schoolboy, for he had kept the fine Edwardian manners of his youth. He had been tall then, who had become hunched with age, something which, with his beak of a nose, made him look like a very old bird of prey, added to which he wore a hearing aid which screeched and whistled, so entering his room was like entering an aviary. His name was Percy Mansell Jones, formerly professor of modern French literature at the University of Manchester, who had retired to his home town of Carmarthen, which, like me, he loved. We had been introduced by our doctor, who thought I might find him interesting. Mansell Jones was then in his late seventies, living in Oak House in Priory Street. I was sixteen, and I had never been in anything resembling Oak House.

It was old. From the outside it was just a house at the corner of a street of terraced houses, so it took a second glance before you realised how different it was from the others, being so much bigger

In the Dream-Time

'You had this Welsh accent, I remember that. And a full head of hair.'

'You don't remember anything else?'

'No, you must have made a big impression on me.'

DAVID MASTIN, formerly crime reporter, the *Sheffield Star*

I HAVE TOTAL RECALL on a single period of my life, when for once it is not a matter of dredging faces, moments, sayings, from the sludge of memory; I know to the day what I was doing for three years, five days a week. From 1965 to 1968 I wrote a column in a Northern evening paper.

It was called 'By the Way', and, as its name suggests, it was meant to be a commentary on little items in the news. You know the sort of thing: you see these served up like yesterday's roast in most newspaper columns, then carved. When I inherited the column I gradually dispensed with this. I began to write essays, on paintings, poetry readings, the Dead Sea Scrolls, anything that interested me; then I dispensed with that altogether and wrote on what interested me most of all. For five days a week, 1500 to 2000 words a day, I wrote about myself in the *Sheffield Star*. I was twenty-three.

On the other pages of the paper life went on as normal. People divorced or attempted to divorce ('A Sheffield mother of 10 was like the old woman who lived in the shoe, said a judge, dismissing her petition on the grounds of her husband's excessive sexual demands'), they got run down ('Two Women Hurt') or promoted, were told to pay off rent arrears, won contests for their looks or their parsnips, suffered injury, in one case when a man walked under a ladder ('By Heck, Broken Neck' was the headline by a mad sub, removed at the last minute, though he was known to his awed colleagues as By Heck, Broken Neck for the rest of his time on the paper).

But while all this was going on, at the heart of the paper, opposite the editorial, one man wrote about his childhood, the comics he had once read, even the boys who had bullied him in a small Welsh town 300 miles away. He showed off, smugly quoted Sir Maurice Bowra (that for contemporaries of the *Iliad* most of the excitement came from seeing in how many different ways the heroes could murder each other), and had you met him, or sold him a car, you would have appeared in a paper where just about everything else that happened to him did. The one thing he did not write about was girls, which was as well, for then the whole thing would have dissolved into farce, or psychiatry.

'What's this?' asked a young domestic-science teacher.

'What d'you mean, what is it? It's a bath towel.'

'How long have you had it?'

'Three or four years, I don't know.'

'How often have you washed it in that time?'

'It's a bath towel, silly, you don't need to wash bath towels. When you get out of a bath you're clean. What are you looking at me like that for?'

When she did speak her voice was calm but distant. 'Look, I don't want to get personal, but what planet are you from?'

The only published news story I had ever written ('Boy rams runaway van into lamp-post'), and with it my time as a reporter, had fallen away. I was in uncharted space in which there was just me, floating on and out of reach of any suspicion that the column might have been of no interest whatsoever to the half-million or so people (the *Star* had a circulation of 210,000), almost all of them from the working class, who each night bought the paper to see who was dead or had a secondhand car for sale, or both. Not that I would have bothered with sales figures. Indulged by the paper's editor (who liked 'writing'), inducing near-dementia in its news editor (who did not), I wrote on, and on, and on.

I passed my driving test (at the third attempt, a fact hidden from my readers). I prowled round car showrooms marvelling at the descriptions of colours (El Paso blue, Goodwood green, Ulan Bator pink). I turned up at a finance company, trying to arrange hire purchase.

Being then addicted to French cigarettes, to show my aplomb (and credit worthiness), in the offices of the finance company I passed one across the desk to the young man in the black suit. He leaned forward, tried to inhale, then said, ominously, 'Of course you're not a British national.'

'Sorry?'

'You're not British.'

This was clearly not a question but a statement of fact. 'Yes, I am,' I said.

'But your accent.' He had clearly not met a Welshman before. 'Those cigarettes…' There was a long pause. 'You're not a foreigner then?'

And so I became the owner of a red Volkswagen Beetle 717 DWE. Have you noticed how you always remember number-plates from ten cars ago, never the current one?

'God, that car,' said Sandra Brown, a physiotherapist who had the misfortune to be my girlfriend at the time. 'We were going down a hill, it was the first time you'd been out in it after that crash, and you were going on about how new it looked, when, BANG, somebody'd run into the boot.

'I turned and saw this car careering across the road and into a retaining garden wall. Nothing happened for a moment, then first the wall, then the garden, collapsed around it, burying the car up to the windscreen. Amazing bloke, he said you'd reversed up hill at great speed, and tried to claim off your insurance. You of course wrote about that.

'When Princess Margaret came to Sheffield you got wet because she was late, and you said it would be the last time you waited in the rain for a photographer's wife. This got into the paper, and all Hell was let loose in the letters' page. I remember because you got me to write in, saying it was a refreshing new approach to Royalty. The readers swarmed all over me then.'

For the rest of the time I indulged my own interests.

'Got that hot off Doncaster Abattoir,' said Mrs Jepson proudly.

The little pig was in a jar, very pale and crumpled and dead. It had one eye, in the centre of its forehead, below which was an oddly lengthened nose, but Mrs Jepson had no doubts. On a card she had written 'The One-eyed Pig with the Elephant's Nose'.

Next to it was 'The Smallest Baby Born Alive'. A little grey thing, a bit longer than my thumb, it floated in fluid. Through the glass I could see its minute fingers and the expression of utter peace on the wrinkled little face. 'Got that off a university,' said Mrs Jepson.

All the exhibits in her freak show, with the exception of a fat and malevolent African monkey, were dead. It was the vets, she muttered; they no longer let freaks live. And all were very old. But she wasn't going out of business yet. 'Anyone with a bit of common sense will stop and look,' said Mrs Jepson.

And they must have done, for twenty years later, near Liverpool, I caught up with her nephew who had inherited the show, and wrote about it, nostalgically this time for the *Daily Telegraph* Magazine. The One-eyed Pig and the Smallest Baby had not changed at all.

Occasionally I stumbled on something. Driving through the town of Matlock I noticed a car, an Austin A35, in the lower branches of a large ash tree at the side of the road, put there by a flash flood that had ripped through the town. But driving through again, three months later, I saw the car still in its tree, which was odd. This time I stopped.

Now there was a road, a wall and a river, all three within a few yards of each other. Had the car fallen into the road it would immediately have become the responsibility of the Ministry of Transport, which would have removed it. The wall had been built by Derbyshire County Council: had the car fallen on that, it would have been the responsibility of the council. Had it fallen into the river it would have been that of the Trent River authority. But instead it was in a bureaucratic no man's land, in a tree alongside the road, behind the wall, above the river, and every morning its owner, a young man who lived opposite, looked up and saw his car against the rising sun. He only had third-party insurance, he told me, and could not afford to retrieve it.

I wrote about that, and, in a series of one-sentence breathless paragraphs, phoned the story through to the *Daily Mirror*, and, in long paragraphs with adjectives and adverbs added, to the *Guardian*. The *Guardian* paid me two guineas, the *Mirror* £15, and I hoped the car would be there forever, yielding me an annual tithe. Alas, a month later, during their Rag Week, some students from Sheffield University, like infuriating spaniels, retrieved it.

I had similar hopes of the Last Man to see Lord Byron. I was sitting in the *Star* offices one morning, reading the morning papers, when I came on a story about a Russian scientist who had dug up Tsar Ivan the Terrible, and, working from the skull, had reassembled his face. Staring at those grim features, I remembered I had read somewhere that in the late 1930s someone had opened Lord Byron's coffin in his family vault at Hucknall, just down the road from Sheffield. I rang the vicar of Hucknall, who confirmed this had indeed happened, and that one man among his parishioners had been there at the time.

I drove to Hucknall with Yann Lovelock, who had been at Oxford with me. Then, as president of the University Poetry Society, he had dressed in full Guards regimentals, something that turned every head in the High Street, for Lovelock, with his lank black hair and beard, looked like Rasputin. Now attached to the Sheffield English department, he dressed conservatively, that is to say like Rasputin in a suit, which if anything made him look even more strange.

But the vicar, a short, abstracted man, took this in his stride, as, I had the distinct impression, he would have done had I turned up with the King of the Zulus. He suggested that before we met history's witness we should call at the town library to read the account written by one of his predecessors, a Canon Barber, the man who had had the vault opened.

As we walked there all three of us were smoking, and I put my cigarette out just as we got to the library, as did Lovelock, and, I assumed, the vicar. Barber's account was fascinating. I learned later that he had been a man obsessed by the possible Saxon origins of his church, who, whenever repairs needed doing, got his churchwardens, quietly and at night, to dig into the foundations, so for him the Byron vault was a heaven-sent archaeological opportunity when somehow he got the permission of the then Lord Byron, a sheep-farmer in Australia, and of the Home Secretary, to open it. The only thing was, as I read on I noticed skeins of smoke rising.

They appeared to be coming from the vicar, who had not noticed them for he was talking to Lovelock. And suddenly I could feel the giggles coming in a tidal wave, the way they did in school, for the vicar's head was now wreathed in smoke. Beyond speech, and at the same time worried he might take offence, all I could do was point. 'Cripes,' said the vicar. He leapt to his feet, beating at his coat, and ran for the exit. 'Hello,' said Lovelock, who also hadn't noticed and thought the man had merely gone demented, apparently not such an unusual occurrence in his world. The vicar had put his cigarette, still alight, into his coat pocket.

The Last Man to see Lord Byron was a retired bank clerk called Arnold Houldsworth. Then churchwarden, he with twin brothers called Betteridge had done the actual digging, whilst some local dignitaries looked on, the canon having turned the event into something of a social occasion. The three broke into the vault through the roof, then lowered a ladder. Byron's coffin was easy to find on account of the coronet which was still on it, and, nearby, the various romantic little caskets in which brains, heart and tripes had been brought back after the embalming in Greece. And with that the party dispersed for high tea, leaving Houldsworth and the Betteridges in the vault.

'We didn't take too kindly to that,' said Arnold Houldsworth. 'I mean, we'd done the work. And Jim Betteridge suddenly says, "Let's have a look on him." "You can't do that," I says. "Just you watch me," says Jim. He put his spade in, there was a layer of wood, then one of lead, and I think another one of wood. And there he was, old Byron.'

'Good God, what did he look like?' I said.

'Just like in the portraits. He was bone from the elbows to his hands and from the knees down, but the rest was perfect. Good-looking man putting on a bit of weight, he'd gone bald. He was quite naked, you know,' and then he stopped, listening for something which must have been a clatter of china in the kitchen, where his wife was making tea for us, for he went on very quickly, 'Look, I've been in the Army, I've been in bathhouses, I've seen men. But I never saw nothing like him.' He stopped again, and nodding his head, meaningfully, as novelists say, began to tap a spot just above his knee. 'He was built like a pony.'

'How many of you take sugar?' said Mrs Houldsworth, coming with the tea.

And there the story would have rested, sinking into myth, except ... One night at Sheffield University for a poetry reading, I was desperately trying to find a lavatory, having stopped in a pub on the way, when I opened a door into a pitch-black room and, groping for the light switch, touched what felt like a big glass jar. The light came on, and I saw at eye level, about a foot from me, penises cut from corpses. My hand had clearly disturbed them, for they were dancing in a stately sort of way, and each, having been injected with embalming fluid, was the size of a rolling pin.

In Sheffield I had found myself in the profession I was to follow for the next forty years, rather in the way the men pressganged into Nelson's Navy found themselves aboard a man of war.

'What sort of career do you see yourself following?' asked the harassed chap at the Oxford University Appointments Board.

'Well, I write.'

'Sounds promising.' He made a note. 'What sort of things do you write?'

'Poems mainly.'

'Ah.' He made another, much shorter, note. 'Had any printed?'

'No, but I've got one on me. Would you like me to read it? It's about Joan of Arc.'

He looked at his watch. 'Perhaps not right now.'

A few weeks later a letter came, inviting me to apply for a graduate training scheme being started by two newspapers in Sheffield.

Journalism had not occurred to me, but then neither had anything else. Still I had had two articles printed, the first sentence of one, across almost fifty years, is still awful. 'Sober, anonymous, vaguely phallic, the Picton monument is oddly untypical of a Victorian public memorial . . .' This was in the *Carmarthen Times*, and I was writing about the old Peninsular War general, a local boy. I read the sentence out to my cousin in a pub.

'What's with this vaguely phallic?' he asked.

I tried to explain in graphic terms, as I was a university man and he a builder. As I did so I noticed some girls at the next table had stopped talking.

'Then it doesn't make sense, there's nothing vague about something like that. As you know,' he told the girls, who all started talking at once, though not to us.

Had he just said it was overwritten, which it was, I should have been indignant. But when a writer gets told, and by someone he is not entirely sure can read, that his first printed sentence is nonsense, it is something he never forgets.

My second article was written just before the letter came from the Oxford careers people. I had read in a paper about a Chicago cinema usherette who had been fined for appearing on a beach in a new swimming costume. This exposed her breasts, and I used this moment of social history to explore the new vistas it offered bad novelists, the sort who write about weak chins, humorous mouths, you know the sort of thing. What would they do with new areas of the body on which to drape characterisation like washing? Shy, forceful, defeated tits? Actually one American bestselling novelist had already jumped the gun with his references to 'her big, brown, forthright areolae'.

I wrote on and on, with quotes from Kilvert and the lunatic Shelley who once had a panic attack when he saw his wife's nipples over one of those low-cut Regency dresses and thought they were looking at him. 1200 words. And all 1200 appeared in the *Western Mail*. £10, money for old rope. I applied to Sheffield Newspapers.

'Why exactly do you want to become a journalist?' Michael Finley leant forward. A young man in a bow-tie and a hurry, he was the editor of the *Sheffield Telegraph*, a morning paper.

'Well, it's my literary style, I have this tendency to over-write, I need to see what effect the discipline of being on a newspaper will have.' I was being helpful.

But the effect on Finley was immediate. He, who until then had done most of the talking, stared at me through his black-rimmed spectacles. The second man at the table facing me began to chuckle. Not laugh, chuckle. Tom Watson, the editor of the evening paper, the *Star*, did everything slowly and softly.

That was why I got offered a job. Not by Finley, who by then had recovered the power of speech, and was asking me about what I had had published, which was when I told him about the *Western Mail* and the breasts, after which life seemed to lose all meaning for him. But Watson, who all that day had watched the ambitious young men come and go, men who knew about linage and layout from the student newspapers they had edited and about fees from the gossip columns of the nationals to which they had contributed, had met the biggest bloody fool he had ever come across in journalism. I think he offered me a job just to see what I would say and do next.

<hr />

Three of us were given jobs on the *Star*, four on the *Telegraph*, which still takes my breath away. For though they were part of United Newspapers, a very profitable chain which also owned *Punch* and would later own the *Observer*, they were still just two local papers which were taking on, not one or two, but a whole graduate intake, most of us from Oxford or Cambridge. But then Sheffield Newspapers had always taken themselves very seriously indeed.

Donald Trelford, later editor of the *Observer*, but a leader writer on the *Sheffield Telegraph* in the 1950s, remembers his editor Bill Lythe coming back to the office after what had clearly been a good lunch. 'He called me into his office and said he and his friends had decided the World Fair was to come to Sheffield. He wanted me to write a leader on it. "I've got the headline," he said. "SHEFFIELD, CENTRE OF THE UNIVERSE. Now you write the rest." And went home.' Trelford wrote the leader, but the World Fair did not come to Sheffield.

Then there was Michael Finley's Drang Nacht Osten, his drive to the East. Dropping the *Sheffield* from its title so it became the *Morning Telegraph* 'serving four counties' (though in the office rag magazine this became 'serving four houses', for its circulation was already shrinking), Finley campaigned in his paper for a larger regional identity, and actually sent his four graduate trainees out like medieval heralds into the four counties to claim their allegiance. One of them, the *Guardian* journalist John Cunningham, never forgot the expression on the faces of Lincoln people when they heard that they were part of the lost lands of a Greater Sheffield.

The graduate intake was part of this folie de grandeur. The training course lasted about six weeks, the papers hiring tutors, amongst them a lawyer who introduced us to the laws of libel and to bits of Hollywood gossip. There was also a motherly lady who had the nightmare job of trying to teach shorthand to seven young men who strung her along by querying pronunciation, like the variants on the shorthand for the word garage, which the upwardly mobile pronounced as gar-ARGE, and others (the Welsh) as gar-RIDGE. We were bored, we were superior, we were a pain.

We were also lectured by people from the papers, like the crime reporter who swung his arms like a higher primate as he walked, and talked with relish about his hero Lord Goddard, whom he had heard deliver four death sentences in as many days. And the executive who wrote letters to his own paper about the need to arm the police with what he described as 'real man-stoppers'. This remarkable man had been either the hangman or assistant hangman at Changi Gaol after the War, and was said to have a nostalgic photo album to remind him of his expertise. We, who had only met schoolmasters and dons, listened in fascination.

And then there were the tele-ad girls, who sat in a large hall, and were forever on the phone as they took the classified advertisements from members of the public on which the papers' profits turned. They were tolerant and beautiful, walked around in clouds of cigarette smoke and perfume, and most had a past of some kind, being young divorcees or university drop-outs. In pubs I listened open-mouthed to their stories.

'I was taking A-levels, and my brother arranged some extra geography coaching from a teacher at his school. When I got home he said, "How d'you get on?" How had I got on? He'd had me three times before the *News at Ten*. I was only seventeen.' She blew a perfect smoke ring. 'Got an A in my A-levels though. In what, d'you think?'

'Geography.'

'No, English.'

I was among the most interesting people I had ever met.

The *Star* and the *Telegraph* shared a large open-plan office, into which Finley would burst, slamming the door to show his dynamism. He was given to public tantrums, something made even more dramatic by the long, completely silent figure of his deputy Barry Askew, always two paces behind like a sinister Duke of Edinburgh, always in black. Later, as editor of the *News of the World*, Askew would become known as the Beast of Bouverie Street, advising the Queen to her face that if she was worried about the press harassment of Princess Di it might be an idea to send a footman out to buy her wine gums.

I watched the comings and goings of the extraordinary pair with interest, for this, just eight desks away from me, was real journalism, and in such contrast to my own editor Tom Watson, who never slammed a door, never raised his voice, merely stopping from time to time to whisper to someone as he ambled between the desks.

I did not realise that the *Telegraph* had been dying for as long as anyone remembered, and was only kept going by the profits of its sister evening. Its day, like that of all Northern morning papers, had been over by the First World War, when the nationals built their Manchester presses. The end was an unconscionable time coming, but it duly came three-quarters of a century later, by which time the *Telegraph*'s circulation was down to 30,000. And when it did come it was overnight, when Sheffield estate agents decided to remove their 'det bng lge lnge CH' adverts from a paper which in my time had its own Foreign Editor (though he was the whole of the foreign staff as well). It died as casually as that. Yet once it had had a nationwide reputation, when, a few years before our arrival, David Hopkinson, Finley's predecessor, had broken the story of the interrogation practices of the local CID. These in the early 1960s included the use of a rhino whip, acquired God knows where; the whip passed into folklore, and the chief constable resigned.

Since then great efforts had been made to re-establish relations between police and press, and we seven graduate trainees were given a guided tour of police HQ. They showed us their Black Museum, where we stared politely at a small black nose floating in a glass jar. This, it was explained, had belonged to a Somali, and had been bitten off by one of his countrymen during a fight, which was curious enough in itself, only the police then picked it up and pickled it.

At this point I felt a sharp pain. I had been playing with a stapling machine, and, looking down, saw I had stapled two fingers together. The chief superintendent, who was our guide, looked at me, at the blood dripping onto his desk, at me again, then massively away.

I envied my colleagues who had been taken onto the *Telegraph*. I envied them the hours they kept, for while on the evening paper we stumbled in out of a Northern dawn at 8.45 a.m., they swanned in at eleven o'clock, and even then left, or, to be precise, went to the pub at about the same time as we did. But most of all I envied Ian Sainsbury, an Irish actor who had jumped ship, or, I suppose, stage, to become the *Telegraph*'s full-time book and film critic.

He had come to Hopkinson's attention by writing letters to the paper whenever something got up his nose, and something was always getting up Sainsbury's nose. These letters were so long and so well written he got taken onto the staff, first as a reporter (until it was found it could take him a day of sifting through his metaphors to write a seven-paragraph news story), then in his present incarnation. Dear God, the man read books and went to the pictures for his paper, and later drank for it as well, getting the Glenfiddich Trophy for his wine column.

The books were glossy and new, and, when they came, he arranged them in piles on his desk, later rearranging them thoughtfully into smaller, or bigger, piles. Not only did Sainsbury not like anyone picking them, he did not like you even looking at their dustjackets. But, scurrying between sad police courts and even sadder inquests in chapel vestries, I had had a vision of the good life.

I was later made the *Star*'s film critic and saw something of Sainsbury. Previews were put on in Gaumonts and Odeons for the two of us in cinemas capable of seating over 1200 people, for cinemas were still enormous then, their managers waiting on us with toast and coffee. But I was still a general reporter, and engaged in a running battle with the news editor, for whom every film preview was an inquest lost. Sainsbury did nothing else except write stylish book criticism, only he was under the impression that his was an embattled existence and told bitter stories of his battles with the subs, one of whom had cut the word 'inspissated' from his copy on the grounds that it was indecent.

Life on the *Star*, on the other hand, was a startling introduction to news, or what passes for news, which in the end is little more than the fortunes of the famous and the misfortunes of the rest. Each day one of the three of us would be driven by an old gentleman in the office car, an Austin A35 which had done well over 100,000 miles, to the ambulance station (to check on what might have befallen our fellow citizens overnight), the fire station (ditto, on their houses), and the police (on their misdemeanours). Anything out of the ordinary was to be followed up, in other words written about, but it was death we were really after.

Every day the news editor would scroll through the family bereavements in the classified ads section of the paper, and if the deceased was under forty we had to follow this up as well. This meant we were to turn up at the house and ask a family still in shock what had happened, an intrusion beyond belief, but it was expected of us. Famine, Pestilence, War, Death. And the Fifth Horseman of the Apocalypse, the man from the *Sheffield Star*.

Nobody liked us very much. The other reporters who had worked their way up from weekly papers disliked the fact that we had been parachuted in, and appeared to make such a mess of what to them were such simple jobs, like the day two of us were told to do what were called *vox pop* interviews. This was when you went out with a photographer and in the street stopped members of the public to ask their views on some issue of the day, which then appeared in the paper under a photograph. In our case it was the decision of the Wilson government to raise pensions. Easy.

Except that we had with us a photographer who, like everyone else, thought himself our superior. So he wandered off while we were asking our questions, and photographed anyone who took his fancy, so when we got back to the office we found we had no quotes at all for some, and for others just a line or two. With time ticking away and the lay-out complete, each face to be accompanied by 150 words of comment, we began to make these up.

We thought we were on safe ground, for pensions were a popular issue, and we might have got away with it, except that one photograph was of a woman who said she had welcomed the increases, but that was all, just the one sentence. So under this I wrote something to the effect that she approved of everything the Wilson government was doing, and that might have been that for the city was overwhelmingly Labour. Unfortunately she was the vice-chairman of a constituency Tory party, which in Sheffield was as eccentric as being vice-chairman of the local Jacobites. And she had a telephone.

The news editor, quite literally, went out of his mind. He had never been averse, even in an open-plan office, to displays of temper (which he called bollockings), but this was off the scale. The only sentence I can remember was that we were being paid good money, a concept which intrigued me, as though there could be such a thing as bad money. But it was an unpleasant experience, as neither of us had been shouted at like this since school. Of course he couldn't hit us but we were hauled in front of the editor who tried hard to be almost as cross. Everyone was cross, I remember. Even I was cross, for I had given the old bat some good lines.

———◆———

Sheffield had been a shock. It appeared to have no past beyond a hundred years, when it was still on the branch line from Rotherham, and then virtually overnight had come roaring out of the Industrial Revolution. Its centre was tiny, its main buildings crowding in on each other, the cathedral a parish church let out at the seams to accommodate growth. The result was that on the rare occasion when I found myself staring at anything older than late Victorian times I felt I had stumbled on prehistory.

I remember the night I was shown Paradise Square, not far from the paper's offices. No factories, no housing estates, this time, and no pork butchers, this was an eighteenth-century square on an incline of one in seven. No families either; they were long gone, whoever they were. Paradise Square was all offices, mostly those of solicitors, but I used to go there often just to wallow in the elegance.

But the city's oldest building was much, much older, hundreds of years older. Elsewhere the oldest building would have been a church or a guildhall or some town mansion, but this was a pub, and by pub I mean pub: the Old Queen's Head was not a grand coaching hotel, its exterior picked out by spotlights, it was a small, half-timbered building with a jetty, or protruding first floor, and it wasn't in a street or anything like that. The Old Queen's Head stood on its own in the city's bus station like some parked time machine.

Dating back to the fifteenth century, when men still ran around in armour, it had probably survived because the council and the brewers had forgotten about it. Inside it looked like any rundown pub, with lino and fruit-machines and a juke box, though there was one room with panelling; this room was not popular with customers.

I must have looked almost as out of place myself, for my idea of dress then was a long hacking jacket in a violent check, tight cavalry twills and high laced boots: in an industrial city I must have looked like a groom who had had a good run on the horses.

In the three years I spent in Sheffield I lived in six different places, once in a council house, sharing with a tenant whose young wife had died (I slept in a room which was to have been their nursery, surrounded by cartoon kittens on the wallpaper), once in grandeur with four dental students, once in a rooming house where one morning a matching set of transparent bra and crotchless panties came through the post for me. I of course wrote about this, and was met that night by one of my fellow roomers. 'I think you have something of mine,' he said, quite unabashed. 'We … er … share a name.'

My last bedsitter was in a house owned by a Christian sect which worshipped there in strange robes, and where I was politely asked not to cook curries at the weekend as the smell clashed with the incense.

In the 1960s the city of Sheffield was a sociologist's dream, for it would have allowed him to draw the neatest of the neat little diagrams of which his breed is fond. Think of a circle: in the east was industry, the steel works and the terraced streets which housed their workforce; in the south-west, a thin segment, there was money. Also trees. Money and trees have always gone together, and in the south-west there were whole woods within walking distance of the city centre.

In one of these was the grave of a charcoal burner who, setting his cabin on fire in the 1780s, had been buried in its ruins. A century later, Sheffield's poet laureate chanced upon this.

> In the midst of a wood, not far from this city.
> There is a solitary grave. And if you'll listen to my ditty
> Its history I'll try to explain ...

And explain Edward Price did, for three pages and twenty-five verses.

> I have gone to the wood at different seasons,
> My journeys have been for different reasons;
> These visits to me have proved recreative,
> And against troubles that come a fair palliative.

The charcoal burner had sold his charcoal to the steel owners, whose successors were to follow him into the west, building their mansions in what had become what estate agents refer to as 'a leafy suburb'. They went on to build their grammar schools there. Six of the city's eight grammar schools were in the south-west, and in some of its primary schools the 11-plus pass rate was over 50 per cent. In the east the pass rate was often one per cent.

The circle was completed after the Second World War, when the biggest council-house sprawl in Western Europe was built in the north of the city to join the south-west with the east. When this happened the rich moved out to the villages of the Peak District, and their mansions were converted into flats, in one of which I lived with the four dental students. Here I moved through huge rooms, crossed vast lawns, to catch the bus every morning and, with it, the descent to the city's inquests and police courts, a descent into sadness.

'When I entered the house I found I was obliged to keep walking.'

'Can you tell the court why that was, officer?'

'Because otherwise I'd have stuck to the carpets, sir.'

The Welsh working class from which I came was house-proud and ambitious for its children. In the courts of Sheffield the industrial working class was paraded in all its misery. 'The vagina, I found, admitted two fingers,' said a police surgeon in an incest case, with no more emotion than if he had taken a barometric reading. The lawyers were smooth in suits, everyone else small and confused. The latter trailed rent arrears, gave evidence of emptied bottles of sleeping pills, and were without hope. And every night I returned to the huge rooms and the vast lawns. From all this I was rescued by the French Foreign Legion.

An old gentleman of seventy-one, living in the terraces of industrial Sheffield, where he still worked part time for one of the city's many cutlery firms, had written to the paper, and in his letter, by way of introduction, had mentioned the fact that he had served longer than any living Englishman in the Legion – the old Legion of *Beau Geste* and desert forts. He was, if I remember, complaining about the lack of buses, or bin collection, in his part of the city.

Which was how, much later, I found myself in a Soho drinking club, deep below ground and hung about with, of all things, fishing nets, listening to a Polish gentleman. For though editors may not care much for buses and bin collection, they do know what sells papers, or at least they did then. I had been told to write up the old soldier's experiences in the Legion, in which the Polish gentleman had also served. In Soho, now a window-cleaner, he was talking about the good old days.

'Once I drink three litres of red wine. And then I eat one-quarter of a pound of soap, after which five black slugs.'

'What happened then?'

'I am not sure what happen then.'

A little later I was listening to a Hungarian legionnaire, an information scientist from Woking, who had been at Dien Bien Phu. I was asking him about hard men, a term which seemed to come easier to someone whose one experience of violence was being caned by the headmaster of Carmarthen Grammar School, than it did to veterans of the French Foreign Legion. But the Hungarian was a courteous man.

'Well if by that you mean someone who scares me, there was such a man ...' I listened, for he was a ringer for the old film star Jean Gabin, and probably the toughest-looking individual I had ever seen.

He was Hungarian also, and in the Legion, where I had known him very slightly. Quiet man. We met again in Budapest during the Uprising in 1956, when the Russians were coming back.

Now this man, he puzzled me, for he had no gun, and he was wearing this old raincoat. Me, I was wearing a steel helmet, I am a great believer in the steel helmet.

And we were in this room when we heard Russian armoured cars, and this man, he walked to the window. I saw him reach in his pocket and he brought out a bottle of something which he flicked into the street below us, just like that, like you throw a cigarette away. After that was darkness.

The blast, it had caught and thrown me, and the steel helmet, that was rammed down, breaking my nose, which is how it looks the way it does. And of course I couldn't see. When I got the helmet up again there were no Russians alive in the street, and

one of the armoured cars, it had been twisted like washing. But the man in the raincoat, he was reaching into his pocket for another bottle. Which is when I realise what it was. For two, three days, I had been with someone carrying litres of nitroglycerine. I think you could call him a hard man.

Earlier I had watched as, near Victoria Station, he had stood in line with four others, the Pole, a Lithuanian and two Englishmen, one of them the old gentleman who had written to the paper. They were there to be reviewed by a French officer under the statue of Marshal Foch, for it was the anniversary of the Legion's proudest military achievement, that siege in Mexico in 1863 when forty-six legionnaires were besieged inside a farmhouse by 2000 Mexicans, and where, with only six left alive, they fixed bayonets and charged. Sheffield, with its bins or buses, was a long way off.

◆ ◆ ◆

I would go round to see the old gentleman, usually in the evening, and in the kitchen of his small terraced house, his wife knitting placidly in a corner, he would talk about siroccos screaming out of the Sahara so that if you closed the windows you suffocated; if you left the windows open everything got covered with thin, fine sand. It was the detail, the incidental and concrete detail, of his narrative that fascinated me. In the background there was the click of knitting needles, the sound of a cat purring, the odd coal falling from the fire, and all the time the old gentleman talked.

Kipling's 'The Finest Story in the World' is a startling historical narrative because it is grounded in such detail. When he evokes the wretchedness of life below decks on a slave galley he does so by a single image of the darkness, 'the sunlight just squeezing through between the handle (of the oar) and the hole and wobbling about as the ship moves'. That is all, but you feel the man was *there*. With Kipling this was the product of his imagination; the old gentleman was describing things he had known fifty years before.

On guard duty one night he had had his throat cut, and was not killed because he was standing to attention, and the bayonet on his long Lebel rifle had stopped the knife going right through. He described the sensation. 'I scarcely felt it. If you have a knife, put it in warm water and draw it across your throat, that's the feeling. Their knives are sharp, and then the blood comes and that's warm.' He was taken down to headquarters with his head strapped forward, and lived.

Other details: legionnaires were not issued with socks until the film *Beau Geste* got made, when tourists started coming to the great Legion base at Sidi-bel-Abbes. The Legion was transferred to Vietnam, and when the ship went through the Suez Canal the men were battened below deck like cattle, sergeants standing on deck with revolvers to prevent desertion. Even then a man deserted three miles off Bombay, swimming through cross-currents to land, for conditions in the Legion were terrible. As he put it, they could complain to no one, having neither a family nor an MP in France ('they used to say that a legionnaire was just worth a sack of flour').

Each man was expected to carry a 100lb. pack, the heaviest in any army, thirty-one miles a day under the North African sun. In that pack was rifle and bayonet, 200 to 400 rounds of ammunition, a two-litre flask of water, two extra uniforms, tent canvas, tent stakes, a blanket, mess plate and fuel, also a shovel or a pick or a cooking pot.

Still there was always the mobile brothel provided by the French government, where ten women were expected to service five thousand legionnaires. The ten survived because each charged three francs, the equivalent of twelve days' pay. When the Arabs captured a deserter they hit pay dirt, for the French authorities paid them 200 francs for a man whom usually they dragged in half-dead behind a horse. In the Legion the old gentleman had served with Laplanders, Red Indians, Chinese, negroes, even two Eskimos, everything and everyone except Australians and New Zealanders. He met White Russians, American gangsters on the run, Jewish refugees.

'Once I spent six months in a tent with two others. We had the Bible, a copy of the Tatler, and P.G. Wodehouse's *Ukridge* to read. We used to pass them round. I know the Bible well, but there was a time when I knew *Ukridge* off by heart.'

Those weeks in winter were extraordinary. Sometimes the old lady would fall asleep to the rhythms of that soft voice, which made the horrors it conjured up even worse. Four Vietnamese students, thought to be revolutionaries, were beheaded one by one by native troops on the grounds that four living prisoners were a nuisance when the reward was 200 dollars a head ('Nobody screamed, they're a stoical people'). A long-dead, and mummified, camel stood in the sands with footsteps leading away ('They seldom went far'). The widow of the English consul at Rabat lived on in a bungalow surrounded by barbed wire, had an Arab servant push her around on a tricycle, and each week presented the locals with a prize for the best-kept local donkey. Occasionally, he told me, the Legion was sent out to look for lost civilians.

'It was hopeless, it was like looking in a full ashtray for a grain of sand. But the desert could be beautiful as well, you could see purples and greens in it in the evenings. I saw a mirage once, we all saw it. We were on the march and I looked up and saw minarets in the sky. They were very white. It was probably something from up near Cyrenaica, it lasted about ten minutes.'

He was a very bright old boy, and was ambivalent about the Legion, ashamed of the orders he had carried out, yet at the same time fascinated by the institution of which he had been part. Their motto was *Legio Patria Nostra*, the Legion is our Fatherland. No mention of France, which was merely their employer, and until 1931 the Legion was not even included in its list of army regiments; and later, when it was, was placed below the penal regiments.

'I suppose it was no kind of life really, we never knew what day it was, Sunday, Friday, Pancake Tuesday. All we knew was the Legion's feast days because we stopped work then and got drunk. There were a lot of feast days.

'And yet there was a sense of comradeship I don't think you'd get anywhere else. But we were on the side of the burglars. The French government called their policy in North Africa "peaceful penetration by the bayonet". If I live to be a thousand I'd never serve in an invading army again.'

I wrote his story up in five long episodes which the paper serialised across a week, as the result of which I was moved over to features. Farewell, the inquests and the police courts, and hello, bullshit. I visited a cat shelter, and quoted, happily, from its annual report. 'In spite of many tragic happenings 184 kittens were placed in good homes, and 85 full-grown cats. One hamster was put to sleep, likewise four rabbits, one monkey and five sparrows. Three tortoises came for their holidays, and settled down quite well during their stay ...' And would have gone on quoting forever, had I had the space.

Len Doherty and I were the features staff of the *Sheffield Star*. He wrote the leaders, I the column which appeared on the same page;

together we were a bit like a public park. Len had his soapbox, from which, each morning, pale and sweating, he delivered 600 words, then disappeared, usually to the pub. I had the shrubberies and the bandstand where daily I wandered, hoping to come on some tableau or cast-off out of which I could coax 1500 words. Len, under the name Vulcan, thundered; I, under the title By the Way, waffled. My afternoons were long, his were non-existent, and so it was, day after day, for three years. It was an odd time.

Our desks faced each other, away from the open plan of the main office, which meant that for me every morning, from a quarter to nine on, there was Len six feet away; for him there was me. Every morning, spring, summer, autumn, winter: like an old married couple we quarrelled and made up over and over again.

When we got on well, after a few pints of beer in the pub, he would hug me and say, 'You're a good old lad', which, particularly the hugging, embarrassed me. When we got on badly, I could hear him muttering 'Fokkin' graduates' behind his typewriter, which he pounded. Len would have been in his mid-thirties then. He was a hard little man, and looked like a lightweight a bit out of condition, but not that much out of condition. He had a reputation for violence, and had once torn the piping from a pub urinal, emerging in a lounge bar with the green dripping copper wound about his neck like a Dark Age torque. 'Woke up quite a few bastards, did that.'

Like a director of Western films he had this slightly wistful belief in a clean-cut violence that solved everything, as, curiously enough, did the editor Tom Watson, a Territorial Army officer. Tom whispered, Len blustered, and each morning they dreamed the dreams that became the paper's leaders. For Len all this would one day have a terrible irony when he stepped through the looking glass and found himself in a world of real violence.

What gave our rows a dangerous edge was that he did not have much sense of humour, particularly when he had a hangover, which was often. I liked him but there were so many Lens: the showy Len, the sensitive, the over emotional, the fatherly (he had four children, about whom he never talked), the tense, the kind, the bullying, the vulnerable, that I was never sure which of them I would be staring at across the two Imperial typewriters in the morning. And under all this was a sadness. I was twenty-three, with no past except childhood. Len at thirty-five had nothing but past, many pasts, each of which had closed behind him, each time with bitterness.

A Glaswegian, he had at seventeen entered the pits of South Yorkshire, where, like many another, he had married young and become a Communist. He left the Party after the Red Army crushed the Hungarian Rising, leaving amidst much recrimination for he had been marked out as a rising star, a working-class novelist hailed as a successor to D.H. Lawrence. His first book, *The Man Beneath*, came out in 1957, and was followed a year later by *The Good Lion*, both written in 3000-word bursts of longhand between shifts at the mine, so that sometimes he turned up for work without ever having been to bed. Both books were a success, which meant that, still a miner, he became an object of awe, and curiosity, to left-wing intellectuals, into whose circles he erupted like a Westerner hitting town after a long cattle drive, only in Len's case the town was Hampstead.

In his classic account of Northern industrial life *Weekend in Dinlock*, in which Len appears as the coal miner/painter Davey, the American writer Clancy Sigal described these 'sudden, spurting trips down from Yorkshire to London and of the wild, drunken self-pitying, sometimes cruel ways in which he spent the rare releases he gave himself from the prison of his village'. His startled metropolitan male admirers were forced to watch the fights he picked, and there were even more startled women novelists. Of one of these, a very famous writer, he ruefully informed me, for he was not given to boasting about such things, 'In them days, if I'd had a few pints, I could go on for hours. The old girl, she'd come like a bus.'

The Communists felt he had betrayed them when he turned his back on the Party, his mates at the pit felt he had betrayed them by taking up with his smart new London friends, and these in turn felt betrayed when in 1958 their protégé was offered, and took, a job as a features writer on the *Sheffield Star*. His wife endured much.

I met her once when Len invited me home to supper, an unusual occurrence, for he kept his different worlds apart. She was a nice woman, gaunt and tired, and said little as she served us a meal of steak and kidney in portions a worker at the coalface, not men who merely struggled with typewriters, might expect. She and their four children, all of whom seemed to have been born within five or six years, did not sit with us, but looked on as though to see Len home that early was something out of the ordinary. It was certainly the only time I ever saw him eat, and even then he only picked at his food. It was a sad occasion.

When I knew him the novel-writing had also become one of his pasts, though he talked often about the one he told me he was writing, a historical novel set in Roman Britain. He had done some research, and when we were on good terms we discussed footwear and the stirrup. When we were on bad terms we did not talk.

The worst time of all was when he got me to write about an extension to a golf course, at which the chairman of the local brewery was the leading light. Len saw the possibility of a future lit up by subsidised boozing, in which, he airily informed me, I might share. Unfortunately I stumbled on something, I think it had to do with footpath rights across the greens, and could not resist some mischievous crack. The chairman went up the wall, the future receded, and for months it was 'fokkin' graduates' and blank eyes across the Imperials.

After I left the *Star* for *The Times* in 1968 I did not see Len again. I heard about him from time to time, as when the following year he became Provincial Journalist of the Year, and was given foreign assignments, the sort that never come a provincial journalist's way. Colin Brannigan, the paper's ambitious new editor, sent him to Vietnam and the Middle East, and on 10 February 1970, returning from Israel, he got caught up in a world of violence he had only fantasised about until then.

At Munich airport, he was sitting in a transit bus with other El-Al passengers when a terrorist rolled a hand grenade into it. One man was killed and eleven badly hurt, one of whom was Len. But the psychological hurt went deeper, for, his moment of action come at last, he had tried and failed to kick the grenade away, and so blamed himself for their injuries. In the decade which followed his marriage broke up, he was in and out of hospitals, and made several suicide attempts. In 1983, finally about to return to work, he visited the paper which all this time had kept his job open for him and found the office full of people he no longer knew, and, what was worse, who didn't know him. The following day, he was found hanged in his garage. He was just fifty-three, and it was his birthday.

The Worst of Times

It is ten o'clock on a hot August night, and I am driving through the lanes of the Home Counties on my way to the seaside resort of Eastbourne. It is 1968, I am twenty-six years old, and the last thing in the world I want to do is drive through a hot August night to Eastbourne.

But I am a general reporter (Home News) on *The Times*, and tonight is the night shift, something required once a week of all general reporters (Home News). Usually this means I come on at five in the afternoon, try to look busy like a secondhand bookseller in a heatwave, read the papers, sidle off for a Chinese meal ('You bin Singapore?' says the drunken proprietor, weaving between the tables with a bottle of brandy. 'Have a drink, you look like man bin Singapore'), am polite to the various lunatics drawn out of the dark like moths to the paper, phone girls, and am home by midnight. It is a nice way to spend an evening, and I have been doing it successfully for the year I have been on *The Times*. Only tonight is different. Of late all nights have been different.

The Times had been bought by Lord Thomson, a Canadian money man, and the days were gone when office boys warmed the chief sub's slippers in front of an open fire. Thomson, in an effort to inject dynamism into his new purchase, had transferred some of his executives from the *Sunday Times*, which he also owned, sweaty young men in striped shirts.

Unfortunately the only positions so far found for these had been on the night shift. Days on *The Times* were much as they were. Stately leaders got written, usually by men who had been successful in some Oxbridge examination long ago; public figures were given respectful mention (someone swore blind to me that he had actually seen a reference in the paper to 'the late Mr Rasputin'). It was when the sun went down on Blackfriars that the sweating started, and it spread to diffident old gentlemen on the night news desk, men who had never sweated except among their bean rows but who now jumped every time a door opened in case their new masters burst in and demanded to know why the paper had not covered such and such a news story.

For the new men, equipped with bizarre titles like Assistant Editor (Night), had found that the one way they could be seen to make their mark on the paper was to introduce, at the last minute, sensational news stories of their own. The presses were already turning, the first editions almost ready, yet now *The Times* had virtually to be rewritten. In the daytime the atmosphere was that of a cathedral close; when the sun went down it was that of rural Transylvania. Which was why I was speeding through the Sussex lanes.

The paper had had a hot tip, so hot I had not even been told its source, that an oil tanker was in trouble, with oil expected at any moment to come ashore on the beach at Eastbourne, this at the height of the tourist season.

'I hope you don't mind, old man, but it looks like a big one,' said the night news editor, damp with anxiety, then, enticingly, 'We'll put you up at the best hotel.'

For his world was suddenly one full of disaster and conspiracy.

A few weeks earlier the paper had warned its readers that 'a small army of militant extremists' was planning to take over key installations in Central London. Only there were no militant extremists. It would soon disgrace the memory of a dead Cambridge don in the belief that he was the Fourth Man, the accomplice to the spies Burgess, Philby and MacLean (but when the real Fourth Man eventually did turn up he was given lunch at *The Times*). No matter. Tonight oil was coming ashore.

I was anxious because my car, a Saab Sport, a neurotic two-stroke, because of some fault in the electrics, sometimes stopped dead in rain, often in the middle lanes of motorways, and it had just started to rain. But for some reason the old car was on its best behaviour, I could smell the fresh night smells through the open window, and George Herbert's lines were in my mind.

> And now in age I bud again,
> After so many deaths I live and write;
> I once more smell the dew and rain,
> And relish versing.

Suddenly it seemed that whatever awaited me at Eastbourne, it was not such a bad old world. Or life.

It was half-past eleven when I found the hotel, a vast Gothic pile on the front, its doors already locked. I was admitted by the night porter, a leathery old number in a cardigan who managed to give the impression that nothing in this world would surprise him again. He let me use his phone, and when I got through to the news desk I was answered by Stanley, a barrister who seemed not to need sleep for his days were spent in court, his nights on the last shift of all.

'Excellent,' said Stanley, when I told him I had booked in. 'Hold on a minute.' And I heard the phrase 'He's there' as he relayed this information, after which there was some talk I could not make out. 'Did you get that?' said Stanley. 'Right, what we want to know is, how far's the sea?'

I turned to the porter who was reading *The Devil Rides Out*, a supernatural thriller by Dennis Wheatley. 'Excuse me, how far's the sea?'

'Eh?'

'How far's the sea?'

'You going swimming?'

'No, no, how far away is it?'

'Well, it's just across the road.'

'It's just across the road, Stanley.'

'Excellent, excellent. Now this is what you're to do. Don't ring off – run down the beach and tell us what's happening.'

'I've been told not to ring off,' I told the night porter who, behind a large mahogany desk, was now sitting up very straight.

'That's all right, no it isn't. How long you going to be?'

'Oh, just a few minutes. I've got to have a look at the sea.'

'At this time of night?' He put his book down.

'I won't be long.'

Five minutes later I was back. 'I couldn't see the sea,' I told the telephone. 'But I know it's there, I could hear it.'

'Brian, he couldn't see the sea.'

Suddenly there was another voice on the phone. 'Why couldn't you see the sea?'

'Brian, it's dark.'

The night porter, I noticed, was listening with interest.

'Damn,' said the voice.

He sounded so upset I felt obliged to add, brightly, 'It usually is at midnight.'

The phone went dead. I put it down very slowly, and drummed on the desk. 'Look, I hope you don't mind, but could you possibly get me a double whisky? Have one yourself.'

'I think I'd better,' said the night porter. He was looking a bit jumpy, as anyone might emerging from the certainties of Satanism into the uncertainties of a world in which young men at midnight were ordered to find the sea.

As he went off the phone rang, and I answered it. 'Now this is what you do,' said Stanley. 'You wait for first light, you hire a boat, no matter what it costs, and you go to sea. Got that? And you don't come home until you've found the oil. Also, you're not to speak to anyone, we're hoping for an exclusive on this one. Sorry about all this, but it's what we've been told to tell you.' Clearly one of the striped shirts had been and gone.

'Very nice of you, sir,' said the night porter. 'Cheers.'

'Can I ask you something? If someone wanted to hire a boat in Eastbourne, where would he go?'

'Now?'

'No, no, tomorrow morning.'

'Oh, well it depends on where you were thinking of going, sir,' he said guardedly.

'Well, just out to sea really.'

He breathed out, shaking his head. 'Look, it's no business of mine, but I think you should know the coastguards round here are busy buggers.'

'Good God no, it's nothing like that, just a trip round the bay, that's all.'

'Oh well, if that's what you're after. I was just going to say, if you want to hire a boat this time of year you don't stand a chance, they're all in the trip round the bay business. I've got a leaflet somewhere.'

'Let's have a top up first. Put it down to my room.'

'Very nice of you, sir, very nice indeed.'

------◆◆------

At ten o'clock on an overcast morning I was sitting thoughtfully in a motor launch with an elderly couple, a corgi and two Teddy Boys, trying very hard not to part company with the grapefruit segments, porridge, grilled plaice and full cooked breakfast I had just gloomily consumed. There was of course no sign of oil anywhere.

This time it was the day newsdesk that did not believe me. 'No, don't come back. It could be a matter of wind, it's out there somewhere.'

'What do you want me to do?'

'I don't know, walk up and down or something, buy yourself an ice-cream. But remember, don't draw attention to yourself.'

Don't draw attention to myself? The sky had cleared and it looked like being a very hot day, but amongst the swimwear and the straw hats I was in a three-piece black suit with a watch and chain. When I came on the paper I wore my sports coat with the violent check until it was pointed out to me that as a representative of *The Times* I might with little or no warning be called upon to attend a memorial service or some grand luncheon, both of which activities required a dark suit. On the sea front at Eastbourne, an undertaker stared out to sea.

The undertaker lunched at one, with a bottle of wine he charged up to the paper, after which he was in no pain of any kind, and immune to embarrassment, something which had a bearing on what happens next.

At just after 2.30 I saw stretched out on the shingle one of the most beautiful girls I had ever seen. She was in a brief black bikini, and asleep. She had that slightly wiry auburn hair that goes with skin smooth as ivory, and a line of pubic hair led from her trunks to her navel, so fine as to be almost invisible, but when the light caught it, it was the flight path of the sun.

I am not entirely sure what happened next, except that I crunched my way down the crowded beach and sat next to her. Time passed, and I was aware of people talking and of some laughter, but I ignored all this for I was waiting for her to wake up. Which eventually she did.

What I am not sure of is what I then said. Put yourself in her place for a moment. There you are, a teacher from the Midlands in your mid-twenties who has a holiday job teaching foreign students, and you wake from a doze to find a man in a three-piece black suit staring into your opening eyes, as though Death had popped out for a breather from an Ingmar Bergman film.

And what does Death say? 'Isn't it close?' 'Gosh, it's crowded here.' Or, in a choking voice, 'I can't take my eyes off that line of hair.' Possibly not the last.

These things concern me, for never again will I have that confidence, that directness, that expertise. How was it that within an hour, a smock thrown over the bikini, she was sitting down to tea with me at the hotel? Why hadn't she just turned over or pronounced that inspired formula, 'Fuck off'? I think humour must have had something to do with it, for when I mentioned *The Times* and the oil she roared with laughter, a healthy uninhibited burst of laughter that had people watching us with even more interest.

The laughter took me aback for she was a rather serious young woman, capable later of such remarks as 'I don't think anyone should be ashamed of masturbation, do you? I mean, how else would we get rid of our tensions?' But that, as I say, was later, when we were walking along the sea-front, and I was uneasily aware that

I might be, was, out of my league. And how the hell had we got on to masturbation?

Anyway, it was now half-past-six. We were sitting on some kind of breakwater, and in a scene reminiscent of *The Boyhood of Raleigh* I was pointing out at a sea out of which the oil might still come. And it was then that she did it. As gently as a priest administering benediction she leant across and laid her hand on my lap. 'There isn't any oil, you're going to have to convince them sometime.'

'Yes.'

'They'll have to be told if you're ever going to get home.'

'I suppose so.'

'Perhaps not yet though.' The hand was suddenly heavy.

'No.'

HOME NEWS REPORTING STAFF EXPENSES
Item: lunch (bill) 10s 6d
Item: tea with member of lifeboat crew (bill) 6s
Item: supper with off-duty coastguard (bill) £1 2s 8d

I had not wanted to be on *The Times*, a paper which not long before had substituted news for the classified announcements on its front page. I just wanted to be out of Sheffield, and had hoped to join the *Sunday Times* (I did not know about the sweaty young men then), a paper that seemed to me to be new and dynamic, words it often used, usually of itself. Unfortunately most of my generation on provincial papers in the late 1960s also wanted to join the *Sunday Times*.

So when, after two interviews at *The Times*, first with the Home

Editor, then with the Home News Editor, Frank Roberts, a kindly old gentleman who wore a lightweight gardening jacket in the office, which made him look as though at any moment he might pop out to attend to his geraniums, I was offered a job, I took it, even though I was still reeling from my second interview.

Most of this had been taken up with hints of the honour that could, just could, come my way. Why, Frank could only think of one man who had ever left *The Times* of his own accord. 'Left to write a book, only the book didn't do very well, so he wrote to the editor asking for his old job back. D'you know what he said, the editor that is? "The caravan has now moved on." Never worked for us again.'

'Who was that?'

'Er ... Graham Greene.'

'Isn't he in tax exile now?'

'I believe so,' said Frank vaguely.

Then he stopped and looked embarrassed. 'There's something I must ask you.' He had taken his spectacles off and was polishing them on a corner of his gardening jacket. 'It's something I ask all the young men.'

I stared at that big red benevolent face, which in turn was staring out of the window. *Oh God, he wants to know if I masturbate.*

He squinted through his spectacles, then briskly put them on again. 'Do you drink?'

'No.' How else could one answer such a question?

'Good. I hope you didn't mind my asking you that.'

--------◆◆◆--------

Later I found out why. *The Times*, intent on turning itself into a newspaper, had begun to recruit men from the popular papers, some of whom were seasoned drinkers used to five, six, seven pints of beer at lunchtime, an intake that did not seem to affect them in the least.

It was the first time the paper had encountered such behemoths. They should have known of their existence because when the breathalyser came in the great intelligences which then ruled the *Daily Express*, seeking to alert its readers, sent its news staff out to lunch on expenses, and told them to behave as they usually did. When they came back, the paper breathalysed the lot. Only, not content with that, it printed the results *on the front page*, oblivious to the fact that what was being printed was an indictment of itself. Most of them were well over, there were young women who had knocked back the best part of a bottle of champagne, but one man, their veteran crime reporter, had put away fourteen straight brandies, if I remember aright. Yet he blew into the device and the crystals were yellow as marigolds.

So when *The Times* recruited such men the problem was not that they could not do their jobs after such a lunch hour, they clearly could: it was the effect they had on the existing members of staff who accompanied their new colleagues to make them feel at home. By four o'clock in the afternoon you saw them slumped over their typewriters snoring as gently as the Seven Sleepers of Ephesus, It was a very strange newspaper that I joined on Monday, 24 July 1967.

On my first morning (mornings started at eleven o'clock on *The Times*), Frank took me aside and told me it was the custom to throw new young men in at the deep end. Was he dispatching me to a war zone? Not quite. His idea of the deep end was the Royal International Horse Show at the White City, on which I was to write a descriptive little essay.

It appeared the following day in the paper, 'Shrine Where the Horse Revives a Vanished World'. I have it in front of me now. 'Horses and girls are everywhere: thin freckled girls, great brown girls who might have come out of a butter advertisement or John Betjeman's memories, and who have "no idearr" where the Japanese horses are . . .' And so on, 700 words of it, except the ending I had laboured over had been cut as abruptly as the last telegraph message out of a Western fort overrun by Indians. That was my introduction to the little ways of the subs on *The Times*. It was also the zenith of my career on the paper; from then on, though I would stay for three years, it was downhill all the way.

Part of the trouble was that I had been brought onto the paper to write descriptive or humorous pieces in the news section. Only the chief sub-editor Leon Pilpel, the gatekeeper to these pages, was a grave gentleman who saw *The Times* as a paper of record, something that ruled out description and humour, for in both a reader might encounter adjectives. The chief sub-editor loathed adjectives because they represented comment, so any news story, to get past him, had to be a fusillade of fact.

Besides, the paper already had a good descriptive writer in Philip Howard, a man licensed, like a game dealer, for adjectives, humour and, in his case, classical allusions. A considerable scholar, Philip was each year allowed out to attend the whole week's proceedings of the Classical Association, much as Judas Iscariot was allowed out of Hell to cool himself on an ice floe, when *The Times* would print his reports, Philip's that is, in full. Once, phoning one of these through, he heard the copy-taker say, 'What tosh.' Philip, thinking he had misheard, carried on. 'How much more of this stuff is there?' said the man, and, a little later, 'You don't think this is going to make the paper, do you, mate?' Stiffly Philip told him that it had made the paper the day before. 'What, the *Evening Standard*?' He had misdialled.

But the most I could expect was a career as his understudy, which meant that for the rest of the time I reported on riots, fires, the deaths of celebrities and the after-dinner pronouncements of politicians. Very little of what I wrote ever appeared, or, if it did, I did not recognise it after Pilpel's boys with their cruel little pencils had swarmed over it like the *dynion y bwyelli bach*, the men with the little axes, the Wreckers on Carmarthen Bay who hacked rings from the fingers of the dying. Rejection for me became a way of life, and what made this worse was that on reporting jobs I met men from the *Guardian,* whose accounts appeared in full (with adjectives), when not a word of mine was in the paper.

Very occasionally something did. 'Someone has been reading *The Lancet* again,' said Frank Roberts, shaking his head as he often did when relaying an instruction from his new masters. 'And on page twelve he has found a story about the dangers of exploding champagne corks. Champagne corks.' He had a tendency to repeat phrases when he wanted to emphasise that the two of you had once known sanity and better days. 'Apparently chaps have been turning up in casualty with eye injuries. Eye injuries. It was thought this might make a hard news story, but I thought you ... with your light touch. You know, the dangers of the moneyed life, that sort of thing.'

I took the cutting from him and started to read it through quickly before he could make his escape. 'Hang on, Frank. It says here there have only been eight cases in four years.'

'Light touch, old man,' said Frank over his shoulder. 'Light touch.'

It was his way of being kind. A light touch meant your name appeared over a news story, and not just the 'by a Times Reporter':

it was the paper's way of dissociating itself from the adjectives and the humour that might follow.

Using two fingers I began to type, 'To the spiritual dangers of the moneyed life chronicled so roundly in Holy Writ there is now added one telling physiological footnote...' Humour could never be too heavy for *The Times*. I stopped typing, for it was half-past two and I had to make this last.

Two hours later, and I was reading over my masterpiece.

In one London hospital alone eight cases of eye injury due to champagne corks have been treated in the last four years. Three patients have been left with permanent defects of vision, and all, says *The Lancet*, could have been avoided by care in opening the bottles. The magazine advances two theories for this, the first being the sheer volume of champagne being drunk now, the second that those natural openers, English butlers...

English butlers? The only English butler I had ever seen was in a film, and he had been a ghost.

... English butlers have almost everywhere gone under the hill. A head waiter at a London hotel...

Called to the phone, he had been Spanish (at least I think he was Spanish) and harassed. 'What you say, pipple having eyes out from corks? You think we in business to make people blind, sar?' I read on. 'A head waiter at a London hotel, where up to 150 champagne bottles a day are opened, told me that his forty-seven years in the trade had not yielded a single statistic.' 'Forty-seven year, sar.'

The Lancet says that a cork shooting from an upright bottle can reach a height of 40 feet. This means it strikes the eye at a velocity of about 45 feet per second, or 30 mph.

The miles per hour I had worked out myself: checking and re-checking had taken me the best part of half an hour. After such an assembly of lunatic facts there was no way it could not have appeared in *The Times*.

And then there were the nights. People were forever calling on the paper, people with grievances, with causes they thought needed support, intelligent people, indignant people, nutters. At night you were off the maps.

An unsmiling young woman in a plastic mack, she had a light moustache, also letters to show she had been seduced by Edward Heath, then Prime Minister. And photographs, she said. I sat with her in the front hall, for we were not encouraged to take members of the public into the office in case it proved difficult to get rid of them.

The Prime Minister for some reason had chosen to write his letters in green biro, with certain words like 'MANHOOD' in capitals, and with the complicated stuff underlined, like what the two of them had got up to on a swing in Ladbroke Grove.

'And this is what the beast sent me.'

The photograph, in colour, showed a turd, presumably human, among the chocolates in a box of Cadbury's Milk Tray. 'He took this?'

'No, no, he sent me the box. You'll notice the caramels and the Turkish Delight have gone, they were always his favourites. I took the photograph.'

'Nice.' I didn't know what else to say.

'Isn't it?' she said, brightening. 'I didn't use a flash.'

'No?'

'No, if you use a flash you don't get the tones...'

I had the feeling that some were veterans of such nocturnal visits, for, just as newspaper offices attracted them, so they always had some reason for their calls, something that attracted us, and reeled us in like trout.

She was elderly and genteel, and she wanted to talk about her experience of the horrors of nursing homes for the elderly, and, by implication, genteel. Such homes were in the news at the time, and I was taking copious notes to the dictation of that unhurried voice, when suddenly she interrupted her catalogue to say that one night in her despair she had opened the windows on the fourth floor, intending to throw herself out. 'And I'd have done it too, had the great hands not come.'

'"Had the great hands not come..."' My shorthand being non-existent, I was repeating the phrases as I wrote them down. 'Hang on, what hands?'

'What's that, dear?'

'The hands, whose hands were they?'

'God's,' she said quietly.

But the strangest of all was Primo. I was late getting down to reception and the commissionaire was reproachful. 'Gentleman's been waiting for you, sir,' he said, clearly in awe of one of the best-dressed men I had ever seen. He was wearing a fitted black overcoat with a velvet collar, and was leaning forward on one of the big easy chairs, one hand over the other on a silver-topped cane. He must have been in his early seventies, his white hair worn long like that of a successful Edwardian actor-manager.

'You've called about...?'

'Unemployment,' said a voice so silvery it had a tinkle in it. He did not seem inclined to say more.

I was so startled by this vision of elegance that had blown in from the winter night that I then made a big mistake. 'Look, it's a bit bleak down here, perhaps you'd like to come upstairs, Mr...'

'Primo,' he said.

'Is that your first name?'

'It is my only name. I am supreme in the Universe.' But we were in the lift and it was too late now.

The only other reporter on duty was Peter Waymark, who looked up in surprise as we came in. And then it started. Speaking very slowly and looking into my eyes, Primo began to talk about how the Wilson government was dealing with unemployment. Harold Wilson and George Brown were gassing the unemployed.

In the corner of my eye I could see Waymark walking very quickly towards one of the sound-proofed phone booths, only he didn't close the door. He wanted to hear.

Buses, Primo went on, were bringing the unemployed down at night from the North. Would I like to make a note of their numbers? No, it was no trouble at all, he had them with him. And he took a small leather notebook from his pocket. In order to distract myself, for I could hear muffled explosions coming from the phone booth, I began to write. And still the voice went on.

The gas chambers were under Heal's, three floors under, and the unemployed were first given a meal cooked by the best chefs. With wine, very good wine, all paid for by the taxpayer. And then at three in the morning, no earlier, no later, they were ushered into the gas chambers.

At first I could cope, but then Waymark peered round the phone booth door, a handkerchief stuffed in his mouth. And of course then I was gone. But the amazing thing was that it did not affect

Primo in the least. He waited politely until I had finished making my rainforest noises, then, his voice as even as before, he offered me a peppermint. 'And perhaps your friend would like one too.'

I watched him walk away into the night, his stride vigorous, his cane swinging, a happy man.

I watched my editor too, not such a happy man, on the rare occasions I caught sight of him, for the paper's library was on the same floor as its corridor of power and I would look up over the cuttings, like a man in a fairy tale watching from a thicket the passing of a fabulous beast, as William Rees-Mogg, then in his early forties, glided towards his lavatory. Harold Evans, the editor of the *Sunday Times*, rushed about all over the place, pursued by his staff who managed to corner him only in the lavatory; in his time most of the important editorial decisions on the *Sunday Times* took place in its pissoir. But Rees-Mogg had a private lavatory; in the three years I was on the paper I did not meet him once.

I saw more of his predecessors, for their portraits lined the walls. National newspapers do not usually commemorate their editors, having generally parted with them on bad terms. But *The Times* did, or at least *The Times* did then. Since 1817, when the great Barnes was appointed, there had been just ten of them (and fourteen Popes, as Rees-Mogg once reminded his reading public).

We talked about him a lot in the newsroom, for few of my colleagues had met him either, and Frank the News Editor, it was said, had taken a holiday in Somerset to gaze, like a plane spotter at an Iron Curtain airfield, at the Palladian outline of what was then his editor's country house.

But then *The Times*, like the Ice Age, had two species of hominids, and, unlike in the Ice Age, they did not mix. The grandees, the executives, the foreign correspondents, the leader writers, the parliamentary people, were rarely seen by us, though on occasion they did walk among men, as when one of them, in the build-up to a general election with Parliament suspended, was sent on a sort of Cobbett's Rural Rides tour of the country. His reports were remarkable. Towns which should have been in the Mendip Hills were identified as being in the Cotswolds. 'Do you think he knows where he is?' asked the deputy editor at conference. He went to Carmarthen where a friend of mine, then suffering a breakdown, was in the habit of running through the town in the small hours to write, with a black felt pen, graffiti like 'Nixon, Madonna of Napalm' and 'John X for Pope. Give the boy a chance' on the walls of phone booths. The *Times* man, passing through, reported gravely, 'This is a town remarkable for its political sophistication.'

--------◆◆◆--------

Meanwhile the night shifts became more and more demented as the old gentlemen on the newsdesk, who had never rung anybody after ten o'clock at night, began tipping people like the Archbishop of Canterbury out of their beds at one in the morning to give some reaction to the news.

Philip Howard was told to ring Lord Goodman, who then ran the Arts Council, to check out a story that the Council intended making a grant to Bertram Mills' Circus. It was nearly midnight, and, wistful for his bed, he was only pretending to do so when the Assistant Editor (Night) burst into the office. He handed a phone to Philip and stood over him as he dialled, this time the right number (for he had only been going through the motions before). To Philip's horror Goodman answered.

When he had finished speaking, Goodman said, very slowly, 'No, we are not making a grant to Bertram Mills' Circus. What we are doing is making a grant to the Regent's Park Zoo so they can train chimpanzees to become reporters on *The Times*. Good night.'

------◆◆◆------

Most of the time I was on the paper I felt I'd strayed into a situation comedy which we were making up as we went along. *The Times*, intent on moving into the newspaper big league, had sponsored an expedition into the Matto Grosso, hoping this would yield reports of lost cities in the jungle, giant snakes and news of the disappeared British explorer Colonel Fawcett. What it got was relentless, and very detailed, catalogues of butterflies and plants. So when one of the expedition returned it was suggested, rather delicately, that to justify the expense, I should try to add some ... I think the word was drama, or it could have been spice.

At first things went well. Very well. Where, I asked were they staying?

'Oh, quite near the River of Death.'

River of Death. I wrote it in large capitals, for this was where Fawcett was last heard of, and, anyway, you can't go far wrong with the River of Death. 'You've made your base camp there?'

'Oh no, we're in a rather nice Brazilian government guesthouse.'

Bugger.

'Meet any Indians?'

'Oh yes, the Xavantes.'

The most terrifying tribe of all, thought to have been responsible for Fawcett's disappearance. Never seen until the sudden *ff-utt* of an arrow. Head-shrinkers all. I had practically written the piece in my head. 'You actually *saw* them?'

'Couldn't miss them. They spent most of their time playing association football.'

Pilpel's boys did their best, giving it the headline 'At the End of Civilisation'. But it didn't quite ring true.

———◆———

Then there was the night the mangoes came. Philip Howard is a remarkably good-looking man, something that has never occurred to him, though it has to others. Persuaded by the fashion editor to model her idea of male elegance, for he is also good-natured, he appeared in the paper in velvet knee-breeches, posed on some stairs and staring nervously at a great light above him as though about to be kidnapped by aliens; you could feel the embarrassment coming off him. But not half so much as when, sent to cover a boat-race on the Nile, he attracted the interest of an Egyptian gentleman. Howard is six foot three, the son of an England rugby captain and of a Wimbledon champion; the Egyptian gentleman was tiny, but in love. In the end Howard was forced to retire to his hotel room and lock the door against his demon suitor. After that the presents started to come.

I was on the night shift when the box, addressed to Philip, was carried in by two commissionaires. I rang him.

'Where's it from?'

'Egypt.'

There was a groan, followed by, 'What's in it?'

'Hang on.' I began to prise the lid up using a large pair of office scissors. I was uneasy, having seen too many films about what happens when such a box turns up. Then, 'Philip, I've never seen anything like this, it's full of...'

'Oh God, what?'

'Mangoes.'

'Mangoes?'

'Hundreds of them, layer after layer.' Mangoes then were very rare in Britain; if you saw them anywhere it was in Harrods Food Hall, where they were very expensive. 'What d'you want me to do with them?'

'Oh, stick the box under my desk if you can. And help yourself.'

Now I had never eaten a mango, but by a couple of hours later I had eaten fifteen, and was crouched over the crate, the office scissors in my hand, my face as sticky as flypaper. That was when Philip came in to collect his crate, but the damage had been done. For me, for a whole week, solid motions, like mangoes, were a fond memory.

<hr>

But there were times when the merry-go-round crashed to a halt. There was the night one of my colleagues rang in to check on whether the list of casualties had come through from a train crash; he thought his girlfriend might have been on the train. She had been, and was dead, and I had to tell him.

And then there was the night Basil and I found ourselves talking about the Nazis, or at least I was talking, he was listening.

'I saw them hanged, you know,' said Basil, but with no more emphasis in his voice than if once in his long career he and they had found themselves in the same bus queue.

Basil Gingell, the oldest reporter and a man well into his sixties, was the Church and Naval Correspondent, a conjunction of responsibility remarkable even by the standards of *The Times*. He was considered too venerable to be asked to do the night shift, but on that occasion, the staff being depleted by illness or something, he and I were on together.

Basil was a tall, reserved gentleman, rather like one of those retired senior army officers I was to meet later who were called in to help with crowd control at royal garden parties; he was one of nature's courtiers. I never once heard Basil swear, get in a temper, or gossip about any of our colleagues, so I was in awe of him, and of his imperturbable range of small-talk. And now, having thrown this fact like a hand grenade into our conversation, he did not seem inclined to say any more. What follows is the result of my questions.

Basil had been a war correspondent for one of the press agencies, and was covering the Nuremberg Trials when at the last minute he was called in and told that later that night he would be the official British press representative at the hangings of the ten Nazi leaders condemned to death. At eleven minutes past one a.m. on 16 October 1946, said Basil, his memory branded with details. The creaking steps to the specially built gallows. The waiting American master sergeant who had never hanged anyone in his life before. And the silence, the awful silence broken only by the last speeches of the condemned.

The first was Ribbentrop the foreign minister who pompously wished for Germany's unity to be preserved and for an understanding between East and West. Keitel the field marshal called on Almighty God to have mercy on the German people, and then, turning to the chaplain, an American, he said, 'I thank you and all those who sent you with all my heart.' Streicher the fanatic was brief. He just shouted, 'Heil Hitler.'

Basil remembered every word. But he remembered other things as well, the jerk of the rope and the way it stopped dead, though not on every occasion. In the case of Streicher it continued to jerk and plunge for something like twenty minutes. Basil was remembering these details across twenty years, I am remembering them across forty. It would have been impossible for either of us to forget.

And then there was the third time the merry-go-round stopped, in my case forever. It was just before twelve noon when the phone rang on the one direct line in the reporters' room, CEN 9662; I have not forgotten the number, for it was the one on which girls, wives, relatives called. But this time when I answered it a voice I didn't recognise said, 'That is Byron, isn't it? This is Mrs Bowen next door. Your mother would like to speak to you.' I didn't recognise it because it was so formal and slow. And then my mother was on the line.

'*Oh Byron, mae e' wedi mynd.*' Oh Byron, he's gone. Aged fifty-eight, my father had died.

When I stumbled out of the booth everything was going on as before. Phones were ringing, people were walking about, yet where I was there was nothing, just this huge flat fact, and it was the flatness that floored me. The thing I had dreaded ever since he had had his first heart attack five years earlier had finally happened. In the years which followed that first attack I had quizzed every doctor I came across about his possible life expectancy, for we were a small family, just the three of us; I endlessly imagined what form the choreography might take, strangers crowding round the one figure suddenly the centre of attention, which he would have loathed. But he had died, as he did everything, neatly.

Feeling unwell, he had had himself driven home from work, lunchbox under his arm, to die in his own bed, my mother downstairs at the time making him a cup of tea. There was no long illness, no leave-taking, just the pain, as he described it to me of his first attack, of a huge wheel coming over him. It was the detail that brought it home to me, for he could make wheels, had made many. I was twenty-five, and I had come to love my father.

I loved his fine good looks, his humour, and was just beginning to appreciate that this was someone I could talk to, as when, having crashed my car, I rang him and he had said, 'Now, we'll keep this from your mother.' She had a tendency to hysteria. But, more than anything, I loved his sense of values, for this was a cultivated man. Not by the standards of most of you; he had not been out of his country except for the odd holiday in England, and then perhaps six times, had only worked outside his own county once, had read at most half a dozen books, was never at ease in English. But he was a craftsman. He could make Regency sideboards, Welsh dressers, Bible chests, he could make claw and ball legs until you saw the terrible claws tightening their grip: this man, who never used a handheld power tool, could make anything.

In the years before his death, when things were closing in on him, I bought him things I knew he had always wanted. In the Burlington Arcade I bought him a single-bladed small German penknife, horn-handled, as perfect (and expensive) a knife as I could get. When I gave it to him he said something that broke my heart, that he would look after it so I could have it back. And in a small shop in the East End, after a day of telephoning, I got him an Arkansas hone.

This, a natural stone occurring only near hot springs in two areas in Arkansas, is the ultimate whetstone. If you know your archaeology you will have read that one of the most treasured, and most mysterious, objects in the Sutton Hoo burial was a whetstone; in the Dark Ages kings took such things into the next world to sharpen the swords of the heroes. My father made a beautiful box of mahogany into which he fitted his; I have it on my desk as I am writing this, and had our burial customs been different I would have put it in his grave. The passing of a crafts-man in a world that has ceased to value craft requires ceremony.

After his death I oiled his tools, something that appealed to my sense of history. I wrote a poem about it.

> I cleaned your tools today.
> They lay in green baize
> and along the oak racks
> of your chest, the way
> forty years of craft had them lie.
>
> No weapon hoard
> could be more legendary.
> I lift the pale-handled saw
> a liner steward brought,
> a long Diston, Pittsburgh forged.

The plane for mortising
bought in your youth, used
just once, the great black plane
I unscrew and grease, a thing
you never would allow me, living.

You knew your peers, were
at the end the last
among them in our town
to turn a wooden stair.
Among the living such small fames endure.

Stamped on a chisel haft a name,
D. John, your own below it.
Defying the anonymity
of craft, hands in time
honour the paler hands beneath them.

My mother kept his coffin open in our darkened front room so friends and relatives could view him, and it was only with difficulty that I managed to persuade her to have the lid closed on the fourth day. She would die in hospital, unviewed in a morgue. But his passing was in the old Welsh way.

Three days after the funeral the merry-go-round started up again. I wrote,

> The first award for the After-dinner Speaker of the Year was made yesterday. Meeting at the Dorchester in London, the Guild of Professional Toast-masters, who between them had heard some 10,000 after dinner speeches last year, chose Lord

Redcliffe-Maud, Master of University College, Oxford, as the man they would most like to hear over the walnuts and the wine ...

But at least that appeared in the paper. Most of what I wrote in those three years never did. On the *Sheffield Star* I had written whole pages daily and seen these appear; now I was lucky if I saw something appear twice a month under my name (all my yellowing cuttings for those three years fit into a single foolscap envelope). But I took a revenge of which my horse-dealing ancestors would have been proud. *The Times* had started a *Diary* column, fully staffed by four writers; I now started rewriting and trimming my rejected stories, and sold these to them, items for which of course, being on a salary, I had already been paid, so the paper was printing, and paying for, the contents of its own wastepaper basket. And for well over six months nobody noticed. Of course when they finally did there was a row, but not a big row; there was more embarrassment than anything.

Most of the news stories which did appear under my name were elegaic in some way or another. 'A century and a half of outraged English morality came to an end yesterday when the name of Lord Byron was entered among those of his peers in the Poets' Corner of Westminster Abbey' ... 'The great princes usually stay in exile, but on Wednesday Godfrey Evans of the 91 Test victims again keeps wicket for Kent after eight years of retirement.'

Dear God, I even managed to be elegaic over a fucking machine-gun. The last British Army 303, 'last used in Borneo', though the PR man was vague as to when and on whom, was handed over by a general to the directors of Vickers, which had made it. Fat men in pin-stripe and lean men in uniform crowed over the thing. 'Gleaming and polished, it ends its days amid the walnut and electrically operated curtains of the board room . . .' I wrote that; looking back, I have never been so ashamed of anything. *The Times* put it on the front page.

But I did have one small moment of triumph in those three years. The paper sent me to report on something called the International Arthurian Congress, a gathering of scholars, which, meeting every three years, was held in 1969 in Cardiff. With some 200 delegates from all over the world, it was the sort of event to which its organisers felt obliged to invite *The Times,* hoping it might make three paragraphs at most. Except it got someone obsessed by the Arthurian myth. My first report of 800 words across three columns was printed in full, as a result of which, on the second day, the *Guardian* sent a girl; she did not know much about Arthur so I wrote her report as well as my own. On the third day the *Sun,* of all papers, sent a man who knew even less, and asked me to brief him on the old king as our bus accelerated through the Somerset lanes to Glastonbury.

'What you must remember is that if Arthur existed, which some doubt, he was fighting immigrants.'

'Great, the newsdesk's going to like that.'

'Only these immigrants were the English.'

'Hang about, how come?'

'Arthur was Welsh. The Welsh are the original inhabitants of this country.'

'Oh shit.'

At Glastonbury something odd happened. The most venerable of Arthurian scholars, Prof. Jean Frappier of the Sorbonne, had always been vociferous in denying that Arthur had ever existed, arguing that he had been a character out of fiction not history. But now two of his students gleefully came up to me to say they had seen him in the Abbey ruins stand at the reputed site of Arthur's grave, and very quietly remove his beret. As we puffed up the hill to South Cadbury, which may, or may not, have been Camelot, I asked him, *pourquoi avait-il levé son chapeau at Arthur's tombeau?* He said he did not believe in Arthur, therefore he could not believe in Arthur's tombeau, then in English, 'I took off my 'at because my 'ead was 'ot.' *The Times*, respectful of eminent men, cut the last sentence.

I also met a tall, graceful American girl whose father was a Texan oil millionaire. Later in London she introduced me to her parents, to Daddy Bigbucks and to Step Momma number two or three, who seemed very suspicious of me. Over lunch at Wheeler's this woman, who had the sharpest face I had ever seen on a human being, tried to make small-talk.

'Tell me, Mr RAH-giz, how d'you reckon we're going to get out of Viet-nahm?'

Just like that, over the Dover sole. Jesus. All three faces were looking at me.

'By night,' I said firmly.

Which is how these memoirs are being written on a cold winter's afternoon in Northamptonshire, not Dallas.

———◆◆◆———

I left the paper as the result of an interview I had with Michael Cudlipp, the Assistant Editor (Night), one of the sweaty young transplants from the *Sunday Times*. Not having had a pay rise in three years, I felt neglected.

'Why?' asked Cudlipp. 'What have you done for *The Times*?'

And for one mad moment I felt like adapting Anthony Quinn's speech in the film of *Zorba the Greek*, 'I have fought for my country, I have raped for my country', but I didn't.

I left to join the *Daily Telegraph* Magazine as its staff writer.

Colour magazines relied on freelance journalists but they usually had one on the staff as a dogsbody, rather like a tame Indian in a Western fort, and there must have been a vacancy at the time. There usually was; staff writers on the *Telegraph* Magazine under its editor John Anstey had the life expectancy of a Great War pilot, and I was warned I'd be lucky if I lasted three months. In the end I was there for twenty-five years, on the staff and as a freelance.

I had one last contact with *The Times*, when, something like two decades after I left, I was offered the job of the paper's obituaries editor. I think they must have been alarmed at the success of the obits columns on the *Telegraph* which, for the first time in newspaper history, its editor the great Hugh Massingberd had made not just readable, but, ironically, full of life. I hesitated because of the tax problems involved in going on the PAYE system again.

In the end I rang back and asked if it might be possible for me to do the job part-time. I was told, very politely, that death was not a part-time activity.

7

Death of a Friend

'THAT YOU?'

'This is *The Times*,' I said.

'Don't muck about, I know it's you.'

'Oh shit . . .' I knew that high, hoarse voice, and the telephone manner. Speaking quickly, I said, 'Listen, the Foreign Office has been on to me about you. You know that reference I gave you the time you went for a job at the UN? They've been in touch, asking whether I'd like to reconsider what I'd written. I thought, fuck it, what's he done now? What's happened?'

'Hughes . . . is back.'

He was in his thirties then. He looked just as he had looked at school and always would look: he had one of those faces that are out of place in modern times. If you have ever seen a film about the Middle Ages you will know what I mean; about 95 per cent of those taking part look like chaps in fancy dress, but amongst them may be one, perhaps two, no more, who look the business. Hughes was like that. Put him in a cowl, and you could see him against the flames, urging the loonies to destroy in the name of God. In 1958 Savonarola was in the Upper Sixth Arts of the Queen Elizabeth Grammar School for Boys, Carmarthen.

His face was a pale wedge tapering from high cheekbones to a long chin; there was no flesh on it, and no lips, so when he laughed it was as though someone had opened a zip; he lacked the equipment for smiling. As for the rest of him, he looked as if he had been dug up after a week. He wore a black suit at school when the rest of us were in the statutory blue blazers, later adding a black mackintosh, and, later still, a black shirt. 'Wonderful thing, black,' he told me. 'You can wear it for a month.'

When I got to know him I was the scholarship boy, showy, shallow, knowing exactly what would please the various examining boards at which I was pointed, but little else. He was a legend, the oldest boy in the school, in either his eighth or ninth year; none of us knew for certain, for he had gone through it like Rimbaud's *Bateau Ivre*, a boat that had slipped its moorings, drifting on and on and on. Becalmed in the fifth form, he had taken his O-levels two or three times, and then, the current quickening, found he had accumulated enough of the things to make a landfall in the sixth, which is where I met him.

When I think of him I remember those lines from Nathaniel West's *Miss Lonelyhearts*: 'At school and perhaps for a year or two afterwards they had believed in beauty and in personal expression as an absolute end. When they lost that they lost everything. Money and fame meant nothing to them. They were not worldly men.' Had I quoted that to Hughes he would have laughed, for he liked to think of himself as a very worldly man indeed.

At school he hadn't cared what anyone thought of him, which was extraordinary at our small Welsh grammar school where the town clerks, the lecturers, the doctors to be were already assembling the various acts that would be required of them. We were careful and wary, went around in groups, knew our place in the pecking order, mocked anything that made someone in the least unique or different. But nobody mocked him, and that was what fascinated me about him, and would always fascinate me. For even then he didn't seem like a schoolboy at all, there was a quality of stillness about him that you get in the very old. He was bleak, funny and totally original.

As a small boy he had known fame briefly when a car stopped and a man tried to invite him into it, at which point Hughes said he would have to ask his mother first. Of course the car then accelerated away, leaving him to the plaudits of the mothers who told us this was the right response. 'I made a big mistake there,' said Hughes. 'That car was full of sweets.'

The son of a small, and grubby, public house in the town, called ironically the Sun in Splendour, he would turn up from it every morning in the black suit, and then disappear into it at lunchtime and in the evenings. He was rarely seen at weekends until some whim got him to take up cross-country running and he was good at it, for he carried no weight, a pale figure coming out of the rain, his face clenched. He had no friends, had never sought any, for a friend to him would have been large and complicated and useless.

He had mooned away his adolescence, he told me much later, in the attic of the pub. There was an old record player there, one of the wind-up ones, only they just had the one record, and this was cracked. He played it over and over.

> Life goes on
> Just like a song.
> Why waste your *click* days
> In foolish ways? *click*
> You can't regain *click*
> Lost plesh-uhhhh. *werrrk*

Years later he was still singing that, adding the sound effect of the scratches himself.

The pub was hunched and dark inside, a place of old hide chairs and small stuffed animals in glass cases. It had changed little in a hundred years, and, as the windows were never opened, stank of old tobacco and spilt beer, which is actually an interesting smell. Everything was old: the drinks advertisements from defunct breweries on the walls, the fading photograph of the old Duke of Windsor as a boy midshipman. Hughes's parents, whose only child he was, were in their sixties. As a result, he told me in a rare moment of intimacy, he had missed out on childhood. He dressed like an old man, tucking his shirt into his underpants.

'My mother bought me a piano once. I was given lessons for years, but she would never let me practise. "You can't now, we're open." Then she'd say, "You can't now, we're shut."'

In the town his parents had the reputation of being mean, which, considering how much money he was eventually left, must have been true. Years later, one Saturday lunchtime in a pub in London, I remember him telling me that they had never bought him a train set. It was three weeks from Christmas, and he said he was thinking of buying himself one, and he meant it. He would have been about thirty then, and all afternoon we trailed round the crowded toyshops, winding up large clockwork trains, watching the small electric ones buzz on their rails. Of course he did not buy a train set, the years of rural poverty his people had known saw to that. But he did seriously think about it.

This was one of the things that fascinated me about him, and which made him so different. What the rest of us lacked, being on the make, and always would lack, was joy. And this, in his strange way, is what Hughes sought. The other thing was his black humour.

The only things in life that amused him, really amused him, were his own misfortunes. He was good at essays, the sort where the examiners provided a topic on which you then had to write, something that required no preliminary swotting, just originality and a way with words, but the year he was due to sit A-level English the essay was dropped from the syllabus. 'Typical,' he said. The wanton gods were a non-stop variety act; nothing they did surprised him.

The essays on the set books which he did produce were very short, and very odd. At the time he had a great enthusiasm for the Western novel *Shane*. This ends with something like 'He rode into our valley out of the heart of the great, glowing West. He was a man, and he was Shane.' Hughes used to end his essays like this: 'He strode out of the mountains of the North into eighteenth-century poetry. He was a man, and he was Wordsworth.' And so on: for Wordsworth read Browning (there was a lot about fresh air in this one), and once, in an astonishing tour de force, Bacon. The English master gave up after a while, and would just draw a tired red line under these final paragraphs. There was something unfinished about Hughes; with more work or concentration there was no telling what he might have done, but the effort never got made. He would have broken the heart of a more conscientious teacher.

He was a good watercolourist, though it rained in all his paintings. In the sixth form, he entered one of them for the National Eisteddfod, and when it won didn't tell anyone, so the news broke only when the local paper phoned the headmaster.

Naturally he failed his A-levels, and we lost touch. I heard he had gone to the local training college, where he distinguished himself by failing his teaching diploma. No one ever failed a teaching diploma at the local training college; to make the examiners that aware of you must have been a considerable achievement.

⸺ ◆ ⸺

'Hello, mush.'

It was eight years later, and I was at the dance then held every Saturday at the London Welsh Club in the Grays Inn Road. That is to say, I was nearby, in a pub, because the chapel-going, cinema-owning Welsh millionaire who owned the club had imposed an absolute ban on drink. The result was that on Saturday nights all the pubs in the Grays Inn Road bulged with young men with Welsh accents, most of them with degrees, who then emerged at stop-tap, did their best not to be sick and staggered across the road and onto the dance floor where bored young women, also with degrees, who had been dragging out a conversation with each other for something like two hours, did their best to keep them upright.

So the *jeunesse dorée* of Wales met, and the relationships started which would end in captioned photographs in some local weekly paper.

> Glyn Yorath Ph.D., eldest son of Dafydd and Glenys Yorath of Cwmgerwn farm, Cwmtwrch, and Gladys Pugh BA, LRAM, youngest daughter of the Rev. James and Anthea Thomas of Meidrim, have married in Las Vegas, Nevada. The happy couple will make their home near Porton Down, Berkshire, where the groom is taking up a research post in anthrax research.

I did actually read something very like that; it was headlined 'Local Man's Success'. Welsh weeklies, like Oxbridge dons, worship success, whatever form it takes.

'You going to buy me a drink then?'

Hughes was in what he called his heyday. With both his parents dead, he had come into his inheritance, and there was a Triumph Herald, by which he would later measure time ('Let's see, that was the year before I bought the Triumph Herald'). We used to go drinking in it.

He was a schoolmaster, having, he sniffed, passed his diploma, and considered himself a London sophisticate. He certainly knew its pubs, in which he drank nightly, mostly on his own, a habit he had got into at school when he was the only boy entitled to by law. We trailed round London in the Triumph Herald, from small, expensive pubs in Belgravia to caverns in the East End where under strip lighting old men looked up from their dominoes. What we were after, said Hughes, was atmosphere. It was one of his two quests, the other being for what he called 'contacts'.

It was a matter of logic, he informed me. Contacts were people with friends, friends gave parties, and there was free booze at parties, which it was possible to steal, or at least exchange a bottle of Bulgarian red for one of gin, say.

'But you don't drink gin.'

'I do now.'

At such moments you saw the joy his ancestors must have known, cheating each other over wills or over a few square acres of moorland.

He had somehow acquired the lease of a flat in Marble Arch, a pokey place in a mews, but the address fascinated Hughes. 'I live in W1,' he told puzzled girls in parties. 'Next door to Prince Littler's garage actually.' Littler was then a well-known theatrical impresario. Hughes had two sub-tenants who paid four-fifths of the rent, and for whom he advertised in the better class of news-agent. If after a month one of these turned out not to be a contact, Hughes would take him aside and tell him, sadly, that he didn't really fit in. And they, big rugby players, left without a murmur.

I stayed there once. 'You'll be all right in the morning,' he said. 'I've got some bacon in for you. It's like the Ritz here.' I was up before him and went into the kitchen, where on the table there was an opened baked-bean tin with a spoon in it. The washbasin was full, the bin was full, but in an otherwise empty fridge there was the bacon. Or at least a kind of bacon, a streak of red against a hinterland of white fat. I thought I had better open the window before attempting to cook this.

But as I did so something rustled in the wind, something on the sill just out of sight. It was a neat brown-paper parcel which, when I opened it, contained three thick red slices of salt-cured gammon. I cooked all three on the grill. The white bacon I wrapped carefully in the brown paper and put the parcel on the sill, closing the window when I had finished.

About half an hour later I heard coughing from the next room, and the sound of a match being struck for the first cigarette. Finally he got up and I heard sounds from the kitchen, of the window going up slowly, and then no sounds at all, a silence I thought would last forever until I heard fat popping and bacon being fried. He looked at me when he came into the living room and nodded, but in the way he looked there was something that hadn't been there before. But that was it; he didn't say anything, nor did I.

There were girls in his life now, one of them a nurse whom he persuaded to miss her last bus by telling her he had a spare bed, which turned out to be the lumpy sofa in the living room. He told her he had no spare blankets, then quietly turned the gas fire off at the mains. At some point in the small hours, anaesthetised by cold and discomfort, the poor girl tottered into his bedroom where, patient as an anaconda, Hughes lay waiting. 'Half-past three,' he said. She exacted a revenge by pretending to be pregnant, sending him invitations on hospital paper to classes for fathers to be, one of which he actually attended, and had midwives combing their records for his name. 'Not a bad trick, I should have stuck with her,' he said.

It was impossible to censure him; he was so outside any recognisable code of ethics it would have been like slapping a parking ticket on Geronimo. And it would have been cruel, for Hughes took such pure joy in his trickeries. These apart, he valued nothing, least of all himself; he dressed like a scarecrow and ate like a prisoner released from a medieval dungeon, going without food for days then ordering two plates of chicken and chips at his local chippy.

We lost touch at this time, for suddenly, saying he thought it time he saw the world, he upped and went to the States, and Hughes did not write letters. But the Foreign Office did. They wrote a month or two later to say that a Mr Hughes had applied for the post of security officer at the British Mission to the UN in New York, and had given my name as a character referee. I got a secretary at work to write one, a panegyric on *Times* notepaper, and it did the job. A year later, when the FO wrote again, they said they were doing a routine check, and would I care to reconsider my reference. Nervously I wrote again, this time with a more honest description of his character, saying there were those who would consider him a bit on the mean side, but that this might be no bad thing in a security officer, for it meant he had no expensive tastes. I heard no more until the night the phone rang.

--------◆◆◆--------

He was a landlord now, having turned the remainder of his inheritance into a large Edwardian redbrick house in North London. It had five bedsitters, all occupied. Hughes was an odd landlord, too odd even to give offence. He tried to see as little as possible of his tenants, who pushed their rents, in cash, under the door of his room which none had ever entered. But he entered theirs, moving heaters and curtains from room to room when they were out and a new tenant was expected. New tenants were given the best heater, and, in the case of a good-looking girl from the Home Office, the best curtains as well, but the good-looking girl moved on, and the curtains and the heaters resumed their orbits. The tenants I met on the stairs looked bemused.

His own room had its curtains drawn all the year round. Against the Income Tax, he said. He did not declare his rents and argued that its inspectors would not call if they thought there was a death in the house. Logic was always hanging about somewhere. Inside, the room looked as though it had been burgled, the floor covered with socks, ashtrays full of stubs, and the mail of long-gone tenants he had never forwarded. Nightly he would return to this rubble, chain smoke, and drunkenly scribble in a school exercise book in red marking biro, 'It is midnight. I am alone. The fire has gone out and I have no more shillings. This is where life ends. I HAVE RUN OUT OF FAGS.' He was, he told me, in decline. It did not seem to upset him.

He was drinking more, in local pubs now, the quest for atmosphere having been abandoned. In these, nightly, he drank seven or eight pints of beer, and, nightly at home, pissed in the line of antique pewter pots on the dresser left him by his mother. He pissed in a different one each night, and emptied them at weekends. When you called on Hughes you stepped delicately.

There was a Mini at this stage, the clock of which had stopped recording mileage, and the wipers worked only when they felt like it. When it rained he perched on the edge of his seat, wiping the windscreen through an open window with one of the many bar-cloths he had salvaged from the pub. The exhaust had fallen off so the car sounded like a tractor, and Hughes had kept the pipe in his car, encouraging his passengers to hold it. 'Keep it warm, I can tell the police it's just fallen off.' The interior also contained the remains of old Cornish pasties, rotting radish leaves and empty milk bottles, for he was fond of picnics in his car. When he braked (for the brakes still worked, just) the interior crashed like a milk float.

Later the brakes became very dodgy, so he often bumped the cars in front. When this happened Hughes would leap out, inspect the damage with great care, then tell the other driver that it was too small a matter for insurance, and offer him ten shillings. Sometimes the man would be so confused, but so impressed with the exactness of the sum, that he agreed. 'Bumped a bloke in Trafalgar Square, gave him the ten bob,' said Hughes. 'As he went round the corner his bumper fell off.'

About this time I made a note of his conversation, for he had begun to sound like a character in a play by Beckett. 'Life's all rubbish. Finis. Kaput. In the rooms the women come and go, talking of Michelangelo. And what would they want to talk about him for? That's all the modern poetry I know. Fucking drab. But that's the crux of the matter really. I'm so bloody ignorant, I don't even know the difference between *sensuous* and *sensual*. Pity, it came up in class last week.

'You go to parties, dance with a girl, not dancing at all, just clinging together. Great, man, that's harmony, but where does it get you? You can't regain lost pleasure. It's the flux that gets me. Drink, fags, petrol. I get aspirin half price off a woman at school, her sister works in a hospital. Yes, I know aspirin's cheap, but however cheap it is I get it half price, right? It's all flux. I must get married and eat roast meat.'

But he did nothing. He told me he would like to paint watercolours again, but didn't; said he would decorate his room, but never did. He paid no bills and was once taken to court twice in three days by local newspapers in which he had advertised for new tenants. I had come to think of him as indestructible, but now I began to think that all this had to come to some kind of point. He himself told me so often enough. 'I can't go on like this, drunk every night. Can't get any lower.' He was sitting in an armchair cratered with cigarette burns. 'And I should know, I've tried.' He laughed.

Things were not going well for him at the secondary school where he taught. There were complaints about books not being marked, about his appearance and that of his Mini in the car-park. Daily he turned up in some shape or other.

'Why are you making those faces?'

'It's your breath, sir, you bin on the razzle again?'

'Be quiet, boy. I had kippers for breakfast.'

He could cope with such things, but there was something else now, something that unnerved him. His colleagues, he told me, were very left-wing. Quite what form their left-wingery took I don't know for he said little beyond, 'God, you should hear them talk in the staff-room.' Hughes had no interest in politics, had never voted, had not even registered himself to vote ('It's my business, not theirs'), but he began to be jumpy. 'You watch, something's going to happen here. Just you wait.' I would laugh, I had no idea how frightened he was. Then things did happen.

I hadn't seen him for a week or two when I called on him one May morning. The trees in his street were in blossom, and, looking up at these, I saw his curtains had been opened. The last time I had seen this was when, trying to light a fag, he had set some papers on fire.

In his room the mess had been cleared, or at least had been pushed back to the walls, and in its place there were library books. I picked one up. It was *The Beginner's Guide to Seamanship*. On the floor were *Small Boats And You*, *Last of the Clippers*, *The Lonely Sea and the Sky*, *Navigation and the Small Boat Owner*.

'I'm going to get one,' said Hughes, who had been watching me.

'What, a boat?'

He nodded. 'Boats don't depreciate. They're not like cars, boats are made of wood. Wood is going to get scarce.' He stooped, and, making himself a quill from an unopened envelope marked 'URGENT', lit a cigarette from the gas fire. 'I'm serious.'

'Got any idea what it involves?'

'I'm going to give all this up.'

He gestured grandly around the room, as though some great sacrifice were needed. My eyes followed his hand across the pewter jugs, the unwashed coffee cups, the ashtrays and the crumpled letters. 'I'm going to sell up, pack the teaching in, and buy a boat on Cardigan Bay.'

I tried to reason with him. What did he know about boats? He pointed to the books. But what practical experience had he had, what about money, how was he going to live, where was he going to live, what ...?

His expression was gentle. 'I was thinking the other day I haven't had much fun in my life, I don't think my parents had either. It's an odd way to go through life, careful with your cash, not wanting anything too much in case you don't get it. You know, I don't think anyone in my family has ever done anything silly. I mean really silly. And then one day it's over.'

'Life?'

'Yeah, life.'

For a moment the only sound was the popping of the fire.

'I want to show you something, it's here somewhere.' It was a photograph in a magazine of a sailing boat in rough seas. Standing at the tiller was some maniac, a pipe clenched in his teeth, grinning as the spray hit him: the thing was a pipe ad. 'Look at that, man.'

I was suddenly embarrassed, for I had never heard him talk like that before. Something had broken through to what until now he had always kept locked inside himself in the way of his people, and for a moment I saw them, farm servants, chapel-goers, fornicators in fields, mourners, hats in their hands in cold front parlours. Lust they would have known, avarice, even glee, but nothing like this. They had never been dreamers.

'You think I've gone mad, don't you?'

A few weeks later, he rang to say he was thinking of joining a yachting club down on the Essex coast, and would I give him another reference? I did so, again on *Times* notepaper, and it did the trick. We drove down together at the weekend, to a club not on the coast, but some miles inland, a creek surrounded by glistening mudflats. Here we spent the afternoon in the club bar, a large wooden shed, where elderly men in blazers stared out at beached dinghies scattered here and there as though thrown down by some huge child. He did not appear to know any of these men, but assured me he was picking up a lot. 'Practical things,' he said.

A month later, during the school holidays, Hughes went mad.

--------◆◆--------

What happened went something like this, and I should know for he told me the story often enough, embellishing certain details until the two of us were helpless with laughter. But what neither of us knew was the shadow these events would cast. That Saturday morning in August the last chapter in his life began.

It was about ten o'clock, and he was only half awake, listening to a records request programme, when he heard 'Jingle bells, jingle bells, jingle all the way.' There had been no preamble, but then the announcer's voice broke in. 'We are playing this as a special request.' There had been no humour in the man's voice, he said. Whoever he was, he was being very serious. And then the music started up again. Hughes came wide awake, and was frightened. Very frightened.

'I thought it had to be a signal of some kind. And then I realised what was happening. They were coming.'

'Who were coming?'

'The Russians, it was a signal to those bastards who were waiting for them.'

'Like your colleagues?'

'Yes.' (The curious thing is that years later, when the Khmer Rouge were closing in on Phnom Penh, the American authorities broadcast *Jingle Bells* as a signal to its personnel in the city to gather at the Embassy from which their evacuation, by helicopter, would begin.)

'What did you do then?'

'I got up, and it was then it occurred to me that when they came money would have no value. So I got the biggest suitcase I could find, went to Sainsbury's, and filled it up with tins of corned beef.'

'Not sardines or peaches?'

'Piss off.'

'Any special brand of corned beef?'

'Fray Bentos, they were on special offer. Hell of a weight, I was pouring with sweat by the time I got to Paddington.'

'Paddington?'

'Logic, I wanted to get as far away from Russia as I could. I was off home.'

Hughes was telling me all this a few months after it all happened, and I found it so funny I kept asking for repeat performances: 'Do me the Cardiff bit again.' He obliged, for by then he was finding it funny too.

'You know I've got a cousin in Cardiff. Well, I hadn't seen him in ten years mind, but it occurred to me I'd better warn him, he was family after all. So I got off the train.'

'He must have had a hell of shock.'

'Wouldn't you if someone you hadn't seen in ten years comes in through your front door, asks how much corned beef you've got in the house, and you're watching *Match of the Day*?'

'It would have to be *Match of the Day*.'

'Yes, and he didn't switch it off when I told him the Russians were coming.'

'What did he say?'

'Didn't say much. Said it was odd there'd been nothing on about a Russian invasion, he didn't think the BBC'd miss out on something like that. And, this is the lovely bit, his wife said he didn't like corned beef.'

'What happened then?'

'Well, I wished them good luck and went. On the train a guard told me to put the case on the rack, but I said I wasn't strong enough, so he had a go and he wasn't either. "How far you going?" he asked. "Carmarthen," I said. He left me alone after that, but I started to think, he'll have rung ahead to warn them, so I jumped train at Ferryside. It was getting late, but I got a lift in a van. And then of course the bloody suitcase had to fall over in the back. What had I got in there? Corned beef, I said. Killed the conversation stone dead, that did.'

He ended up in Cardigan where another cousin, who kept a pub, put him up.

At the beginning of September, having heard nothing from him for some weeks, I got a card postmarked New Quay. On one side was a photograph of a racing yacht in a blue blue sea. On the other Hughes had written, 'Have dog and cottage. IT'S ALL BEGINNING.' There was no signature.

He came back at the end of the month, leaner than ever, but very brown. Around his neck he had knotted a silk muffler, so he looked like one of those blokes who tell fortunes in women's magazines. He had resigned from his school, he said, and was back to sell the house. Whatever dreams were now leading on he had decided on a swansong to the old life, and put the house in the hands of three different estate agents, not telling any of them about the others, and gazumped as many would-be buyers as he could. 'Funny old world,' he told me. But he sold it, and in a rising market.

I saw him in Wales. The cottage was very narrow, set in a terrace above an estuary. It was beautiful, with roses climbing its whitewashed exterior, and had belonged to an old sea captain. 'Last man around here to go to sea under sail,' said Hughes. The dog was a plump and silly Labrador his cousin had given him because it chased sheep, but Hughes said it had never had a chance to show how intelligent it was. 'Bit like me really.' He called it Dog. Instead of a kennel he had given it one of the cottage's downstairs rooms, while he used the other as a sitting room. Dog's was tidier.

We walked along the cliffs. It was such a clear day we could see the Lleyn Peninsula sixty miles away. 'There's rocks there,' said Hughes, pointing at a patch of placid sea. He was spending his time in pubs, he told me, which were bursting with old sailors, very knowledgeable old sailors, which was handy, he went on, as he was negotiating to buy a boat from a retired Englishman whose wife had told him he was too old to go sailing any more. It was quite a big boat, with a three-berth cabin.

'When I get the hang of it I shall sell the cottage and live on it,' said Hughes. 'And when it gets cold Dog and I, we'll follow the swallows south.' The dog wagged its plump bottom. 'You can see it, can't you? Some small mooring place in France, or Spain, then who knows?'

Hughes went back to supply teaching, and also to his other career, buying a large house in Cardigan that had already been converted into bedsitters. I saw him from time to time. We used to call on a farmer we both knew, a man trying to perfect the brewing of beer from raw materials, so he took delivery of sacks of hops. It was wonderful stuff, and we drank it from wooden barrels in a stone-flagged larder, sympathising with the farmer when he said he had been unable to get it down to less than 9 per cent alcohol, more than twice the strength of ordinary beer, which irritated his wife as this ruled out his more respectable neighbours as guests. 'Help yourselves, boys, you'll be doing me a favour.' Unfortunately we did him so many favours we felt guilty, and one night we called on him with a bottle of whisky, the 105 proof Glenfarclas. Our visit coincided with the moment a new brew, a wheat beer, was ready.

We tasted the whisky, then we tasted the beer, then we tasted the whisky and the beer together, after which we were offered beds for the night, but Hughes refused, saying he had things to do in the morning. The farmer and I watched him and Dog leave, we heard the car start, heard it rev, and then there was silence. 'Quiet engine,' said the farmer.

The next morning when I got down the farmer said, 'I think you'd better see how far he got.' There was a large midden at the end of his yard and Hughes had driven into it; the car was up to its windscreen in dung. 'Must have been going fast to get in that far,' said the farmer. Hughes and Dog were asleep in the front seats.

Another time, when drunk, he crashed into a much-loved old family doctor, which in a small Welsh town is like crashing into one of the royal family. He was put in gaol overnight, and caused consternation by demanding to produce a written statement.

'They were glad to get rid of me. They'd been quite happy when I offered to make a statement, brought me out of the cell, gave me a cup of tea and a biro. I was still writing when the dawn came up, I'd covered thirty sides of A4 paper, which was all they had.'

'What were you writing?'

'Oh . . .' And he stopped. 'Well, it started with what had happened, and then . . . well then I got a bit political.'

It was then I realised that things were not well with him. He had grown wily.

--------◆◆--------

At this stage he stopped making jokes about what had happened. In fact he stopped talking about it altogether, and when I did he just heard me out, for I had this idea that if I could break through to his sense of humour then his troubles would be over; I wanted to believe in what I hoped was just eccentricity. One day, talking on board his boat, which he had brought up river for the winter, a plane went over, a military jet, and it seemed to waggle its wings. I said, 'Hey, did that plane salute you?' He stared at me, and, whereas a few months before, he would have laughed or said something, this time he said nothing.

Now, following the collision with the doctor, his behaviour began to attract the attention of people who didn't think in terms of eccentricity at all. Suddenly there were policemen and doctors, and he was sectioned for a short time. In one of these incidents, coming home from the pub, he left his car in the middle of the road and went to bed. He was roused from this by the police, only he was convinced they were trying to invite him to a party. He called down to them, 'Look, it's nice of you but it's too late, boys.' Like just about everything that happened to Hughes this was both horribly funny and not funny at all. The police steamed in through his front door, grabbed his keys and parked his car. Of his stay in hospital, he said, 'If you want to meet some really boring people, get yourself sectioned.'

He was beginning to seem odd even to me. He asked me to lunch, and when I got to his house the table was laid for three. 'Right,' said Hughes, putting a tape in his video player. It was a porno film, with a man and two women, set in a boat yard. As it played Hughes brought in three tins of corned beef, one for me, one for him, and one for the dog. 'You can open your own,' he told me.

He talked about his boat most of the time now, and kept trying to get me to come out with him, but I was too frightened to do that.

'Can you read maps?'

'I've been to night school.'

'Yes, but have you been out of sight of land?'

'I went to Lundy the other week in fog.'

'Good God, you plotted a course.'

'No, I saw this other boat, and followed him.'

'How did you get back?'

'You can't miss Britain, you fool.'

Later, pointing to the dog, he said, 'You know I told you him and me were going to go south, that's still on, that is. You know Tennyson's poem *Ulysses*?'

'A long time ago,' I said. He and I were the only ones from the Sixth to read poetry after the examiners had ended their sport with us.

'Pass me that book. Listen:

> The long day wanes; the slow moon climbs; the deep
> Moans round with many voices. Come, my friends,
> 'Tis not too late to seek a newer world ...

'That's what we're going to do, me and him. If I were you, I'd come with us. Things could get a bit ... nasty here.'

'Oh, not the Russians again.'

He switched the video off (all this time the moaning and the squelching had not stopped) and resumed his reading.

> There lies the port; the vessel puffs her sail;
> There gloom the dark broad seas.

'How safe's your boat?'

'Boat's in good nick. I've had a bloke check it out.'

'Yes, but there's a hell of a lot of difference between trundling round the Welsh coast and the dark broad fucking seas.'

'Not really. We're on a journey, and the worst thing is that I won't come back. That's it.'

It was the last time I saw Hughes.

I wish it had been as he said it would be.

> For my purpose holds
> To sail beyond the sunset, and the baths
> Of all the western stars, until I die.
> It may be that the gulfs will wash us down:
> It may be we shall touch the Happy Isles,
> And see the great Achilles whom we knew,
> Tho' much is taken, much abides ...

Three months later, his neighbours, alerted by the howling of his dog, broke in and found him hanged in the attic of the cottage above the estuary. The terrors must have closed in again, and been far worse than he had let on or I had imagined. The journey was over.

8

My Thirties: A Pot Pourri

IN MY THIRTIES I was on the *Telegraph* Magazine, which is to say I was

> Like one that on a lonesome road
> Doth walk in fear and dread,
> And having once turned round walks on
> And turns no more his head;
> Because he knows a frightful fiend
> Doth close behind him tread.

Only what was stalking me was reality, or what remained of my sense of it. I was a writer on a colour magazine, my workaday world one that to most people would be the stuff of fantasy. Step into it for a moment and meet…

The face of all men feared

Someone on the Magazine had had the idea that I write an article on Kensington Palace Gardens, that mysterious street which, behind great gates, runs from Kensington to Notting Hill Gate. It was an interesting idea, but the sort of interesting idea that comes to someone sitting in an office. Three of the houses in the Gardens are embassies, and the others are all the size of palaces, huge gloomy palaces. I asked the features editor how he thought I was going to go about this one?

'Just call on them.'

'*Call* on them?'

Calling on them would be like calling on the royal family, some of whom lived just round the corner. One of the inhabitants of Kensington Palace Gardens was in fact a member of an imperial family, the daughter of the last Sultan of the Ottoman Empire.

'Yes, you know, knock on the door,' said the features editor, whom until then I had not associated with a sense of humour. I decided to start with the Sultan's daughter, who, I hoped, would call the police and kill the project stone dead.

Awed by the great front door, I went round to the side and pulled a bell I heard ring deep inside the house. Three or four minutes went by, and I was about to give up when, slowly, after drawings of bolts, the door was opened, and an Indian man stood there, dressed in some kind of military tunic buttoned to his throat. He did not say a word as I explained my business, and then, cocking his head as though listening for something, raised one finger above his head. 'She comes.'

Far away I heard the sound of shuffling feet, of soft-soled slippers on stone getting nearer and nearer. And then in the dark corridor a figure glided into view. She was very tall, and swathed in loose silks, so she looked like an illustration for Rider Haggard's *She*. And the face! I had seen it in portraits, when this was what Chesterton called 'that face of all men feared'. It was long and very pale, and out of it reared the terrifying hawk nose that had been there in generation after generation of one family, in the conqueror of Constantinople, in Suleiman the Magnificent and Abdul the Damned. In Kensington I looked upon the face of the House of Osman.

'Bugger off,' said the House of Osman.

Well, she didn't really say that. What she said, in a whispered monotone, was 'Sorry, so sorry' after I had told her why I was there. She then turned, and the shadows gathered around the long, gliding figure. The expressionless major-domo closed the door.

Later I called on the dowager Marchioness of Cholmondeley, a lovely bright-eyed old lady who asked me in, and over tea complained about her neighbour, the Nepalese Ambassador, who, according to her, had once killed a goat on his doostep. 'Bit of a shock, that. I mean, next door.' As I left she said, 'It must be nice to meet someone like me, so old, and so *spry*.'

Nobody else, not even the embassies, answered my call. I never did write about Kensington Palace Gardens.

Dr Crippen's little friend

It was a summer's afternoon, and in a house on a modern estate in the West Country I was listening as the crime writer Jonathan Goodman told an elderly couple, brother and sister, that their mother, old Mum who never wore her false teeth except to go out, was once the most notorious woman in the world. As Ethel le Neve she had been Dr Crippen's mistress.

Delicately, for neither had known anything of this, he described how the Scotland Yard detective entered the cabin where their mother, disguised as a boy and reading a novel called *Audrey's Recompense*, promptly fainted. He waited for their reaction.

'Mum was a great reader,' said the old gentleman.

The abbot and the demons

In a Tibetan retreat in the Scottish Borders a man was telling me about his life as an abbot in Tibet, when he rode everywhere on a white horse.

'Sad that, you must miss the horse,' I said. 'But what other changes have you have known, coming to this country?'

'I tell you. When I was a boy my mother told me stories about demons. The demons were very tall, had long noses and their hair was red.' He was staring at me fixedly. 'Then I come to your country and I meet people like you.'

A maharajah in Chelsea

The Maharajah of Baroda stood beside the cheetah, one hand on its sleek head. The cheetah was made of ceramic, and was life-sized. The Maharajah was made of pin-stripe and amiability, yet it

was easy to imagine the silks and the pearls, and see the yellow eyes under his hand.

'I suppose that came from some ancestral vault,' I said.

'Yes, Harrods,' said the Maharajah.

Social work in Streatham

'You'll remember all this when you're old, and nobody wants you,' said the hostess. 'Many of the old boys who came here had lost their wives, they were lonely. And they'd sit here, eating their sandwiches, watching pretty girls, knowing they'd never have to take them out, girls who'd never make any unpleasantness about their marriages. They were in paradise, my old boys.

'They'd come at two in the afternoon and they'd be nervous. So I'd usually put on a lesbian act for them or I'd have this university lecturer put on an exhibition with his girlfriend. He almost pulled my washbasin out once. But it did put them all in the mood.

'And it was so respectable. A solicitor friend once told me it was like a regimental dinner-dance without the dinner. And of course nobody danced. But they'd be there all in their suits, and then one of them would go over to the girls, stepping over the naked bodies on the floor. "Excuse me, would you mind coming upstairs?" And the girl, pleased to be asked, would say, "Yes." It was all so polite. The difficulty was trying not to laugh.'

Mrs Cynthia Payne, party-giver.

On Mount Sinai with tablets

Mr David Hicks, interior designer, has invited me to be his biographer.

I'm so glad you could come. It is nice here, don't you agree? You come into this building, you have the impression of great dignity, then you come up here and it's the perfect antidote to today. I'm excited by tomorrow and I did love yesterday, but today's different. You have to work at today.

Of course people in my profession would recognise this room as being *me*. They'd see the geometric patterns, the festooned curtains. But do you know why these are festooned? It's because the people opposite haven't replaced their windows properly; I've had to cut out the view. I'm an extraordinary mixture of – well, perhaps not genius – but quick thinking and practicality. When I'm in a tight corner aesthetically I'm at my best, I have to fight to get out. Would you like to see their windows? No, I couldn't do that to anybody. They're such dreadfully *suburban* things.

But what's really *me* are the colours, the *vibrating* colours. Before I came along people said that colours clashed. The carpets magenta, the chairs scarlet. 'Is my wife going to like that?' Your wife, I tell them, will find it *exciting*.

Some colours I don't like to see together, like peacock blue and orange, but even then it depends on how they're used. There are so many definites in life and so many 'I should prefer not' situations. Don't you agree? I knew you would. I hate everything which matches up, it's so *suburban*. Is there anything worse than suburban? Not in this world . . .

As the result of seeing the above, part of a specimen chapter, Mr Hicks, whom I had found more fascinating than any character in fiction, withdrew the invitation to write his biography.

The end of the world

At Dropshort Lodge, a farm near Kettering, the farmer John Hunt was recalling a fine autumn morning in 1962, at the height of the Cuban missile crisis. There was then, just across the road, a top-secret American air-force base.

> This chap had called to sell my father a tractor. They were talking prices, and I was listening, when suddenly all talk stopped. Across the road and beyond the wire this huge rocket was coming up against the sky. We'd seen this before in practice, what we hadn't seen was another coming up, then a third. And as we watched we saw something else we hadn't seen before. Fumes were beginning to pour down their sides.
>
> The next thing I remember is that father had turned to this man and was saying very quietly, 'Well, Mr Armitage, I think you should lower your price. I don't expect I shall get much use of that tractor now…'
>
> And the other man, also very quietly, said, 'I'm sure you're right, Mr Hunt. I think this is the end of the world.'
>
> I didn't say anything at all, I just couldn't believe how calm they were about it, and I was staring at them, not calm at all. I was seventeen years old. I didn't want it to be the end of the world…

Men went to Agincourt

The *Telegraph* paid for the longbow, which must make it the first one bought on expenses since the Middle Ages. The mighty McEwen made it, he made the bow of red yew in the old way until it stood taller than a man, a curving beautiful instrument of death. Originally it had been his, with a draw weight of 120

pounds, something McEwen was probably the only man in England capable of pulling. In the Middle Ages he would have been a holy terror for the ruling class, today he was something that terrified some newspaper managements even more: McEwen of Wanstead was a hot metal printer on the *Daily Express*. But to accommodate mortal men, me that is, he had shaved the bow down to fifty pounds.

'One question, how d'you reckon you'll get that through French customs?' he asked.

'It'll be unstrung. I'll say it's a fishing rod.'

'Oh no, they'll remember, you watch. They'll remember.'

And they did remember. At Calais a customs man said, *'M'sieu, c'est an arc ...'* and suddenly he was holding his chest, his fingers

wide as though clutching the arrow that was sticking out of him. 'Oooooh.' And there was a second customs man also holding his chest and saying 'Oooooh.' They were so pleased with their performances they just waved us through.

So men went to Agincourt.

The daring old men in their flying machines

The plane, a light bomber, was the last of the Kaiser's air armadas still flying, though that day it seemed reluctant to do so as the mechanic swung the propeller and nothing happened. There were two men in the plane, a pilot and, behind him, a machine-gunner who for some reason had both arms around the gun as though he had just met a long-lost relative. Under goggles both his eyes were shut fast.

The pilot turned to the machine-gunner. 'I forgot to tell you, I'm seventy, it's my birthday tomorrow.'

'Oh fuck,' I said.

'Sorry, missed that. Ah here we go.'

There was a gargantuan fart, blue smoke poured from the exhausts, and this extinct assembly of wood and canvas was moving, at first no faster than a lorry, for its top speed in the air was under 80mph, but there was a hop, another hop, and then there was no ground, only a sky into which it was clawing itself.

A hangman remembers

'When I retired I bought a gallows,' said the hangman. 'Bought it off a doctor who'd had it out of the old Cambridge gaol. Came in a furniture van. I installed it in my cellar, I was keeping a post office then. 'Course the cellar wasn't high enough to install it properly so I had to put two blocks of wood underneath it. Just enough . . .' He smiled. 'Just enough for the trap to creak.'

He rummaged in a drawer. 'Here it is.' The photograph showed the gallows in the light of two green spots, a tailor's dummy on the trap with a white plaster bust balanced atop of that. There was something familiar about those beaky features.

'Hey, that's Dante.'

'Who?'

'That's Dante you're hanging. Italian poet.'

'That who it is? Doctor threw it in with the gallows. What amazed me was the way news got round. All sorts turned up. This managing director called. "I understand you have a gallows in your cellar." I took him down. "I understand you have a rope." He stood there. "May I have the rope round my neck?"

'In the end I had certificates printed for everyone who wanted that done. Some had them framed and put on their walls. A lot wanted photographs printed. And then this chap came to read the electricity meters.

'My wife was ill, and her cousin had come to keep house for me. When this meter chap came I was in the post office, I was stamping pensions or something. I watched him walk up the path. Then a few minutes later my front door banged open and he came through it, running. I watched him go up the road, running faster than I've ever seen anyone go, which was odd, considering he'd come by car.

'What had happened was that he'd introduced himself, and of course my wife's cousin didn't know where the meters were, so he said to leave it to him, they were probably in the cellar. So he must have opened the door, switched on the lights, and . . .

episode, the two girls put on a lesbian show. 'Go it, hen.' Then something extraordinary happened: the girls turned on their tormentors.

They grabbed one of the Scotsmen, pushed him to the floor, and, while one sat on him, the other pulled off his trousers. Suddenly there were thin pale legs under the brown, and cries of 'Gurrls, gurrls, there's too many folk aboot.'

The second Scotsman had shrunk into his chair, both hands over his eyes, and was groaning, 'Alasdair, Alasdair, I knew we should a gone durrect to Tokyo.'

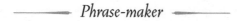

So, with the unreal as a travelling companion, my thirties passed. But the unreal had not ended its sport with me.

Phrase-maker

The Assistant Private Secretary's embarrassment was evident, even on the telephone. A civil servant transferred to Buckingham Palace (and a 'high flier', according to a press which has yet to identify a low flier in the civil service), he had always been careful of speech to the point where you fancied you saw semi-colons form in the air. But this time he sounded as though English were a foreign language in which he was taking an oral exam.

'It's about the ... er, speeches. D'you think ... umm ... it might be ... possible ... for you ... to stop using the first person singular? I've been asked to pass this one on. In future, could you ... umm ... remember to use HRH?'

'You mean, I have to remind myself I am not the Prince of Wales,' I said helpfully.

'You could put it like that, yes.'

In the mid-1970s I began writing speeches for the Prince of Wales.

Pronouns were always a bit of a problem. Until the late twentieth century, English royalty moved in a narrow social group, the members of which had been schooled in the old ways of deference. Royalty was 'ma'am' and 'sir', and I remember Lady Jane Wellesley telling me that she had never called the Prince of Wales anything but 'sir', which struck me then, and still does, as one of the saddest little confessions I have ever heard. It did not matter that royalty, ambitious to involve itself in social issues, found itself increasingly among people who had never called anyone 'sir' in their lives. Royalty was secretly a stickler for the old forms. The first greeting of the day, I had been informed, was to be 'your Royal Highness', thereafter 'sir'. It was hard to keep this up in conversations.

'Who was this Aleister Crowley?'

'The Wickedest Man in the World ... sir.'

What complicated things even more was that royalty when it signed letters (which always came by registered post) did so with a single Christian name, which suggested an intimacy that never was. It is only on marriage certificates that royalty has a surname, and even then it is a matter of debate as to what this is.

Sighing, I pulled towards me the draft of a speech to be delivered to the Highland Society. 'It is a matter of some poignance that I should address a society formed because one member of the family raised the Highland Clans, and another blew them to bits in thirty minutes flat ...'

I began to change the pronouns.

It had all started late one summer's night when the phone rang. The caller was a man I had not spoken to in thirteen years, when he had been the editor of the *Sheffield Star* and I one of his graduate trainees. Since then, Tom Watson had become a director of United Newspapers, a chain of provincial papers that at that time also included the *Observer* and *Punch*. I was a freelance journalist in London, and as we talked I kept wondering how he had managed to get hold of my home number.

Tom was affability itself, chatting about people we both knew, and then, abruptly, he said, could I give Lord Barnetson a ring? Lord Barnetson? I had heard of him, a mysterious press lord about whom nobody knew very much except that he was chairman of United Newspapers, of Reuters, and of just about everything else. What was I to ring him about? Tom was suddenly vague, and said that perhaps a letter, yes a letter, might be better. What was I to say in the letter? Oh nothing much, just that my old editor had suggested I write. He then chuckled (Tom, you will remember, was a great chuckler), and rang off.

I was thirty-five, unmarried, and a few minutes earlier had been sitting in a chair wondering whether to go out to the pub or to bed. Now I found myself thinking about the novels of John Buchan, which often started as quietly as that, and the next moment, bang, you were being chased across a moor. As a freelance journalist, the moor sounded interesting, as anything might that would rescue me from the blank white paper and the loneliness. A few days later I wrote to Barnetson. The next morning, quite early, his secretary rang, first to arrange an interview, then a second time to ask for a CV, which I grumpily sent.

It rained the day of the interview and I was soaked by the time

I had cycled to the United Newspapers offices behind Fleet Street, where a commissionaire was waiting for me. He showed me to a lift, which went up all of one floor to where a secretary was also waiting. Philip Marlowe would have wisecracked his way through this; I followed her, clutching my cycle clips, and was shown into a boardroom dominated by a large oil painting of Barnetson, a man with a small moustache and hooded eyes; he was smoking a pipe. A door opened and a smaller version of the painting came in, shook hands, sat down, smoked his pipe and looked at me; he seemed at ease in silence.

Except that then he made all this inconsequential chat, talking oddly enough about John Buchan (whose election agent he had once been), so I began to think that, what with him and Watson, there were either a lot of company directors with time on their hands or who just felt lonely. But then he laid his pipe down. He had some questions to ask, he said. Was I interested in politics? No. Good, he said. Had I ever written for *Private Eye*? No. (A lie.) And that was it.

He began to talk about something he referred to as 'this position', which was, he said, to write speeches for a public man. No, not for him; he was a mere go-between, but whoever took 'this position' would find himself a shoulder for an unnamed man to lean on. He could not say more, but this would involve meeting prominent men, a consummation, he implied, devoutly to be wished. There might be a book in it, he said, showing me to the door, suddenly the young hack again with his way to make.

But what could the man be? Not a politician or a captain of industry, such men were thick as thieves with journalists. It had to be someone who, despite being famous, was isolated and, from Barnetson's remarks, vulnerable. Suddenly I began to suspect where these trails converged, and I remembered the very young face I had seen eight years before, at Aberystwyth beyond a scrum of journalists – but that seemed absurd. Why me?

A week went by, two weeks, and I rang Barnetson. He laughed and said I would have to get used to the pace at which this group of people worked. And then he said it. Yes, it was Charles, and the next thing would be lunch with his private secretary, David (now Sir David) Checketts.

In the 1970s, you must remember, before the TV films and the divorces, royalty was the most secret, and thus the most mysterious, force in society. Biographers kept their distance, and opponents like the Labour MP Willie Hamilton regarded it as a regressive but horribly efficient piece of machinery at the centre of things. Yet nobody really knew how royalty operated: it was another galaxy, among the outer rings of which I now found myself, my journey just beginning. What would I find at the end of it? Would I be Buckingham to the Prince's Charles I?

------◆◆------

Barnetson arranged a lunch at the Savoy Grill. Checketts being late, Barnetson sat wreathed in pipe smoke, nodding to famous men. 'Hello, Harry,' he said, and then to me, 'That was Chapman Pincher.' Then Checketts came. 'Big boy, aren't you,' he said as I stood to shake hands. I remembered him from Aberystwyth, from that strange interlude when the Prince was given a term's crash course there in the Welsh language. Checketts had seemed then like one of nature's gym masters, forceful, tough, not over-troubled by humour.

Over lunch he and Barnetson talked about their country houses while I ate everything on the table, feeling like the Dormouse at the Mad Hatter's Tea Party. But when the coffee came Checketts got down to business and began to talk about what he called 'a possible role'. There was no mention of shoulders. If things worked out I would be a machine, just as he was a machine, for when he had outlived his uses even he would be gone. There were no pension rights in his job, he volunteered. But he would like to say a few words about what the Prince actually did. A few months before, he said, he had lent his name to a campaign to have bicycle theft stamped out in Cornwall, and was also passionately interested in having old canals re-dug. Barnetson's vision of great events was crashing about my ears as Checketts got to his feet. The next step, he said briskly, was to meet the Boss, 'to see whether the chemistry worked'.

That was August. A month went by, and I wrote to Checketts saying the chemistry practical seemed to be taking an awfully long time to arrange. The letter from Checketts contained no jokes in return: the earliest possible time was in October, he wrote, somehow managing to give the impression that it was I who was seeking the interview.

<hr>

I cycled to the Palace on an autumn morning. There were still a few tourists at the gates, and they looked at me curiously as the policeman on duty scanned a list of names, then pointed towards the Privy Purse door, the right wing of the façade. I was finally inside. A sentry's boots crashed into the gravel as he turned a few yards from where I crouched, chaining up my bike despite the troops and the police, for old habits die hard and bicycle theft was large in my mind.

A man in a tailcoat was expecting me and I sat under Frith's *Derby Day* (there are no prints in the Palace) as he phoned through. There was no sign of a living soul as I was directed across the inner courtyard to the Prince's offices. There, incredibly, was a line of luggage as far as the eye could see, enough to equip a battalion for embarkation, except that each case, each hatbox, bore the Three Feathers. The Jubilee was just over and I had read many articles on the monarchy as a force in the modern world, yet here was the sort of kit an eighteenth-century aristocrat would have taken on a Grand Tour.

This time there was nobody waiting for me. In the end I knocked at a door and the young man who appeared seemed pleased at the interruption. He was an army officer, the Prince's military equerry, and took me to Checketts, who occupied a large office opposite. This looked like an Oxford don's sitting room, but with a big black Labrador asleep on the floor. Checketts rang through and we walked to an old lift which took us to the second floor. He raised one finger, knocked on a door and disappeared as suddenly as the White Rabbit.

I was left amongst the red and gold: red carpets, gold-framed old paintings almost touching, a décor which could have been masterminded by the man responsible for the Gaumont and Odeon cinema foyers. The sheer amount of stuff on display was remarkable; come the revolution, someone could go out of his mind trying to produce an inventory of Buckingham Palace. But my journey was ending. Like Pompey I was about to enter the Holy of Holies.

The door opened and I was beckoned in. More oil paintings, more reds, more gold, a leather-topped desk and the Prince of Wales coming round from behind it. He was wearing a double-breasted blazer with bright brass buttons, and looked startlingly like his photographs, only smaller. He had a high colour and good features, which nevertheless looked as though they had been assembled in a hurry, from memory. But what I remember most is the hand I shook, which was completely at odds with the rest of him; it was massive and strong, and my own hand disappeared into it.

It was a very peculiar job interview. My prospective employer seemed ill at ease, licked his lips a lot, played with a signet ring, and kept giving those eerie social smiles where the eyes crinkle a fraction of a second before the mouth moves. It was I who asked the questions. Did he see it as a full-time job? No, part-time. Was he looking for a researcher or, I searched for the word, a phrase-maker? A researcher, said the Prince; he would write his own final scripts. But, curiously, when Checketts introduced me to other members of the staff it was as the new phrase-maker. Phrase-maker. Rain-maker.

Little of this registered at the time, for the Prince kept saying the strangest things. He said he was not an ambitious man. All people seemed to want, he explained gloomily, was to see him; as far as speeches went, it was of no matter what their content was. There was a marked melancholy in everything he said. He found it hard to remember faces, and people were so annoyed at this, for they forgot how many faces he saw. Asked whether he was looking forward to America, where he was soon to go, he said no, not really; he had made it a practice not to look forward to anything, so that anything, if it happened, could surprise him. And then he said the strangest thing of all.

The bands were playing outside the window when the heir to the throne informed a man he had only just met that, until the year before, he had not believed in the monarchy. I looked across at Checketts, but he was examining the backs of his hands as though he had caught sight of them for the first time. It was the public response to the Jubilee which had changed his mind for him, the Prince went on, and the way crowds had greeted him and the Queen. He now felt the monarchy had a function.

Checketts got to his feet. Downstairs he introduced me to Michael Colborne, the Secretary as he called him. I had expected to find an office run by tall public-school men and here was a man who was a dead ringer for the Cockney comic actor Alfie Bass. Colborne had been a petty officer on the Prince's first ship when, to his bewilderment, he found himself whisked out of the Navy overnight. I liked Colborne, who seemed to have trouble with reality as well. After Checketts had gone, he told me mischievously that, contrary to appearance, he, Colborne, ran the place, then roared with laughter. He had even written speeches, and when the Prince opened a sewage farm had contributed the fact that the average British family produced thirty pounds of the stuff a week. He had felt proud, he said, when he heard the Prince actually say this.

I cycled thoughtfully back along the Mall, my mind full of the story of Pompey who, when he finally penetrated the Holy of Holies, had found nothing there at all. Everything to do with the job, except the man at the centre of it, seemed so happy. No one had mentioned any of the problems associated with what a constitutional monarch-in-waiting could, or could not, say in public. But then, as I cycled under Admiralty Arch, I realised that nobody had mentioned money either.

⸺ ◆ ⸺

The story broke in the Londoner's Diary of the *Evening Standard* under the headline 'Charles Takes On the Son of a Carpenter'. My wife, coming on the cutting the other day, said this made it sound as though the Second Coming had been at hand.

Prince Charles has taken on an aide to help him with his speeches. Until now everything he has said in public has been all his own work, but in future he will be able to call on the services of Byron Rogers. Rogers is a freelance journalist from humble Welsh origins – his father was a carpenter – and his engagement by Prince Charles indicates the change in attitude at Buckingham Palace. There is now, I understand, a determination that some appointments should be made among those of lowlier stock.

Odd lot, the English: snobbery, like damp, always shows through somewhere. I knew the writer, I had met her at parties, yet she would clearly have had no trouble at all in describing the Virgin Mary as upwardly mobile. I had in fact pleaded with her on the phone not to use this particular story, and even the pleading, I noted as I read on, had been incorporated into the tosh.

The Times speculated about the nature of the job ('part-time rhetorical consultant and teller of shaggy-dog stories'), while the *Evening News* burbled about 'an unprecedented honour' (I was writing for the *News* at the time). I was also introduced to the interesting little methods of my colleagues.

'You married, Mr Rogers?'

'No.'

'I see, confirmed bachelor then?'

'Hang on.'

Confirmed bachelor, like 'he was unmarried' in obituaries, casts a shadow. But the *Daily Telegraph* gave the story the full treatment it reserves for truly mysterious events like the death of the Glastonbury Thorn: a one-sentence paragraph. 'The Prince of Wales has appointed as speech writer Mr Byron Rogers, a colourful Welshman', as though being a colourful Welshman was a job, like a bus driver.

'I don't think it is generally known that Britain is self-sufficient in blackcurrants.' It was a month later, and I sat up in the bath, startled by the familiarity of those words. The voice was even more familiar. I had switched on the wireless, forgetting that early on a Saturday morning Radio 4 has a farming programme.

'In fact we lead the world in the production of blackcurrants. No imports disturb our trade figures, no foreign price rises threaten our economy ... Every year the wind blows through ten thousand acres of British blackcurrants ...' The Prince's timing, I noted, was very good.

The speech to the Farmers' Club was the first I had worked on, and it set the pattern. The Palace, usually Michael Colborne, would ring to tell me where the speech would be made, to whom, and under what circumstances. This was to be an after-dinner speech; but the themes and the character of the speech were left entirely to me. At one point I wrote to the Prince, complaining that I felt like a duck-gun being pointed in an approximate direction in the hope that the scatter pattern might hit something, anything. He wrote back and said the duck-gun appeared to be working.

But it meant I had to rely on my wits even more than I did as a journalist. For the Farmers' Club, meeting in St James, what was I to write about, the Common Agricultural Policy? I went to see the Club's officers, read through a Club history (from which I extracted the little gem that the last Prince of Wales to address them had done so in 1923, 'to an unceasing chorus of cheers and applause, saying, it is sad to relate, nothing whatever of substance or importance'). This must have appealed to my employer's sense of melancholy, for the little quote duly turned up in his speech and in others as well.

Then I remembered that odd fact about the blackcurrants from some otherwise forgotten article I had written long before, and I was up and running. The rest followed, with the irony of an agricultural club meeting in the middle of London which in the past had been addressed on such subjects as 'Slurry'.

From the start I was aware of the comedy involved in writing speeches to be delivered in places where I had never been, to people I would never meet, about matters of which I knew absolutely nothing. It was worse for my employer who had to go to these places and meet those people. I had been hired, a member of his staff told me, to stop him starting speeches along the lines of 'Ladies and gentlemen, what on earth am I doing here?' when the ladies and the gentlemen knew exactly what he was doing there.

So time passed. The Anglo-Venezuelan Chamber of Commerce at Caracas. The Burma Star Association, And, the ultimate unreality, something that had me walking round the room touching the furniture, an address to a gathering of engineers at Zurich University. For that I stole a column about engineers from my colleague Peter Simple, in whose fantasies I by then believed I had taken up residence.

I fell back on my own experiences, which then of course became the Prince's, so he would come out with anecdotes like this, 'A friend of mine was doing market research on the brewers.' Can a Prince of Wales ever have had a friend doing market research on the brewers? Anyway this man, my friend Fletcher Watkins, had to find the lowest social category of all, and, in a moment of inspiration, went into a municipal garden and met a tramp. He got him into a pub, bought him a pint, and the tramp opened like a rose. What did he think of Charringtons? Oh, very good. Marston's? Wonderful. But surely, said Fletcher, there was some brewer he objected to. The tramp got to his feet. 'You see in front of you someone who once had a family, a job, someone who once had a future. You see in front of you a man brought down by Bass.'

If the Prince's speeches ever get published, historians may ponder over a period in his life when Welsh headmasters confided in him about the relaxed entrance requirements of the new polytechnics ('If you've got anybody there who's not yet been fixed up, just send him along'), and when he could describe eighteenth-century Highland society as 'the Masai, grown white and articulate, at the end of the Great North Road'.

The last remark was dropped, without preamble, into a speech, for it was the Prince's method to use a paragraph here and there (he still liked his 'What on earth am I doing here?' openings). There were of course things he, or his advisers, felt he could not say. He presided at a press awards ceremony and I wanted him to end the speech by looking quizzically around him: 'But I see only a section of the British press in front of me, and the more poorly paid section at that. Ladies and gentlemen, where is the Linotype Operator of the Year?' His father, he said later, had raised no objections to this, but the event's organisers had.

I also wanted him to poke fun at Anthony Holden, known at the time to be writing the Prince's biography and thus accompanying him on every royal tour, by saying that his own job was bad enough 'without my Boswell padding behind me in the Economy Section', but he chose instead to be nice to Holden; his attitude changed dramatically when the book appeared. He later showed me a second book which Holden produced at the time of the royal marriage. Inside there was a fulsome handwritten inscription in, I think, green biro, at which he pulled a face. But the press speech he enjoyed, in particular the conceit I had worked up in which he compared his own presence to that of a pheasant handing out prizes after a shoot.

Only once did the shit hit the fan, and that ironically enough was the one occasion when I had really done some research. It was on British industry, and I used the comments of the American and Japanese businessmen I had interviewed on the stultifying social divisions they had seen in this country between the executive restaurant and the works canteen. The Prince made the speech, and that night on the television news I listened to something extraordinary: a CBI spokesman denouncing a member of the royal family. Even more extraordinary, I met that weekend in the pubs of Carmarthen working men who remembered what Edward VIII had said in the Rhondda during the Depression and felt they might again have a prince who understood.

The question of payment took months to work out, and required a meeting with Checketts, who in a memo had said, 'I rather thought he was going to do this work for nothing.' They were not quite of this world, these men, and I remembered the remarks of one member of staff when the Prince, seeking to intervene in the social problems of South London, called a conference. 'They all came but at a certain point HRH got up and said, "Well, I'm afraid I have to go now." Which left all these policemen and teenagers staring at each other round a table in Buckingham Palace.'

Checketts asked what was the going rate in journalism, and I, plucking a figure out of the air, suggested £125 per thousand words. That worked for a while except that if something interested me I wrote on. And on. Then the Assistant Private Secretary, newly transferred from the Foreign Office, came up with an impeccable Civil Service compromise: speeches were to be graded according to their public importance, the fees to range from £65 for a post-prandial jolly to £125 for Sermons on the Mount. I could of course have quietly trebled this, as the *Daily Mirror*'s James Whittaker suggested one night at a reception; it only required a phone call, he said, scribbling a number on a piece of paper. I never did, not only out of loyalty but because the reality of life on the other side of those gates was just too bizarre.

A remarkable young man, more camp than Julian Clary, once minced into Michael Colborne's office. When he had gone I asked who he was, for Colborne, I noticed, had not introduced us. 'That,' he said heavily, 'is the best reason for getting the Prince of Wales married as soon as possible.' It had been the Prince's valet. On another occasion I walked in to find Colborne's desk covered in knitted woollen socks: someone had called, hoping to get a Royal Warrant.

It was a nice place to call, the Palace. I used to break cycle journeys there for a cup of coffee and a chat, and, more than once, to cash a cheque. Once I had the idea that I write an article on the Prince's mailbag. Nobody had any objections to this so I spent an afternoon sorting through his post, through the knitted scarves and the fruit cakes which got delivered daily. The letters were very odd. There was one from a very cross girl in the American Mid-West, saying she had waited for him all day in some bus station in South Dakota. In others people poured out their hearts, but the article was never written; someone in authority pulled the plug on it, which was more or less what I expected would happen.

The Palace, like everything else, was not what it seemed. Entered from the Mall, it was a Palace, but entered from the side, the

Buckingham Gate entrance, it was a storehouse, with men wheeling trolleys and a noticeboard on which the footmen sought to sell each other secondhand cars. But then you went through a door, the carpet started, and you were in the Palace again.

There were so many corridors on so many different levels that occasionally I lost my way, and once, below ground, came on something out of the Brothers Grimm, a door marked 'Royal Clockmaker', which I could never find afterwards. Below ground I saw people going about their jobs, but above not a soul, so if you kept your nerve you could wander at will. Once I surfaced in the Throne Room.

There was the odd social event, like a Garden Party. I was invited to this, but when I asked if I might bring my mother, on the grounds that she loved a day out, this caused a kerfuffle among the Prince's people. It was explained that guests could bring a spouse or a daughter, but nobody else. Still in the end they agreed, although, for fear of creating a precedent, they said she would have to be invited as a guest in her own right. In which case, they went on, she would for some reason have to be presented to the Prince. This is some kind of special honour (the Chairman of Carmarthenshire County Council, invited at the same time, was just one of the guests, though the local paper announced this on its front page), and at Garden Parties you see retired officers rounding up the presentees, then like sheepdogs in the TV programme *One Man and His Dog* forming them into neat little queues, hovering to see they do not stray.

The conversation between the Prince and my mother was unforgettable.

'Do you live in Carmarthen or outside it?'

'I now live outside it,' said my mother, speaking with more

care than I had ever heard her use, 'but I have lived inside it.'

'Have you really?' said the Prince, who seemed to be under the impression that she had somehow come out of the Matto Grosso.

He then said, 'You have a clever son.'

And she, taken aback, said, 'Do you think so?'

Through all this, ignored by both, I stood looking from one to the other, like an umpire at Wimbledon.

'What a nice man,' said my mother after he had gone.

'Can you remember anything of what was said?'

'No.'

Then there was the Ball before the Wedding in which, wearing the white tie and tails I had inherited from my Uncle Jack, a ballroom dancer, I saw the bride-to-be, the youngest of all there, run through the room like a hunted thing. The guests included the Cabinet, the members of which talked warily to each other, foreign royalty, including the King of Nepal, in strange uniforms, two of the Goons, and Mrs Nancy Reagan. Nobody, I noted, awaited her at the door, so the Empress of the West entered, very small and alone.

Princess Margaret, looking upset, sat on the stairs being comforted by the Archbishop of Canterbury in gaiters, and, with the smells of kedgeree drifting through the State Rooms, it could have been any wedding in Britain. Some guests got extremely plastered, for there was a bar serving the strongest cocktails I have ever drunk, and had the police in the courtyard who had checked every car on the way in ('What's this then?' said an officer prodding the sack I had in the boot of my Cortina. 'Potatoes,' I replied), checked them on the way out all their targets would have been met and the magistrates' courts of London full for weeks. I caught one tiny dowager as she fell down the stairs and she weighed no more than a piece of cardboard; her make-up, close to, was pale green like that of one of Dracula's Brides. In the cocktail bar queue a huge bull in regimental scarlet turned to me. 'No finer sight in the world than a young Catholic girl with hair under her arms, dontcha think?' Up to a point, I said carefully.

I went to the wedding, a fact mischievously recorded by Peter McKay in the *Daily Mirror* gossip column under the headline 'Byron The Writer Will Be There', this despite my asking him not to use it. I borrowed my friend Philip Howard's old morning coat and the fancy waistcoat he had worn as a member of Pop at Eton thirty years earlier, and in this, for it was a very tight fit, I walked up Ludgate Hill to St Paul's like a man in plate armour.

'Who's that?' a man in the crowd asked his companion.

'Fuck knows.'

How did it end? My wife was asking me that the other day and all I could tell her was that, just as in Hollywood, the phone stopped ringing. I was not sad, because the Engineers' Speech in Switzerland represented a final marker of lunacy for a man who had never met an engineer in his life. But there was no final letter of thanks, not even a row, nothing at all after five years. My own idea, for what it is worth (God, I am beginning to sound like the Prince in the speeches he was then making), was that an article may have contributed.

It had become known that I was doing this work, so editors had been keen on getting me to write about royalty. I usually turned them down, but the idea of writing an open letter to the Princess of Wales intrigued me. 'People will talk about you endlessly, about your appearance and your imagined relationships with other members of the Family. In some households you will be like a relative who never calls …' It was kindly meant, and Colborne told me it had been much appreciated.

But then I wrote for the *Express* an open letter to the infant Prince William (and probably would have gone on writing open letters to all of them, down to the corgis), and halfway through this quoted two paragraphs from Einhard's ninth-century biography of the Emperor Charlemagne. The writer is describing the lot of the earlier Merovingian kings of France.

> Nothing was left the king except the name of king … He sat on his throne and played at government, gave audience to envoys, and dismissed them with answers he had been schooled, or rather, commanded, to give. He had nothing to call his own except one estate … and a not very numerous retinue. He travelled when occasions required it in a wagon drawn by oxen … in this guise he came to the palace or to the national assembly of his people. The mayor of the palace controlled the administration and decided all issues of policy at home and abroad.

The parallels were obvious, but I helpfully spelt them out at length, even to the State Coach.

'You must have been completely off your rocker if you thought you could go on writing speeches for royalty after that,' said my wife.

The last time I saw the Prince was at Highgrove where he seemed happy, talking about the DIY he was doing, about Nitromors, and the piece of celebrated modern furniture he had been given and quietly relegated to his detective's bedroom. I also met an old Irishman he was fond of, a character

Colborne told me would make a funny profile. The Prince gave me a piece of cake to take away, and I never saw him again.

⸺ ◆ ◆ ⸺

By then the unreal had given my thirties one last spin. Aged forty, I got married.

9

Exits and One Entrance

I AM NOT entirely sure how I got married. I know I proposed; it was on the M40, on its easterly approaches to Beaconsfield, for I remember seeing a sign on an embankment: 'DANGER. DEEP WATER'. And I remember what the proposed-to said: she said, 'All right.' It is just that in the background there was a purpose quite apart from us, and much invoked, a bit like the Schlieffen Plan for the German general staff in the years before the Great War.

For, alerted to the fact that we were living together by my friend Geraint Morgan, a Methodist, my mother had not let up in her efforts to hound into matrimony a couple in early middle age co-habiting quietly in Islington, far from the chapels of Carmarthen. Apart from asides to me in Welsh ('*Uchafu*', the ultimate expression of physical disgust), she kept bringing the matter up, once in a pub under the Cleddau Bridge.

This was then kept by a retired English naval officer, who every morning took delivery of fresh fish from Milford Haven and had a small but excellent wine list. Unfortunately the Welsh appeared not to be too keen on fresh fish or small but excellent wine lists, and the pub was deserted apart from my mother, my wife-to-be and me as we tucked into a lunch of brill, new potatoes and Gewurtztraminer. The retired naval officer was leaning gloomily on his bar, staring into space. And then ...

'When are you two going to get married?' said my mother in a

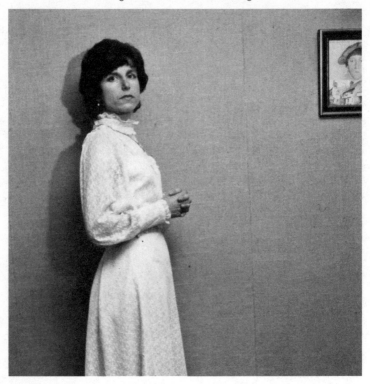

loud voice, and out of the corner of one eye I could see the naval officer start, then straighten up.

'Well, I . . .' But at that moment my mother choked on a fish bone and ran for the ladies, scattering chairs, for she was a strong woman. On the face of our host, I can see it now, there was a smile of pure wonder that Providence should have provided him with this floor show.

A few weeks later my mother presented my wife-to-be with the wedding and engagement rings from her marriage to my late father. And as I write this I am looking at a letter from my mother-in-law which we found among my mother's papers, congratulating

her, in the usual scatter pattern of exclamation marks, on her achievement ('We hope they will get on with it now and do it SOON!').

So I acquired another family, and another cupboard to rummage in.

My wife, on her father's side, had an Anglo-German background. 'You keep that to yourself, d'you hear?' commanded my Aunt Mary. They were bankers and scientists, though a great-uncle had been a professional soldier who had breezily joined the German cavalry when he discovered it was cheaper than the British. The result was that during the Great War he and his brother were on opposing sides, but on different fronts, for things were done like that then, with my wife's grandfather, interned as a British civilian, locked up in a camp near Berlin.

During the Second War one of her two uncles was in the Luftwaffe, the other a Jewish refugee in Britain, whose father had been a German officer killed on the Western Front and whose mother had been murdered in Belsen. The ageing cavalryman, having survived the Great War, was by then the commandant of a POW camp, who by the end of 1944 still believed Hitler would win the War. It was confusing and very sad. This was a little family, as the Yugoslav partisan leader Mihailovitch said, reflecting on his own fate, 'blown away by the gale of the world'.

By the time I met them its English branch had taken refuge in Christian Science, in long walks with large dogs and in the photography of flowers (when my father-in-law died we threw away eighty perfectly lit photographs of roses alone). 'One thing about flowers,' said my wife. 'They do keep still and smile.' Her father's people reminded me of the gentle eccentrics communing with grass cuttings whom William Brown encountered from time to time, though it meant they could end up in the oddest situations.

━━━━◆◆━━━━

The letter I found hard to read. I could see it was not an English hand, for the 'D's were capped, as were the 'U's, and there was an odd squiggle below the 'H'. But there was no mistaking the name. Large and impatient, it was the sort of signature field marshals should have. *Kesselring*. In front of me as I write is a handwritten letter from the Third Reich's last Commander in Chief in the West,

the man who on his appointment by Hitler, in March 1945, observed dryly to his staff, 'Well, gentlemen, I am the new V3.' The letter is addressed to my wife's grandmother.

In 1950, with her son, my father-in-law, a judge under the Allied Control Commission in Germany, Granny had come visiting, and, a woman with a conscience, had expressed a wish to meet people the rest of the world preferred to forget, the German war criminals locked up in Wirl Penitentiary in the British Zone. Strings had to be pulled to allow her to do so.

For inside Wirl were men who had dealt in death, filling the skies with planes and laying waste whole countries, amongst them the Field Marshals Albert Kesselring and Erich von Manstein. Three years earlier Kesselring had been sentenced to death for the shooting of 300 Italian hostages, a sentence later commuted to life imprisonment. 'A smiling and forceful little gentleman', he had directed the Luftwaffe in the Battle of Britain, and wise-cracked to the *Daily Express* reporter Sefton Delmer, 'Next time there is a war they will have to have lawyers in command.'

So in Wirl they gardened, and argued about the war amongst themselves. And then along came Granny, who, persuading the commandant that what these fallen paladins needed was a crash course in British values, *drew up a reading list for them*.

Kesselring's letter, written in English, is a masterpiece of dry irony.

Dear Madam,
It was a delightful surprise for us generals when your book
parcel was handed to us. We are anticipating, Madam, the great
and real pleasure of reading first these books of Bernard Shaw
and John Galsworthy, as they are particularly likely to yield some
profit to our minds in our confined state and to enliven us ...

Granny sent four book parcels in March, more in May, and, in September, twelve volumes of Dickens, also three of Tolstoy, the latter possibly of some interest to von Manstein, who had spent his war trying to kill as many Russians as possible. She seems to have endeared herself to all of them, including the commandant Colonel Vickers, who in his last, typewritten, letter to her wrote, 'I smiled at your postscript about whether I should write anything about my work. This is extremely unlikely.' Under this, in his own hand, he added mischievously, 'I gave your best wishes to Kesselring and his comrades...'

The Colonel, like the generals, had clearly never met anyone quite like Granny: such implacable unworldliness was outside all their experiences of life, and it was something she passed on to her children. On the eve of the First Gulf War her daughter, my wife's aunt, wrote to Saddam Hussein, appealing to his better nature, and enclosing, as proof of her credentials, a photograph taken of her in her youth riding a camel. She got no reply.

My mother-in-law's people were of a different stock; it would have taken more than the gale of the world to blow them away. A cousin said, 'If you came on more than two of them in a room it was a quite terrifying experience.' One, her grandfather, had just one ambition, to ring the bells in every belfry in England; a clergyman and a sturdy man in gaiters, the Rev. Francis Robinson glowers out of old photographs, his name familiar to anyone of you who has ever strayed into a church belfry and read the names on the peal boards.

Men who ring bells are proud if in the course of their lives they participate in the complex permutations of completing just one peal. The Rev. Robinson rang 1,261 peals, the first man to go above a thousand, and in a single year, 1886, *claimed to have spent 4,637 hours ringing bells*. Think of that for a moment. It works out at almost thirteen hours a day, every day, seven days a week, and this was a man who in addition managed to carry out his parish duties, father ten children, eat, and travel from church to church to accommodate that one ambition.

'He had this horse and trap,' a bell-ringer told me, 'in which he and his team of ringers used to drive around the country. If they got through a peal he'd buy them supper. If they didn't, they'd drive home in a huge silence.' Robinson started life as a banker before disappearing into the belfries, and wrote an autobiography which he imaginatively entitled *Among the Bells*.

His son Bill, my mother-in-law's father (whom she always referred to as 'dear Daddy'), looked like a prize-fighter, and in photographs seems about to spring, being out of place in any form of dress other than a mask, a striped jersey and a sack labeled 'Swag'. He was a Harley Street paediatrician, and wrote one book which he entitled *Baby Welfare: A Guide to its Acquisition and Maintenance*, the first sentence of which reads, 'A steam engine and a baby are among the commonest objects met with in our everyday life.'

There is, as you might expect, a family tree which, with its branch lines massively ignored, roars back to that terminus of the old world, the emperor Charlemagne, also to some Viking horror called Sigurd the Snake-eyed. But, for all these roaring boys, the one figure that always fascinated my wife was her great-grandfather on her grandmother's side, another clergyman, the Rev. J.F. Morton. Here silence fell. Nobody in the family ever talked about him, and until six years ago all she knew was that in late Victorian times he had lost his faith, resigned his living at

Ainstable, near Carlisle, and died in poverty in London. What follows is in her own words.

I rang the vicar of Ainstable, and got an answering machine, but I never got an answer. From a reference library I got the number of a churchwarden, but when I rang it I found myself talking to a man from quite a different village. So I decided to look for the answer myself, and drove with my elder sister along the A6 through a strange, open land, the Lake Fells on one side, the Pennines on the other.

The church at Ainstable was a Victorian building, and it was bleak, bleak up there, the wind whipping across from the Fells. Oddly in these times, the church wasn't locked. Inside we found a leaflet that told us the whole thing had been rebuilt, and there was an old photograph with the caption, 'Taken at the time of the rebuilding 1876, during the time of the Rev. J.F. Morgan.' That would have been about the time my great grandfather was there, but J.F. Morgan? Had the church airbrushed him out as well?

I had just started to write in the visitors' book, appealing for information, when my sister, reading from the noticeboard, said, 'Listen to this. "Stained-glass window, SW chancel wall, Memorial to Frederick Darley Morton, infant."' We found the window and, at the bottom of it, this: 'In memory of Frederick Darley Morton, infant son of J.F. Morton BA, vicar of Ainstable, who died Jan 27, 1876.' And there was a verse from Kings II, 4, 26. 'Is it well with the child? It is well.'

This was so moving. I had never heard of this child, and I wondered whether he was buried in the churchyard. Then something very odd: as we left the church we found it locked, which had been open when we came in. Neither of us had

slipped the catch: it was as though some agency had wanted us to be undisturbed.

I started looking on the north side just because the child may have been unbaptised, and it was there I found a small grave. A light rain was falling as I scraped at the lichen, and then, suddenly, a ray of sunshine broke through as though a torch had been switched on.

Now if you have ever tried to read an inscription on weathered stone you will know that to do so it requires a certain time of day, the light falling at a precise angle. Just before that I would not have been able to see anything, and just afterwards it would have gone, but for a few minutes there it was. 'Frederick Darley Morton, born January 20, died January 27, 1876.'

And then on the other side I read, 'I shall not be hurt of the second death. Revelation 2, 11.' Only this is a slight misquotation. If you look up the passage it reads, 'He that overcometh shall not be hurt of the second death.' So a man who clearly knew his Bible backwards had been so moved as to misquote it.

As we drove back down the A6 an intensely bright rainbow came out. It seemed to blaze, even though at the time my mind was full of that poor man and his wife. The child would have been their fourth, but their first son. I had thought, hoped, to find some intriguing scandal, perhaps intellectual misgivings, that had resulted in the lost faith. Instead there was no mystery.

The memorial window, that expensive little tomb, but especially those arcane, terribly moving Bible passages, that misquotation, pointed to someone completely shattered by this death. And it occurred to me how like one of the quests in the old legends it had been: the misinformation, the sudden clues, and the almost supernatural intervention, the angled light, the rainbow. I could hardly believe what had happened. It was as though I had been touched on the shoulder and shown the answers.

———◆—◆———

My father-in-law, a retired judge, was the most mysterious man I have known. In the ten years I was in his company I never heard him once venture an opinion on anything – on the weather, on food, on books, on people. No, that is not entirely true. Once I told him that I did not think the Son of God had walked and talked in Palestine, this to a gentle, reserved man who read his Bible every day. But all he said in reply was, 'Oh, I say.' Nothing more, but it has made me feel more guilty, and embarrassed, than any argument would have done.

He was someone, according to a niece, who ran through your fingers like sand. But he, a full colonel in his thirties, was also a man to whom one of his sergeants at the end of the War felt obliged to write and thank for having got him through it; he was later the chief justice of a large African state, his term of office straddling the awkward years of colonial and post-colonial rule. But he, who had filled so many roles, had run out of them in retirement. It was not his kingdom you entered when you came to his house.

The first I noticed was the labelling of jars in the larder: my mother-in-law labelled everything, even jars of chutney with the manufacturers' names already on them, so on the one side there would be Branston Pickle, on the other, in her handwriting, 'chutney'. I had never encountered such a need to impose control before.

It could only happen in an upper-middle class English family: elsewhere my mother-in-law's dominance would have been challenged by constant rows or imposed by direct commands. Here there were no rows and no commands, just muted endearments, darling this and darling that, but if she said, 'Oh dear, I seem to have left my spectacles upstairs', an elderly gentleman leapt to his feet as though an order had just come through from the *Fuehrerhauptquartier*. He had been schooled to authority from an early age by nannies, prefects, housemasters and the army, and in retirement, as he dwindled, there was just the one authority, an authority once blunted by social life, by parties and menus, the bossing of servants and of dogs which now had nothing to blunt it.

Had she had a job, her energy and will would have been funnelled, but it was her tragedy, and that of her family, that all she ever became was someone's wife. There was no intimacy with her, for mostly she talked, bright cocktail-party chatter as if she and you had just met, telling anecdotes we had heard many times, though we did not dare remind her. When she had a small stroke, a sherry glass falling from her hand, her speech slurring into silence, her two daughters who saw this, both of them middle-aged, felt unable afterwards to tell her what had happened.

Only once did she ever admit to her power, for she had taken a shine to me, thinking me equally monstrous. She showed me an alcove, the size of a bathroom, off her bedroom, where her clothes hung. Her husband, she said, had a little cupboard at the end of a passage, and for a moment there was a grin, so devilish and gone so quickly I had to remind myself it had been there.

Her husband would have been puzzled had you asked him about the roaring ego he had helped assemble. He wore the clothes she chose, went on the holidays she demanded, and at the end slipped away, dying in his sleep. It was the one rebellious act of his life. She had him buried, she who had always known where he was, apart from the War (though even then she had written every day), and on his grave, without irony, which was not something she ever knew, she had this cut: 'Be still, and know that I am God.'

And then the quiet came, when there were only dogs to hear the anecdotes, and confusion came with it, when she forgot names and, as resident carers came and went, thought herself in a hotel. With her driving now a danger to herself and everyone else, her car was quietly taken away by her eldest daughter and son-in-law, though she blamed me ('I never did trust the Welsh'). When her last dog died her daughters took her out to lunch, then drove her to a residential home and left her, just as forty years earlier she had left them at their boarding schools. They waved goodbye gaily, only this time the bewildered young faces staring down the drive had been replaced by a bewildered old one. And two women in their fifties felt this was the most daring thing they had ever done, and the saddest.

I went to see her there, among the solicitors' widows and the retired chief constables, one of whom had, literally, just fallen out of a tree. Each private room bristled with photographs, though the people who occupied those rooms had forgotten of whom. Here, like a very small child, she lived in the moment, singing carols on hot summer afternoons with the other old ladies. And here she died.

I was the last of the family to see her. The circumstances were the usual racketty ones that were then my working life: I had been to see a pigeon called Red Daniel some forty miles away. A champion racer, he had been stolen three years earlier, and on a night of terrible gales when his new roost must have been blown apart, the pigeon, like Ulysses, had come home. My mother-in-law was by then very ill and in a coma as I sat with her and told her about Red Daniel while she slept on. As I left I kissed her, which I had never done before, and then something extraordinary happened. Her eyes still shut fast, she spoke. 'G'bye, g'bye.' It was the old cocktail-party voice, but small, like syllables borne on the wind, as though on some headland she had heard her name called, and turned.

━━━━◆━▶━━━━

A few weeks later, her house sold, we dismantled the life that had been there, its taste in books, records, furniture, the wedding dress in cream and gold silk which had lain untouched in a Chinese trunk for sixty years, a silver cup recording that on one unimaginably golden day she had won the 440 yards, the hurdles and the long jump. I found a photograph of her aged two, a stout girl staring, and it was the face of someone determined to have her own way whatever the cost. Later she learned to smile in photographs. Me on safari. Me with the chief of police. Me skiing. MEEEEEE. Her small children appeared from time to time, once with their nannies, all four staring out from some bleak stretch of sand at the North Sea; their backs were to the camera.

'Odd woman,' her sister-in-law had told me. 'Not a trace of a maternal instinct.' But the letters she wrote to her children at their boarding schools were sticky with 'darlings', and each ended 'Tons of love' or 'Heaps of love', sometimes as 'T.O.L.' or 'H.O.L.'

As we sorted through her boxes I came on a little moment of history, an exchange of letters between the Chief Justice and his new African President. Members of the President's party had taken to bullying their defeated political opponents, and the Chief Justice was incredulous: 'It is as though after a Cup Final the victors are gathering around the dressing room of their opponents, uttering all sorts of abuse and threats.' The President, for there was a real friendship between two very religious men, was conciliatory: 'Our task is not made easier for us when these chaps refuse to respect the National Flag and the National Anthem.' Delicately, for this was a brand-new democratic state, he touched on tribalism.

But most of the letters were those my father-in-law had brought back from three war zones. These letters, carefully bound with string, sometimes with romantic blue ribbon, had for fifty years followed them round the world, box after cardboard box. Hundreds, thousands of letters, packed and unpacked, all of them unknown to their children. My wife was nervous of reading them, knowing this would involve meeting her parents as young people, but in the end did so.

There was a lot of play-acting. At the start of the War, writing to her 'Angel Fairy Princeling', she was the adoring little woman: 'Talking to the Russians through an interpreter must have been too thrilling for words ...' Hers was a breathless war, with nannies to be interviewed (and usually found wanting) and visits to London to be arranged to see friends. The 'nestlings', their children, had walk-on parts, and were sometimes 'sweet', sometimes 'divine'. The War, like them, got a walk-on part.

'Poor little Finland, trying to remain neutral, what a mess. Night, night, my darling.' Hess landed in Scotland in 1941, a sure sign, she decided, that the War would be over very soon. The A-bomb was dropped, and she tried to engage various elderly relatives in portentous discussion, only to be told that the more people it was dropped on the better.

But there was a sudden directness in her letters when, the War over, there was a possibility that her husband might get a job in occupied Germany. How big would their house be? Would there be maids, nannies, gardeners? Looking after children ('nestlings' no

longer) was not quite her thing, confided the Petkin, which was what he called her; there were also references to 'Le Sport', their word for sex, vaguer than his had been, but tantalising, and of course so much easier to arrange with a large household staff.

My wife made a sudden dramatic appearance at this point, a small tearful child pleading with her mother not to send her back to the boarding nursery where, aged two, she, together with her elder sister, had been left while their mother 'packed' for Germany. She was told later that she was there for six weeks. Now in one of the letters she found that she had been there for seven months, and it was a letter she wished she had never read.

Nothing was ever thrown away. There were envelopes marked 'desk keys', 'suitcase keys', 'clock keys', though none of these fitted any desk, suitcase or clock which we had assembled in the middle of the floor. But one key fitted. We locked the front door for the last time, pushed the key through the letterbox, and it was an end.

There were other exits. My stepfather, a retired farmer and traveller in cattle foods, died a happy man. Suffering from angina, he had been three weeks in hospital, his condition worsening, yet when I went to see him on the last day of his life his eyes were shining and he roared with laughter as he told me about two visitors he had had.

'Funny old gals.' He talked broad Gloucestershire. 'Two of 'em, one a small woman reading from a Bible, and the other a very tall old thing in a long blue dress. They came in here, walked round my bed, didn't say a word to me. And then they were off. Here, boy, you don't think I'm seeing things, do you?'

'Perhaps they were hospital visitors,' I suggested.

'Dunno who they were. Bit odd, if you ask me.'

When I asked the nurses about them they said I was the first visitor that day.

Three hours later the hospital rang, and I took the call. 'I don't understand, they said he was poorly,' I told my mother, 'but that there was no need for us to hurry.'

'You know what that means,' she said.

She lasted just three months. She became withdrawn and distant, two things nobody could have accused her of being in her prime. She sat in a window, staring out, so withdrawn she did not even quarrel with me, something that in later years had become a fixture of her life, when she and my stepfather would stand in the doorway as we left, he waving cheerily, she wringing her hands and saying, 'Where did I go wrong, oh where did I go wrong?'

'That's it, I'm never going home again,' I said to my wife in the car.

'And you say my family's barmy,' said my wife, having heard it all before. There were no rows in her family, there never are in a totalitarian household.

What did we row about? The silliest things, most of which I cannot even remember: that is the tragedy of it. Like the night I walked in and my daughter, then seven, was watching the soap opera *Emmerdale* with my mother and stepfather when the characters started to discuss a reversed vasectomy. There was a hell of a row over that, in the course of which my mother said, 'None of it's *true*.' Which was a bit ripe as she was in the habit of giving a running indictment on the moral characters of the cast ('Look at him, he's a real old wide-o').

Then there was the time I was opening oysters, and stuck a

knife in my thumb. My mother came in just as the blood was spurting, actually spurting as though from a water-pistol. 'There you are, see,' she said with an air of wisdom, as if I was being punished. When we had both stopped shouting, she said, puzzled, 'But it's what people say, "There you are, see." It's only words, boy.'

A lot of things puzzled her. To sear the skin of a boiled ham she once stuck a poker into a fire in the old way, only she stuck it into an electric fire. And that was the electric fire gone, with my mother, thrown backwards, sitting, bewildered, on the floor. Gas she understood because there was a flame, but electricity was a great mystery. She fiddled around with a knife inside a toaster until one day there was a flash, a bite got taken out of the knife, and that was the toaster gone. To remind her, I made up a calypso, only I couldn't resist singing it in front of her friends.

> If you wan' to meet a doctor,
> Stick a knife into the toaster.
> Faster than bird fly out of tree
> You fin' yo'self in Casualty.

Hoover motors burned out, steam kettles into which she forgot to put water fused, all quickly tidied away before anyone could notice. 'And don't you dare tell anyone this time.' I never once saw her switch on a TV or a gramophone or a radio, so I never saw what she could have done with these. When he was in hospital the last time I told my stepfather I had bought her a cordless phone. 'Poor Maisie,' he said.

But what hurt me, and her, the old friend of my childhood, was how cross we got with each other. It is what happens when the relationship between a mother and her only child has been too close. He commits the crime of growing up, and changing; she commits the crime of staying just as she was. Had there been a

257

distance between us, as there was between my wife and her mother, we might have weathered it. As it was, we infuriated each other in her last years. People are only infuriated by those they love.

I would drive away, vowing never to return, and three weeks later there we would be again, driving through the countryside to see a church in a dingle where a sixth-century king had been buried. 'I don't know why you bother with these old places,' said my mother in the back seat, refusing to get out. 'You're odd you are. Turn the page, boy.' We would pass through a village. 'Depressing old place, glad I don't live here.' We would park on a cliff, with the full wonderful sweep of Cardigan Bay below us. 'Don't you two ever clean this car? We had pigsties at home cleaner than this. Have you got any sweets?'

My mother-in-law, who liked to impress by talking about her travels ('The Victoria Falls? I know every drop,' she was once heard to say at a party), would sometimes among the anecdotes venture into history, though when she did, whatever she had started with, the Lion Gate at Mycenae or the legend of Atlantis, she always ended up within four or five minutes with Guy Fawkes. 'Poor Guy Fawkes.' On television she had seen his signature after they had racked him.

My mother, with her total lack of interest in any form of knowledge, did not feel this need to impress, which invested her with a sort of invulnerability. All she ever wanted was not to stand out in any way: to fit in with her friends, wear a sheepskin coat, go to coffee mornings, and have a tidy house. Anything else just prompted the comment, 'Who does he think he is?', that traditional Welsh reaction to any form of difference, or achievement. I sometimes think all Welsh wars of independence foundered on this, people muttering 'Who does he think he is?' as

Llywelyn ap Gruffydd or Owain Glyndwr rode by.

My wife puzzled her because, tiring of the wall-to-wall TV soap operas which she and my stepfather watched, my wife would retire to our bedroom to read. 'She's in her flat again,' said my mother. But she felt it her duty to instruct my wife in useful household tips. 'Always be tidy,' she told her once. 'If you don't, and you're brought back in a box, people will say, "Did you see that house?"' Tidiness mattered, the Doulton china figures Balloon Man and the Balloon Lady dusted ('Who will look after these when I'm gone?'), the brass handles on my father's cabinets gleaming. 'People with nice houses never want to die,' she reflected. Horrified by eccentricity, she was absolutely without any suspicion of how eccentric she was.

'Bob?' I had asked on the phone about my stepfather. 'I don't see him, he's upstairs with his old trollops all the time.' What she meant was that my stepfather had been to the library and taken out some novels by Anthony Trollope.

I bought her a secondhand, rather grand fur coat; she had always wanted a fur coat. But she only wore it twice, for public opinion had turned against fur coats. I felt very sad about that. Then there was the time I became interested in a 'paedophile' conspiracy case in Pembroke, something I thought the greatest miscarriage of justice in my lifetime. I was going to interview someone and asked if she'd like to come, thinking she'd refuse for it was a sad occasion, but she said, 'Of course I'll come, I may not get the chance again.' My stepfather had been dead a month. She stayed in the car, and when I got back she was fast asleep, her mouth open, and I found myself looking at a very old lady.

'I do hope He calls me soon,' she said often.

He called her in the month of May. There were three weeks in hospital, most of them in intensive care, during which, after a perforated ulcer and a tracheotomy, she could not speak. And then there was the evening phone call to tell me that she had become 'poorly' since my afternoon visit, but there was no need for me to hurry.

On Boxing Day that year I drove to the smallholding where on a plateau above a mining valley she spent her childhood. This had been landscaped and gentrified (the farm opposite now had a tarmac drive with fountains), where her family, her father reduced to coal mining after being forced to sell their farm, had been so poor she had no dolls except those she made herself from twigs and rags. I stopped the car and looked at the hedge in which, playing at keeping house, a small child had lit some sticks, added coal and almost burnt the hedge down. She was good at fires.

To some extent you can anticipate grief, even though when it comes it still knocks you sideways. What you cannot anticipate, and what nothing prepares you for, no asides from the recently bereaved, no helpful little articles in the family section of newspapers, is the feeding frenzy when bureaucracy closes in on someone's death. And it comes to all of us.

At first there is the interlude when all time stretches before you, when days no longer turn on the early morning phone calls to ward sisters, and there are no hospitals to visit. The worry and the urgency have gone, and there is just the yellow house where the shoes are in line, the coats behind the door, and you have only to open a drawer, any drawer, for it to break your heart. And then the bedlam starts.

Days in glum offices, waiting in queues, reading leaflets, filling in forms, reading, as in a dream, a battered old book someone has left, *The Golden Years of Steam*, which means that for the rest of my life I will associate death with the *Mallard* crossing moorland. And all the time the agencies of the state are nibbling away like minnows.

Death certificate for a council crematorium which charges double at weekends. Signatures from two doctors already on a salary, £82, which, I note, is £4 more than three months earlier when I registered my stepfather's death. This certificate is handed to me in a sealed envelope, along with my mother's belongings in carrier bags, and I find myself signing for a watch that never kept the right time, for three towels and a pair of slippers. The envelope, addressed to the Registrar, is marked 'Confidential', so I open it and see that for their eighty-two quid the doctors are hedging their bets. The cause of death is given as 'Possible cerebral incident'.

Copies of death certificates from the Registrar, £3.50 each, each one run out in seconds from his computer. I pay in cash, and the change comes out of a chocolate box kept in a cupboard, alongside a large doll.

I know this Registrar, we were boys together, and now, as required by law within forty-eight hours, I sit giving him details of a birth which was registered the year of Passchendaele, when the Welsh infantry, advancing against machine-guns, were seen to hold out their hands, palms up, as though walking into a sharp spring shower. All round the walls are signs which say 'No Smoking', and the Registrar looks up as I puff on my pipe for I am beyond niceties this day. 'I gave up seven years ago,' he says pointedly. 'Nasty habit.'

'I'm sure you've still got a few left.'

———◆◆———

And so on and on, this journey through the suburbs of a death. To the Benefits Office to stop my mother's pension. ('I forgot to do that,' said my friend Henry. 'It went on being paid into the bank, and then they found out. Blimey.') The Benefits Office is a brick bunker patrolled by a private security firm, for claimants, I am told, have been known to jump over the counter. The guards walk up and down a queue of people so haggard and so downcast they do not look as though they could jump over a brick. Not that jumping would have been worth their while. When it is finally my turn I find myself speaking to someone through bullet-proof glass.

To the Council offices, to record what will prompt a change in council tax. I sit there for an hour, then I produce the documents and answer all their questions. Six weeks later through the post come forms I cannot understand, which seem to be asking the same questions.

To a building society to close my mother's small account, noting as I do so that she who has not had to pay tax in years has been paying it on her interest, being unaware of the fact. More forms. But the building society could not be nicer. The transfer of the account to me goes through.

Then the undertaker's bill comes, for the oak, the swansdown upholstery and the rest, all consumed by fire a day later, and I ring the Nat West, where my mother has £1200 in a current account.

'Have you been to Probate?' says the woman at the Nat West. Her name is Iris.

'No.'

'Then I'm afraid we can't release the money,' says the Goddess of the Rainbow.

My mother has left me the executor of her estate, also its sole beneficiary. Surely there is no need for Probate, which is just the High Court's permission to distribute assets to the beneficiaries?

Iris is unmoved. There could be, she says, drawing the sentence out for emphasis ... claimants. Claimants for 1200 quid? I see them lining the rails of banana boats or, cold-eyed and snow-shoed, crossing the wastes of the Yukon, all of them making for Carmarthen.

I ring a solicitor who said, yes, they can handle Probate for me. Fees? Hmmm ... oh, just £300, and a court fee of £50. Oh, and VAT of course. So a third would be gone at the outset, just to soothe the fevered imagination of the Nat West. I decide to seek Probate on my own.

In the directory there is no Probate in Northampton, my nearest county town. I ring Enquiries, and find myself talking about wills to a mystified Probation Service. I ring the Lord Chancellor's Office, which tells me to ring the Northampton county court, which I do.

'Sorry, dear. No one here seems to have heard of that. We're unpaid bills and catalogue debts we are, hundreds of thousands of them. Why not ring the criminal court?' Criminal court? I ring the criminal court.

'Oh yes, our local Probate Registry is Birmingham.'

'BIRMINGHAM?'

'Yes, chap comes every Wednesday, always by train, they never drive, and he sits in a room from 10.30 to 2.30. Would you like his number?

'I know, it's so hard to find us,' says the woman at the Birmingham Registry when finally, late in the afternoon, the number answers. 'Sometimes we come under the courts, sometimes under District Registry, depending on which directory you consult.' There is really very little to Probate, she goes on. All you have to do is fill in two forms, then turn up by appointment and swear in a front of a Probate Officer that everything you have written is true. And the cost? On all estates worth over £5,000 there is a flat fee of £130.

It is like Dorothy finally meeting the Wizard of Oz. All those difficulties, that mystery, those rumours of the expertise involved, they end in two forms and an appointment in a rented room with a man who loves trains. Twenty minutes. Plus, of course, £130 on the tiny estate of an old lady who all her life paid tax, even at the end when there was no need for her to do so.

But there is something else. 'You do realise half the estates in this country don't need Probate,' says the man in the Lord

Chancellor's Office. 'And there is no legal obligation on the rest, except certain organisations insist on it for their records. You know, when there are shares or houses involved. Banks? Oh, I think you'll find they can use their discretion.'

Discretion? I have now spent two whole days on the telephone, and when I make the last call my voice is bleak as the Polar ice.

'Hello, is that the National Westminster Bank? I should like to speak to Iris...'

But amongst all these exits there was one entrance, after which nothing was ever quite the same.

It is five weeks later, and my wife and I have entered domestic service, which is much as we expected domestic service would be. We spend a lot of our time in the kitchen now, muttering in the way of servants whenever an interval occurs between the imperious yells.

Like most dictators, our employer seems to find it difficult distinguishing between day and night. She sleeps in the day but then in the small hours or at dawn the summons comes, as Hitler's or Stalin's came to send feet clattering across the halls of serpentine or syenite, or in our case of Marley tiles. So far we have spared the monologues about the New Order. New Orders do not interest her, for she has gone back beyond organised society to an egomania to which not even dictators can aspire. One blue eye opens, and there must be food; it shuts, and there must be warmth. If either is lacking, all hell is loosed.

As servants, my wife and I are out of the reach of any trade union, for we have gone back too, beyond serfdom and slavery, to the wood and the moon. And however much we mutter, we know we are in the service of a living god and there is nothing at all that we can do about it. When last measured, and she is often measured (and will be for the next fourteen years), the god was twenty-two inches long.

◆ ◆

She came in the hot weather, at teatime. My wife and I were both forty, and had assumed it would never happen. Like an aboriginal I had come to believe there was no connection between copulation and death, for men could believe this, in the 1970s, in London. And then it happened. It was as though machinery forgotten in some gallery, being switched on, had come to life at once.

There was just one hiccup in the long nine months, when, two weeks before the expected birth, my wife, because of her age, was admitted to hospital to have her blood pressure monitored. It was an afternoon so hot that when one moved it was like moving in water, and I had gone out into the town to buy her a fan, calling at the fishmarket on the way.

Now in the fishmarket in Northampton then there was a trader in a Homburg hat who had a weakness for two things, cigars and haggling. I asked him how much a pound the dabs were, and I knew I was lost then for the eyes swivelled and he took the cigar out of his mouth. How, he began, how would I like *all* the dabs. There was a long line of dabs. But the cigar was moving in a lazy arc across the stall. *And* the plaice, he said. Ten pounds the lot. No, and this was what did me, nine pounds.

In the streets of Northampton the sun beat down on a man carrying two large raffia fans, and ten pounds of fish in a black bin liner.

They had decided to keep my wife in overnight for more tests, said a young doctor. But then his nostrils twitched, and his eyes swivelled, suddenly no longer the decisive figure he had been.

'That's the fish,' I said. 'Needs eating.' Of course they let her out that night, even the blood pressure admitting defeat for it went down.

On the day when it was due to make its appearance there was no sign of the baby. A friend from home called and I made a hot curry which my wife ate. We then went to the pub, after which, tiring of the gabble of talk, my wife ate some bran and went to bed. Bran and curry. As I write this now I can only record my amazement that the birth did not appear on the radar screens at NASA.

Around two in the morning there were definite signals that the launch was on. I drove her to the hospital, my head like a bucket after all that beer, which was a definite advantage. Hangovers enabled the old Celts to go into battle; now they enable their descendants to be present at births, one of the divides between this and the last generation. They would need two beds, said my mother darkly, one for the birth and the other . . . She let the sentence trail away, something she rarely did.

In the admissions hall a small young man in a short-sleeved shirt was talking to a midwife, and it was a scene of such obvious exegesis it might have been part of a very bad film. His wife was about to give birth, he was asking about the forms of painkillers, and the midwife was telling him, both talking at the tops of their voices. Good, he said, smiling. He was a short-haired, superior young man, and would have been viewed with approval by any panel awarding a Tory candidacy. He would like to be consulted, he said, still smiling, if a painkiller was to be administered. *He would like to be consulted?*

And he was. He refused his wife access to any of them as she screamed and screamed, like a woman giving birth off-screen in a

Western film, while he, somehow neater and more scrubbed as the day went on, strolled up and down the corridors smiling at people, not one of whom thought to hit him with an oxygen cylinder. Inside my bucket I ran a brisk little film of him being publicly vasectomised without drugs.

The only book they had there was a New Testament in an American translation ('You the King of the Jews?' 'You said it,' said Christ). I read the Book of Revelation to my wife, so there were things coming out of the sea when the pains started. It was a terrible day, morning sliding into afternoooon. They had connected her to some kind of machine with a graph recording the intensity of the contractions, and as the needle shook and plunged I saw the nails go into her hand, and into mine when I held it. Then they gave her an epidural, and the quiet came.

In the end it was a forceps delivery, and I watched incredulously as the huge spanners and the tongs were laid out, clanking against each other on green cloth. My wife, behind the green cloth which had been raised to hide it from her, seemed distantly interested.

There was much tugging and then everything happened very quickly. There was a long, bloodstained rabbit which cried. A daughter, said the doctor, putting his tools away. Then, like a butler announcing a new arrival, he said, and here's the afterbirth. Some people ate it, he said chattily, with onions. He had heard of a sect that went round collecting all the afterbirths they could get for this purpose. Where was this, I asked, in the Congo? No, he said, in Islington.

Later that week, that same week, my wife and I walked down the village and this doctor was there, unpacking his cricket pads. The hospital was playing the village. A few days earlier, I would have taken down on stone tablets anything the man had said. Now I stared at him in puzzlement. He looked about nineteen.

We called her Bethan, because my wife liked the sound of the name and thought the English would be able to pronounce it, and then, because her mother tried to intervene ('Darling, Daddy and I have been talking, and we think she should have one English name'), Gwenllian. The name of the baby daughter of the last Prince of Wales whom the English stole, and the spelling of whose name was such a problem to their bureaucracy. Wencilian. Wentliane. Nothing had changed.

Bethan. I spelt it out, letter by letter for the registrar. Gwenllian. He looked at me, we went through the whole process again, and as he registered the birth as 'Male' we had to start again. I was getting irritated by now, the way I get irritated when some idiot newscaster, whose one talent is to read aloud in public and is so proud of the way he pronounces Beijing, says 'PON-DEE-PRID' for Pontypridd. So while I could have given Carmarthen as my own place of birth, I went for accuracy and gave him both barrels. Bancyfelin. He put down his pen and he sighed.

So I entered fatherhood.

<hr />

Left to myself, I should have ended this chapter like that, except my editor, who has met her in adulthood, thinks I should add something about her beauty and the pleasure of her company. As her father I do not feel I can do this, for what I have been most conscious of is being unnerved at having someone around the house who may be brighter, and is certainly wittier, than I am. I have been aware of this ever since she came into a room where I was watching a television documentary on Oswald Mosley.

'What's this?'

'*Blue Peter*,' I said grumpily.

'I see, how to make the Nazi Party out of an egg-box.'

She was just fourteen, and I knew I should be in trouble for the rest of my life.

10

A Gap in My Social Calendar

IN THE 1980s my wife and I moved to a village in Northamptonshire. Why? A good question. On the day we moved in, one of those bleak dead days between Christmas and the New Year, I saw, we both saw, two big red and blue macaws, the colours exploding in the monotone of the landscape, fly steadily over the village as though they, and we, had become one of those dream landscapes by Douanier Rousseau. But if I had to find a reason why we moved it was partly to do with the melancholy and rootlessness of Sunday afternoons in London, partly to do with the appeal of country pubs. The latter gives a poignance to what follows.

◆◆◆

A well-dressed couple stands by the bar. Everyone in the pub that night is watching them out of the corners of their eyes, and listening. Which is how we hear the man ask his wife if before Christmas they can visit someone they know. She purses her lips, rummages in her handbag until she finds a diary, and says, 'Let me see if we've got a gap in our social calendar, dear.'

After they have gone, Joe Carr the groom says, grinning, 'Did you hear that, social calendar?' He turns to my wife and me. 'What about you then? You two must have a gap in your social calendar you could drive a horse-box through.'

271

'What d'you mean?'

'Why else would you be here with the likes of us?'

'Do you really want to know?'

'Well, I wouldn't be asking if I didn't.'

'It's because I've been looking for this place all my life.'

For ten years, in the Old Red Lion in Litchborough, I found the perfect pub. And now it is gone.

The lights go up on a stage where a man at a rostrum is peering at his notes. At first his delivery is academic, but it changes.

The perfect pub made its first appearance in the literature of these islands in that collection of Welsh medieval tales known as the *Mabinogion*. In *The Dream of Rhonabwy*, set in the Powys of the mid-twelfth century, three men on some kind of quest come on a building with smoke coming out of it.

> They could see a floor full of holes, and uneven … and there were branches of holly in plenty on the floor, after the cows had eaten off their tops. And when they came to the main floor they could see a dais of bare, dusty boards and an old woman feeding the fire … When she felt cold she would throw a handful of husks on to the fire so that it was not easy for any man alive to endure that smell entering his nostrils.
>
> And on the dais they could see a yellow ox skin. And good luck would it be for the one of them whose lot it would be to get on that rug.

In short, the sort of establishment which would appear in the *Good Pub Guide* as 'a rural gem'.

Time passes, the yellow skin rug becomes the stool at the end of the bar, the Windsor chair by the window, the seat within the inglenook, for the quest for the perfect pub has gone on. In an essay George Orwell called his The Moon Under Water and compiled such a loving inventory it was a shock when at the end he admitted it did not exist. But it does exist.

He slips the first slide into a projector.

Thirty years ago I had a glimpse of it in Tucker's Grave, a pub near Norton St Philip in Somerset, named after a suicide buried at the crossroads on which it stands. What was it like? Ah, more to the point, what wasn't it like? There was no carpet of the sort that brewers' interior decorators delight in, with their jagged geometric patterns; here there was no carpet at all. No jukebox, no piped music, no fruit machine, no television set with a twenty-four-hour news channel relaying the woes of the whole world. 'This place', observed Charlton Heston of his eleventh-century manor in *The War Lord*, 'hath the dimensions of heresy.' To the brewers Tucker's Grave would have had the dimensions of heresy.

It had flagstones, a fire, a local draught cider which that night was green as emerald, and the whole place felt as though it had dropped out of time. All perfect pubs have this feel, for, however addicted to central heating and insulation men are at home, they prefer to drink in the past. Tucker's Grave was a single room.

And it was here I encountered something I had not known in any other pub. Nobody stood at the bar, for there was no bar. In that room everyone, a couple of farmers, a traveller in something or other, and, incredibly, a dealer in gold futures, talked to everyone else. Nobody boasted, nobody talked down or up, we were on equal terms. Think of that for a moment.

I come from the working class and received a middle-class education, so life, like a career in the Soviet Communist Party of the 1930s, was a series of disappearances. There was the 11-plus exam, after which most of the children I had grown up with had gone. There were O- and A-levels, after which another lot went. I moved away, I went to university, took up a career, married, and suddenly there I was at some dinner party, listening to bright uneasy chatter about concerts and holidays from people with whom all I had in common was work and, I suppose, my new social class. In these circumstances you have two choices: you can do a complete makeover on yourself, and erase the past as Mrs Thatcher and Roy Jenkins did. Or you become obsessed by what you have lost.

In a pool of light two men, one very old in a long apron, one very young, are sitting at a table, a half-bottle of whisky between them.

When I was at Oxford in the 1960s college servants, one to a staircase, cleaned our rooms, washed up and did the beds. Those undergraduates who had never mixed with anyone outside the upper middle class, in short the majority, were distantly at ease with such men; working-class boys like myself made a point, awkwardly, of talking to them. It is eleven o'clock in the morning and we are three-quarters of the way through the whisky my uncle, a butcher passing through to the Smithfield Show, has left for me, and my servant has just told me that Rasputin was once one of his young gentlemen.

'Hang on, George, Rasputin wasn't at Oxford.'

'Naow, not 'im. Bloke what shot him, Mr Prince Youssopov. And he was a funny bugger an' all.'

'You were his servant?'

'Course I was very young then, but I saw a lot of him for he didn't go home in the holidays. Russia's a long way, you know. And every bank holiday he'd stand in his window, Mr Prince Youssopov, dressed in this white uniform he had, and he'd throw gold coins down to the people passing by. Of course then they'd fight, and he'd laugh.'

'Bloody hell, I mean, gosh.'

'Yes. Became very interested in chickens after that. Kept them in his rooms, oh the trouble we had over them chickens. Said he was going to introduce a new breed into Russia when he got back. I often wonder what became of them poor chickens, what with that revolution they had. Yes all right then, pity to waste it, Mr Rogers. Haven't got a fag on you, have you?'

Looking back on such conversations, I found myself wishing there was somewhere, some neutral ground, where it would be possible to meet on equal terms someone like that again, where people didn't refer to such men as characters, who didn't just gossip about editors or publishers, someone, in short, unlike myself. And in Tucker's Grave I found it.

I was there just the once, for I broke up with the girl with whom I'd gone there, who lived not far away. But I talked about it a lot, and one night, in a pub a hundred miles away, I saw one man start as though I had made the Sign of the Fish in the dust. Johnny, the sculptor David Wynne's son, killed last year in a motorcycle accident, had also not forgotten Tucker's Grave.

By then I had found the perfect pub again.

Slips another slide into the projector.

The Cooper's Arms in Lammas Street, Carmarthen, was a rundown little place (all perfect pubs from the Yellow Skin Rug on have been rundown little places). It isn't now, but then it isn't a pub now. When its old landlady, Mrs Bright, died, it became in bewildering succession an ethnic furniture shop, a stationer's, and an estate agent's, where once I remember a stuffed alligator called Algy on the wall, the newspapers of the last week scattered everywhere, and a fire in front of which Mrs Bright sat, prodding it, just like the old woman in *The Dream of Rhonabwy*, while one of the customers served behind the bar. For again this was a single room where, again, everyone talked.

A pool of light, with voices.

A man tells me what it had been like being blown up in a quarry (he remembers a moment of absolute silence), and a farmer called William ignores my warning not to stroke my stepfather's Jack Russell bitch.

'Best leave her, she's older than she looks.'

'Boy, we're all older than we look.'

'No, seriously, she's even older than that, she's twenty-two.'

'Listen, good boy, I have owned dogs all my life, I have worked with dogs, I understand dogs. *Dere 'ma'n ferch fach i.* Come here, my little girl.'

Of course the next moment, as in a slowed-up film by Sam Peckinpah, we see William's blood, caught in a shaft of sunlight, as it falls to the floor. He, the dog Jane and I, we pass into folklore, for such a pub always has its own folklore, and each time she and I go in Mrs Bright asks, 'Poor little Jane, she got the

taste of that old William out of her mouth yet?'

The world goes its own way. Saturday night in Carmarthen, the overweight teenage drunks, who are never allowed into the Cooper's, howl at the moon over Lammas Street, and one man draws the curtains on them and the world. He says, as languidly as a character in Michael Arlen, 'Natives a bit restless tonight.' And then, with Mrs Bright's death, it is over, and this man, a month after the pub closed, goes into the west, taking the boat train to Fishguard, where, with a suitcase empty except for a stash of paracetamol and a bottle of vodka, he books into a hotel and at some point in the night is done with all earthly closing hours.

I never thought to find the perfect pub a third time.

The Old Red Lion could do with a coat of paint. On the inside of the door are deep gouges, level with a man's chest, left by the landlord's Great Dane that died eleven years before, an engraving of its long sad face still behind the bar. All the other pictures are of pigs, which the landlord, an Irishman, loves. Again a single room, its floor is flagged, and there is an inglenook, inside which a fire burns, even in early summer, a framed certificate proclaiming that in 1992 or 1993, I forget which, this was adjudged the Northamptonshire Fireplace of the Year.

Outside is a line of stables not used in living memory. These the brewers have had painted green without an undercoat, so after a few months the old red colours have broken through, and this, together with the tiles that have fallen off the walls of the men's urinal, suggests the whole place could be entered for the Turner Prize. The Old Red Lion, in short, has the complete inventory of the perfect pub.

On the wall someone has painted it as it was fifty years ago with all the detail of a Saturday Evening Post *cover, horse brasses gleaming and, of all things, a vast samovar. All these disappeared long ago with disappearing landlords, and only the painting remains.*

The Old Red Lion is really three pubs in one. Thus the *Daily Mail* reader who comes in the early evening and thinks the poor, like baddies in Westerns, have it coming to them, rarely meets the retired builder who takes the *Morning Star* and is a lunchtime drinker.

The lunchtime drinkers are a retired gardener, some farmers, two builders and an old gentleman who talks with a broad Midlands accent, though never about his time in the Afrika Korps. They talk about wild creatures they have seen and, the older ones, about the man who returned to the village with an Eskimo bride, a woman who, having missed the bus to go shopping (there were buses then), went out into the squire's park (there was still a squire) and shot a deer.

At six-thirty, with the shadows, another cast assembles. Now it is the turn of those returning to the village from offices like pilots returning to an aircraft carrier, and who, if they see wild creatures at all, find they look a bit unreal. They talk about films and food, and the progress of their dogs in obedience classes. Also about lap-dancers, whose names they appear to remember.

The mix now is extraordinary. There is a sculptor, a man who sells beds, one who sells dental equipment, a visiting professor of political theory from a nearby town, a man retired from driving the council's gritting lorry who each night flings open the door like a gunfighter, a merchant banker who comes in so quietly he does not enter so much as materialise, and an engineer, a terrifying man who feels it his duty to explain such modern scientific marvels as fibre optics. Oh yes, and my wife and me.

By half-past eight we are gone, and an hour later the last

performance is under way. The players now come in after supper and have lived all their lives in the village, some being related to each other so the odd slumbering row breaks out. All those in the three performances think of the pub as theirs, but, with the exception of the landlord, few in one performance ever meet those in the other two.

And here they come. People from all walks of life like Chaucer's pilgrims, talking.

Dramatis Personae

Tom O'Shea, an ex-sergeant major, late of the Irish Guards, then of the Catering Corps, to which he transferred on the wistful premise that there might be more of a future to cooking than to killing. *Landlord*

Joe Carr, ex-cavalry trooper, ex-lance corporal, ex-corporal ('sometimes all three in a week, so even I wasn't sure what I was'), and a man of whom Tom said, 'He'd ride anything, that one. If he could get a saddle on her he'd ride the banshee.' Head groom in a racing stables

Bobby Daynes, landscape gardener

Jenny Daynes, his wife

Keith Hurford, engineer, a man given to detailed scientific explanations

Stephen Fielding, a dental salesman

Edward Drew, electrician

David Wynne, sculptor of *Boy with a Dolphin* on the Embankment and of *Guy the Gorilla*

Reg Furniss, mechanic

George Humphreys, ex-engine driver, ex-gritter

Joanna Rogers

Byron Rogers, her husband. Chorus

Tom O'Shea. A huge man, with forearms like hams, which are more tattooed than those of Popeye.

'Before I took on this pub the brewery had a course for about twenty of us, when we were asked to introduce ourselves one by one. Only nobody stood up, so I did. "I was born in Adamstown, a village near Wexford in Ireland. I left school at twelve, and worked on a farm until I was seventeen when I went to London and got a job with a travelling fair. I then joined the British Army, saw twenty-two years' service with the Irish Guards, the Royal Engineers and the Catering Corps, when, cooking with petrol, I made chocolate eclairs in a war zone, in the mountains of Yemen. I left to become a lecturer in catering until I got fed up with the red tape, and got a job with a catering company in London, preparing banquets at the City Livery Companies for up to 1400

people at a time. I loved that until one morning in the small hours, driving home to Aldershot, I found I didn't want to do it any more."

' "Very good," said the man from the brewery. "Now tell us in your own words why you want to take on a pub."

' "I want to take on a pub is because I need access to drink twenty-four hours a day."

' "Oh, I see. Well, perhaps that's enough introductions for now." 'But they still gave me the pub.'

Bobby Daynes, who, winter and summer, sat in the window seat wearing a flat cap which, the more improbable his stories got, was pushed further and further back on his head, his eyes mild with wonder, until, the climax reached, he would look around him then ram it down to just above his nose. The cap was a guarantee of authority.

'When I was sixteen I was a stoker on the Grand Central.'

The Great Central, the last major line in Britain, ran through the landscape which even now, fifty years closed, it still dominates, its embankments, viaducts and bridges built on such a scale they look the work of giants, as the ruins of Roman Britain looked to the first English immigrants. When they talk about the Great Central in the pub the old railwaymen seem baffled that what they had thought would last forever has gone in their lifetimes.

'My first driver, he was a tartar. They all were, the old boys, but mine, he had me keep my shovel so clean I used to fry eggs on it for him. When I look back that's what I remember about the old Central, coal and fried eggs. That, and the day we went to London.

'We went to the old Guinness brewery at Park Royal, where they invited us into this bar they had. I didn't drink much then, I must have had two pints, but my driver, he had ten. He didn't seem too bad at the time but on the way back, soon as we'd got clear of London, he started shouting, 'Coal, give me more coal, boy.' Suddenly the stations, they were ripping by. No eggs, just coal, more coal. [*The cap comes down.*] By the time we got to Rugby we was on fire.'

'How did you stop?'

'How *could* we stop? There were flames everywhere. Well, we did stop, but I haven't a clue where, and all these birds were singing. I'll tell you one thing though, which still surprises me. We were still in England.'

He introduces his wife, Jenny.

'We met she was just fifteen. I was playing for a railwayman's cricket team, and she said to me, "You hit the ball over that chestnut tree, and I'll go to the pictures with you tonight."'

'You hit the ball over the chestnut tree?'

'Must a'done.'

Jenny Daynes lights a cigarette, and does not say anything.

'How high was the chestnut tree?'

'Oh, massive old thing.'

'It weren't that high,' said Jenny Daynes quietly.

Jenny Daynes

'We married when Bob was twenty-one, I was sixteen, and by the time I was twenty-two we had four boys. Things were bad then, the Central was beginning to lay men off, and one year we found we didn't have enough money to pay the electricity. But then I read in the paper that there was to be a women's race, Rugby to Daventry, ten miles, with a first prize of £30. I entered, though I hadn't run since I was in the playground. I won, and it paid the electricity. I entered the next year, and won again. But the third year I didn't run, these professionals had come. Look.' She showed us a photograph in which a woman with strong brown legs is holding a silver cup.

I said, 'What a good-looking girl, I wonder if she's still around.'

'Oh, she's still around somewhere,' said Jenny Daynes. 'I've got her number if you want it.'

CHORUS: Sometimes they talked about their jobs.

Joe Carr

'I worked for a one-legged retired captain whose speciality was training crazy horses, on account of his being crazier than they were. He had a pegleg which he tucked into a leather bucket when he rode. And this day him and me, we were asked to take these two horses out with the Hunt, get them used to it like. When we got to the yard they had sacks over their heads, and a groom was holding each one on a very short rein. I got on one, the Captain got on the other, and then, God help us, they took the sacks off. That was the last I saw of the Captain or the Hunt, or anybody really, until I managed to find my way back to the yard late that night.

'I laboured on church steeples with a young master mason, who played pop music all day long and, disliking scaffolding, worked a hundred feet up, the two of us, from swaying ladders. After that I drove heavy lorries, and one day I was delivering meat to this lunatic asylum. I went round the back, opened the doors, and was just carrying this half-pig out when this rather grand bloke came up. "I'll take that, butcher," he said. Fair enough, I thought. I gave it him, but when I came out with the next one there was no sign of him. He was haring down this avenue with the pig on his back. They didn't see him for three days, the pig they never did see.

'Then there were the circuses, touring with one of which in France I got to know some Polish trapeze artists. I've met some mad bastards in my time, but nobody came close to this lot. "You good man, Joseph," they said to me. "Tomorrow we have breakfast." So I turn up at their caravan, and you know what breakfast was? This great cold greasy sausage and a bottle of vodka. Each. I mean, it was all right for me, I was just looking after the horses, but there was a matinee that day. Two hours later these lunatics were on the high wire.

CHORUS: With each story he would get down from the bar stool, and then there were the mad leers, the spreading of the arms behind him as though anticipating take-off, and the crouching, as he acted out each part.

Joe Carr

'One of my first jobs of all, I was working in a stables and lodging with this awful woman, who had a daughter about my age. And one night the girl did something that annoyed her mother. She grabbed her, pushed her head down onto the table, up with her skirt, down with her knickers, and began to smack her on her big white bum. There was I, sitting at the same table, having me dinner, liver and onions, next to her bum. And I was going out with her at the time.'

Keith Hurford

'I went to Lapland once. It was early morning when the plane landed on this airstrip surrounded by fir trees, nothing but fir trees as far as you could see in any direction. We were the only ones getting off, and there was this black Mercedes waiting. It took us along this road through the forest, so straight so you could see for miles ahead of you. I looked back once, then wished I hadn't, for you could see for miles that way as well – it wasn't so much being at the end of the world as not being in it. There were no landmarks anywhere, so God knows what we'd have done had something happened to the driver. We drove all day and there was nothing, not a house, not a road sign, nothing but forest. And no cars either, just us. It was like being in a James Bond film. But then we turned right and drove for another two hours until we got to the factory.'

'The factory? What factory?'

'I was in the packaging business then, and I'd been sent to see this new machine, only one of its kind. Above the Arctic Circle they'd finally solved the problem of the most difficult thing in the world to package.'

'What's that, Keith?'

'Talcum powder.'

Eddie Drew and rights for rats

'I'd been doing the electric rewiring for a London shop infested by rats. In the old days you just put poison down, and that was that. You can't do that now. This Rentokil man who came, he said to me, "Rats have rights now." You put these sticky pads down, the rats stick to them, then you come alone, knock them on the head, fold them up in the pads, and write a number on them. Honest, that's what you got to do. "Rats have rights," that's what the bloke said.

'It's become an odd old world, there's no fun on jobs now. Nobody makes jokes, everyone's just frightened of losing their jobs. When did you hear someone whistle last? Think of that for a moment, in your lifetime the whistling went out of England.'

Steve Fielding

'I took this dental machine to Bristol Zoo to oversee the removal of a growth from a gorilla's mouth. They made me put on Zoo uniform, then sign a form to say I'd been made aware of the risk, that the gorilla might come round suddenly and attack anyone near her. I was then taken to a cage out of which came this terrible roaring and snarling. One of the vets was trying to shoot anaesthetic darts into the gorilla, but she kept pulling them out. They finally managed to put her under, but a few minutes later, when I was in the cage, I nearly fainted for suddenly the growling and the snarling started up again, only this time louder. It was the keeper making these sounds as a means of testing how deeply she was asleep.'

David Wynne

'When I was making my statue of Guy the Gorilla I went in the cage with him, I wanted to see how he moved and that. Getting in was the easy part. But they get very bored, gorillas. Lovely old chap, he took a shine to me and wouldn't let me out. They had to distract him with a banana and a stick of celery.'

CHORUS: But mostly they talked about what all talk about, moments in their lives.

The blonde at the bar

'I had a pair like that once,' said the blonde at the bar to a woman who had come in wearing a pair of boots above the knee, the sort worn by cavalry troopers in Cromwell's army. 'I wore them in a pub and this man said to me, "Oh, I'd give anything to have those round my neck." I took them off, and put them round his neck. Know what he gave me? A packet of crisps.'

The old man, the greyhound and the duvet

Tom said, 'This old boy, his wife died, so his family got him a greyhound. He was a terrible gambler, so they thought he'd race it or something. But he came in one night. "How's the training going?" "Training? Oh, we've packed that in. That bloke" – he always called the dog that – "that bloke's too clever to race. You know, when we woke up this morning he'd got more than half the duvet again."'

Reg Furniss and the Great Freeze

'I was here in the terrible winter of 1947. The snow was over the hedges, in places it was over the telephone wires, and people had started running out of food. Eventually we managed to get a tractor to the next village, where there was a bakery, and we got a whole lot of bread. When we took the bread round the cottages everyone was that grateful, except this old woman. She stood in her doorway, and all she said was, "But I always have a batch."'

Later the subject of ethnic food came up. 'I tried two Indian meals once, but I didn't want to get involved,' said Reg.

Steve Fielding and the poet Yeats

'Poetry really passed me by at school, but if there's one poet I've really taken against it's Yeats. What happened was that I fancied this girl, and when she moved into a new house I found out that the estate agent fancied her as well. When I went to call on her she had all these cards welcoming her to her house, and there was one from the estate agent. In it the bastard had written, "Tread softly for you tread on my dreams." I think he'd got her a deal on the carpets.'

Violet Jordan, a racehorse trainer's wife, describes Miss Whiplash, a dominatrix living in a house called Handcuffs.

'I knew her quite well. She told me that when she was sixteen she went to Paris to learn her craft.'

'Hang on, Violet, you can't learn much about whipping.'

'Well, whatever it was, she learned it. In Paris.'

'What does she do now, she retired?'

'Yes, she sells duck eggs, but she still does a bit over the phone.'

'How can she do it over the phone?'

'Gives them a good scolding.'

'Who?'

'Farmers mostly, they like it after a day's work.'

'Do they pay for it?'

'Oh yes. With credit cards.'

CHORUS: There were glimpses into privacy.

Married life

'When my wife left me I was so upset I told everybody about it,' said Steve.

Tom said, 'When my wife left me I didn't tell anyone for three years.'

'Me, I had a party,' said Joe.

'How many parties have you had, Joe?'

'Three.'

Reading of the ballade

I found a poem, a sort of ballade, I had written for my wife the year I forgot her birthday, when the only card which came for her was a summons for speeding. I asked if they would like to hear it, then read it aloud.

> My birthday was a day of mist.
> My husband did not send a card.
> Who cares? Officialdom
> Recalled I still was me.
> A summons in the morning post,
> 'No circular', the cover read,
> Established I had gone too fast
> Some weeks ago at Collingtree.
>
> My birthday was a day of mist.
> My husband did not send a card.
> Who cares? At 57,
> Recorded in a camera lens
> So there can be no argument,
> On some diversion in the road,
> I went too fast at Collingtree.

> Prince of the cobwebs and the bone,
> When others have forgotten me,
> Please have this cut upon some stone,
> She speeded once – at Collingtree.

In what other pub, or London gentleman's club, would such a little scene have been enacted, and what other pub or club would have listened?

Occasionally there were arguments. Not many. In fact what fascinated me was the perfect manners in the Old Red Lion, which had a lot to do with Tom the landlord. But one night we strayed into history, and I was talking about the end of Roman Britain, which was a mistake. I said that Edinburgh was originally a Welsh town, Caer Eidin, where the earliest surviving poem in Britain was compiled, in the Welsh language. Nobody seemed to mind that very much. Stuff the Scots. It was when I said that the English were fifth-century immigrants brought over by the Welsh, or the British as they were called then, from Schleswig Holstein as an early version of Securicor that a bed salesman, a fanatical rugby supporter, blew his stack: 'Well, I've heard some rubbish in my time . . .' And things did get a bit nasty.

I kept off book learning after that, for most arguments were over far more important things. What was the name of Dan Dare's superior officer in the *Eagle* comic? (Sir Hubert Guest) What actor played the first Richard Hannay? (Ronald Coleman) Films could be checked out from *Halliwell's Film and TV Guide*, a copy of which like a family Bible sat on the windowseat. One argument alone was a black hole.

'What was the name of the shepherd in "Black Bob" in the *Dandy*?'

'Andrew Glenn.'

'That's it, he had a beard.'

'And he was blind.'

'Blind? How can you have a blind shepherd in the bloody Highlands of Scotland?'

'Andrew Glenn was blind.'

Middle-aged men went home and summoned up the Internet like the Witch of Endor, others looked in their attics for old annuals, and it got to a point where Tom the landlord put an absolute ban on all discussion of Black Bob. The matter was only settled when I got in touch with the publishers D.C. Thomson of Dundee, and a letter on the wildly headed notepaper **DANDY!** was delivered to the pub. They were both right, wrote the editor. Andrew Glenn was briefly blind, having been injured, so the dog Black Bob had looked after the flock, until later, just in time for their next adventure, the shepherd recovered his sight. Peace again reigned in Ithaca.

CHORUS: From time to time there were glimpses of the old world.

Tom O'Shea on the Ireland of his childhood

'God, we were poor. No electricity, no radio. No shoes either. From May the first to October, we children went barefoot, and that was in the late 1940s, De Valera's Ireland. "Bless you Dev," they'd shout, them with their arses hanging out of their trousers. There were old people, men of eighty, still working then. They had to, you took jobs where and when you could get them. One of our neighbours, he had two daughters who drove trains in Nazi Germany throughout the War. Hard to believe. And they both survived.

'What did we children find to do? We listened, there was a lot of listening. Jim Douglas the vet, an old World War One soldier, he told us stories about the trenches and ghosts. We were too scared to go to bed after, just as we were too scared to go out into the lane after dark, on account of the three men shot there in the Irish Civil War. Nobody knew who they were, or even what side they'd been on. They were just brought there, and they were shot. My father was in that war, he was in one of the IRA's Flying Columns. He told me that he'd had a Mauser until one day he climbed up into the roof of this cowshed, left it on a beam, and came home.

'A fair few old British Army soldiers were still around. I remember this old boy talking about how he'd joined. There was some kind of recruiting drive, and he went up to this sergeant to ask what was involved. "Nothing to it, lad. Eat meat and follow the band." Three months later he was on the Somme.

'I never regretted joining up. I was seventeen, and suddenly there were more boiled spuds than even I could eat. I never encountered any animosity at home for having joined up. My uncle Mylee, he was forty-three years in the British army, joined as a private, served in two world wars, left as a private, never learned to read or write, signed for his pension with a cross. Cleverest man I ever knew.

'There were some strange old characters in our village, like this old boy who lived in a cottage, just him and his pig. A lot of people wanted to buy the pig, but he wouldn't sell, said it was his life's ambition to see what the natural lifespan of a pig might be. Him and his pig, you'd see them in the lane going for walks. They grew old together.

'Then there was Mary Ann. She lived alone, had two cows.

When the meal was finished she'd put all the plates on the floor. "Jack, Jack, where's that fecking dog?" The dog would come running, leap the half-door and lick all the dishes, at which point she put them back on the dresser. She made her own butter, only she kept this in her chamber-pot, it was the only dish big enough. "Of course I give it a good scald first," she'd say. People were terrified of working for her, for she was a kind old girl and she'd ask them in for a meal, and of course out would come the butter.

'Anyway, these two, they sat there this day, eating the bread and sliding the butter off their plates to the tomcat when she wasn't looking. When they got outside one said to the other, "Jaysus, Jim, did you see that cat licking its arse? I didn't think it'd ever stop." The other man said, "Poor thing, it was trying to get the taste of the butter off its tongue."

'My father was a reading man. Filled the house up with books he'd found wherever he could. This night he was in the pub talking about them with his friends, and this old boy he was hopping about trying to get in on the conversation. Only everyone knew he couldn't read. Finally he said, "Jaysus boys, I have a powerful book." Stopped the talk stone dead. What book was that? "It's one you wouldn't let out of your hands." Yes, but what was it?

' "*The Book of Kells*." '

Bobby Daynes saves on cartridges.

'Ever tell you about the tomcat?' said Bobby Daynes. 'God, he was a terror, used to attack people in the street. In the street. Anyway his owner gave me money to buy some cartridges and kill him. I'd have been about fourteen, and I thought, this will buy enough cartridges to shoot a couple of rabbits for me dinner. So I killed him with a shovel and buried him.'

'You didn't.'

'Hang on. A day or two later someone said they had seen the old tomcat in the street, covered in earth. He were ever so good after that. Never attacked no one.' The cap came down.

It occurred to me that this was more or less the plot of Stevenson's *The Master of Ballantrae*. But in pubs men who have read too many books are nervous of bringing such things up. 'I read a book once,' I ventured. 'This bloke keeps getting killed and buried, next minute the grave's empty.'

'There you are, somebody else trying to save on cartridges,' said Bobby Daynes.

CHORUS: With so many ex-soldiers there were a lot of stories about military life.

Tom's Army

'I enjoyed the army, I've never laughed so much in my life. Of course you avoided certain people, like the Belfast men, the Wallawalla boys as we called them, little men, liars, boasters, wild bastards. But it was worth joining up just to be allowed to watch the officers. It was a hiding place for nutters, the army.

'There was this General, I knew his batman. Hell of a good soldier, he stopped Mad Mitch turning Aden into a bloodbath. Used to ride naked at dawn through the woods around Sandhurst. His son brought this beautiful girl home once, she came in a red sports car, and next morning she meets the General coming out of the bathroom, towel over his arm, pipe in his mouth, stark naked. "Morning, my dear." Ten minutes later, the red sports car's acclerating down the drive.

'One morning he tells his batman, "Now Peter, dear boy" – he called everyone dear boy – "I'm going to spend the morning sunbathing. Got that, dear boy? No phone calls, nothing." About an hour later the phone goes, and his batman comes out onto the patio. "Sergeant-major."

' "Now Peter, what did I tell you? No, no buts. Me General, you, what are you now, dear boy? Corporal. You corporal. And if you want to stay that, don't disobey me again. But as a matter of interest, who is on the phone?"

' "Montgomery of Alamein, sir."

'*Whoosh*.

'The old boy must have been in his eighties then, but they were still that terrified of him. Funny chap, Monty, used to draw his pension at the post office in town once a week, same time, regular as clockwork. His chauffeur would drive him in. And this feller I knew, who'd been in the army with Monty and couldn't stand him, he'd started work nearby on a block of flats, so when he saw him he shouted at the top of his voice, "Swing your arms, you scruffy old bastard. One, two, one, two. Call yourself a soldier?"

'The first time Monty just stared, but there was a second time, and a third. And of course with the building going higher and higher there was no way Monty could see him. He'd stop the car, and wait, then dart out, glaring around him. Then he'd park in another street, and there'd be this sharp nose peering round the corner, but it didn't do any good. "Swing your arms, you scruffy old bastard!" By the end old Monty'd be dancing in the street in his temper.

'It was the sergeants ran the army. As for the sergeant-majors, they were like gods, the ones in the Guards even had their own batmen. I remember one of them, he'd come into the guardroom in the morning, *Daily Mirror* under his arm. "Prisoner, ten-shun." And whoever was in the cells that morning would come out of the lavatory where he'd been made to sit for half an hour, warming the seat for the sergeant-major.

'We'd built this airstrip up in the Radfan mountains, why I don't know, for no plane ever landed there. But then one did, very early in the morning, great big thing, a Dakota. We all stared, the hatch opened, and this man appeared. Never seen anything like him in my life. He was wearing a bowler hat, a short-sleeve striped shirt with an MCC tie, navy blue shorts, black ankle socks, and these gleaming black shoes. He was carrying a briefcase and an umbrella, though no one could remember when it had last rained in the Radfan.

'I couldn't stop myself, I said, "Who the fuck are you?"

'And he said, "I …" And he stood there, looking around him. "I am the Wogmaster."

'He was the Government liaison officer to the mountain tribes.'

CHORUS: Joe's army was not unlike the wild mob that went to the Peninsula with Wellington.

Joe Carr

'We got sent to Northern Ireland, me and Speedy Quick, to bring back this bloke who'd gone AWOL. Imagine that, going AWOL in Northern Ireland. But when I got there this military policeman said, "Got news for you, sunshine. It's not one, you've got six of 'em." Jesus. I got them handcuffed to each other in this Land Rover, and we're on our way to the ferry when I hear *sssssssss*. "It's a fucking bomb, I'm off," says Speedy. I jammed on the brakes and the two of us baled out. The next thing, these six comedians are grinning down at us from the Land Rover where one of them's let off a fire extinguisher for devilment. So now we're on the ferry and we've got this cabin where I chained them to the beds. But then it occurred to me: "Any of you bastards got any money?" It turned out four of them did, and two didn't. So I unlocked the four, got them to hand it over, and me and Speedy and them, we went on the piss. The two who didn't, I left them to talk things over with the beds.

'We had this bloke, he was that desperate to get out he pretended he'd gone off his head. But it was the way he did it. Pretended he had a bike, cycled everywhere, even on parade, changing gears, mending punctures, the lot, all of it in the air. The old sergeants weren't buying it. "Piss off," they said. But then a new officer came, very young, very keen, he saw all this and got him and his phantom bike in front of a psychiatrist. A few days later he was out. On his last day he cycled up to the guard post, waited until the bar comes up and went through. Now he's on the other side, he's out. "Hoy," he shouts, and they all turn and he makes out he's picking something up which he throws over the bar. "Shan't be needing this now." Oh, he was a clever bastard, he was.

'I had little time for officers, me. I remember this big regimental ball for all ranks at Osnabruck, when the invitations read, "Officers and their ladies, non-commissioned officers and their wives, other ranks and their women."

'We were on parade once, and this general was coming round. You know, the way they do, a word here, a word there. Very embarrassing for everybody, except, of course, the generals. And he came to this chap. "D'you like the Army, my man?"

' "No."

' "What? I've been in the Army twenty-five years, and I've enjoyed every minute of it."

' "So would I, if I was a fucking general."

'The general didn't speak to anyone after that.

'One night Princess Anne came to the officers' mess. I was a corporal then, and in charge of the guard. All we had to do was wait for the car, open the door, and say, "Good evening, ma'am." But I suddenly realised one of the troopers with me had been on the piss, and it was too late for me to do anything about it. I was keeping an eye on him, but when the car came I got distracted and lost sight of him so I assumed he'd gone off somewhere. I was just thinking, thank God, when he burst out of some bushes, flung open the car door for Princess Anne, and said, "Evening, ma'am, you gettin' plenty?" They all jumped on him. Not Princess Anne though.'

CHORUS: But the strangest story about the Army came from Bobby Daynes.

Bobby Daynes goes abroad in the Tottenham Court Road.

'In 1955, I was eighteen, doing National Service, when we were told we were going overseas to Libya. Before that Gaddafi, they had a king or something then. And when the lorries came for us we all thought we were going to the docks. Except that three o'clock next morning they pulled up, one behind the other, outside Goodge Street Underground.

'Down the steps we went, down and down. Deep old place, Goodge Street. At this point we thought we were going to catch a train or something, but then we saw these sergeants standing round an open door, a door in a wall. There was nobody about at that time of morning, but these sergeants were shouting, "C'mon, let's be 'aving yer," as though we were in a terrible rush.

'So we went through the door, and, I'm blowed, there were more steps leading down. And when I say down, I mean down. If you think Goodge Street's deep you should have seen these buggers. One lad, he said, "Fuck me, we're walking to Libya."

'We didn't have time then, but when we came up again I counted those steps. There was 667 of them to street level. Down and down we went, single file, it was that narrow. Finally there were these big rooms, very low but big, but no bugger ever told us why we were there, all we was told was that we had to stay there until we sailed. And there we stayed. For three weeks.

'They fed us, but we wasn't allowed up, we couldn't phone home or anything, even if there was phones, which there weren't. You know, we could hear the Tubes above us. Just imagine that, hearing Tubes *above* you. But of course we were young, we could put up with just about anything. Except the farting.

'I got so bored down there I cut my name into the wall and the village I was from. And d'you know, forty years later my dad told me one day this chap had rung, said he was an archaeologist. Wanted to know was I the R.W. Daynes what had been down there. He could 'a been ringing King Arthur. But what we was doing down there I never found out.'

CHORUS: And there the story might have stayed, yellowing into myth. Except that Roger Morgan of Subterranea Britannica, a society devoted to the study of man-made structures under-ground, confirmed the existence of what lay, and still lies, under Goodge Street, 140 feet below street level.

One of eight huge bomb-shelters hurriedly excavated under deep Underground stations during the Blitz, it passed out of use when the Luftwaffe's attentions shifted to Russia, and later became a top-secret American broadcasting station. Barbara Tadd, another member of the society, was invited down on VE Day by a GI and everyone, she remembered, was drunk, for there was a bar down there, and canteens. With space for 8000 bunks, it could accommodate the population of an English country town, which was why, when the Americans left, it was designated a transit camp by civil servants who had never spent a night down there. Roger Morgan, a practised troglodyte, talked of the cruelty involved in housing young soldiers even for short periods at such a depth. This practice ended in 1956, after a fire in which luckily nobody was killed. It is now used for storage.

One little footnote: another of these shelters, under Clapham, was used to house the first West Indian immigrants who had come over in the *Windrush*. As the result of their experience they rushed off to the nearest labour exchange, which happened to be in Brixton, and so the first ghetto came into being.

Sometimes my wife and I would go for a walk before the pub opened. One evening we walked from the farm near Castle Dykes to the wood at Everdon Stubs. There were rabbits in the farmyard hopping away in all directions, and when we went round a corner there was a small deer nosing in the hedge. It didn't see us for a few seconds, then it passed into the hedge like an exhalation. The last of the bluebells in the wood, and clumps of white stitchwort, shafts of sunlight here and there.

Then back along the small road that follows the ridge from Preston Cape to Upper Stow, and on. In 'a time out of mind' as they used to say in medieval legal documents this was known as the Old Salt Road, packhorses crossing England from the salt mines at Droitwich.

So to the pub, with the fire lit, and we hoped all this could go on forever. But the clocks were ticking. And suddenly there were passings.

The passing of Bobby Daynes

There came a point when all Bobby Daynes's tales were about Bob himself. Diagnosed with cancer, he talked about doctors not wanting to see him for two months, then a month, and we hung on his words. In May, in fine spring weather and just a few days after we had last seen him in the pub, he died. The following night Jenny and her sister came in the pub to make arrangements about the £100 he had left in his will for his last round.

When they buried him there was no room in the church for everyone, and we sat outside, listening to the service being relayed on loudspeakers. It was the first time many of us had seen each other in daylight. We looked shabbier, and older, for, like everything else, the light had been kindly in the Old Red Lion. Both Bob's parents, then in their nineties, were there.

Later Jenny talked about his last day. 'All four boys were there, and he said to them, "Now look, you all get your spades out and dig that grave. You could save a few bob, it's expensive paying for a sexton."'

'And did they?'

'Naow, you've got to be an expert or something. But they carried his coffin as he'd told them to.'

The passing of the pub

By the end it was clear that the pub was on borrowed time. Tom's ill-health, in particular his circulatory problems, meant this large, strong man now had to heave himself along on sticks, which in turn meant his customers had to help out with the running of the pub. We lit the fire. In fact we got terribly competitive lighting the fire, so there were two fire-lighter men, one fire-lighter men, and, the supremo, Jim the gym master, who used no fire-lighters at all. Jim lived in a centrally heated house but loved fires, so he roamed the fields, collecting fallen wood in his knapsack, and, had it proved necessary, would have gone back beyond matches, beyond flints even, for the pure neolithic joy of dried twigs. A huge, fit man, he came in one night looking bewildered after a medical appointment. 'This nurse,' he said as he knelt with his back to the room, ministering to his altar, 'she said I was obese.' The fire caught, and Jim, among certainties, was a happy man again.

As Tom got worse Keith the engineer changed barrels for him, Joe brought in ice, others bottles, and it was like being made a prefect. At the very end Tom just sat in a chair, doing sums in his head, and everyone helped himself, ringing up these sums on the till. 'This is a wonderful way to run a business, I just wish I'd thought of it earlier,' said Tom. But then the brewery suddenly remembered that they owned the Old Red Lion.

Their surveyors called to see how they could convert it and its outbuildings into a gastropub, and when we turned up one evening one of them was still there, a young man in a suit, walking up and down, occasionally talking into a mobile phone. Apparently they had found an old well everyone had forgotten about, but as he looked down the card he needed to start his BMW had slipped from his pocket. For three hours he had been walking up and down, waiting for someone from the company to turn up with another card. We felt a grim satisfaction.

From then on whenever we turned the corner into the village we looked to see if the sign still hung. Keith saw the tenancy advertised on the Internet, but the pub staggered on, though there were moments when we saw how it must look to strangers. In September, 2007, some young men came in, dressed like marooned pirates with trousers to mid-calf in the absurd modern way. Thick hairy legs. Very confident. When they left one of them, Ben Gunn or his brother, told Tom loudly so everyone in the pub could hear, 'I think you should know your glasses are dirty.' Tom apologised. The glass-washing machine was packing up.

But there were still moments of pure comedy. A young man came into the pub. 'Delivery, mate. Sign here.'

'Sign for what?' said Tom.

'Your tent.'

'My what?'

'Your tent. You know, so people can smoke outside.'

'Is there anything to pay?'

'No, mate.'

'I'll sign.'

It was a huge green parasol, of the sort that has gone up all over England and Wales following New Labour's anti-smoking legislation. Now thrive the tent-makers. Only this tent was open to the winds, and some weeks later the autumn gales blew it halfway up the roof, where for weeks it stayed, the one indisputable legacy of the late prime minister. Tom called it his Tony Blair Suite.

So there was a Christmas, and a New Year, and in his chair Tom talked. Until then I had not been aware of how superstitious he was. We had for years been searching for a new front door, having been quoted £1500 for one in oak, but then we found one on the local tip for £10. Tom said, 'You've been searching for one for so long this is probably a magic door. When you pass through it for the first time you'll find yourselves in lands unknown.' And he wasn't entirely joking.

In the hills behind the pub there was in a wood a series of enormous earthworks, eleven acres of ramparts behind ramparts, with a central keep forty to fifty feet high, all this in permanent shadow and silence. One night at sunset, walking past the wood with my wife, we heard the sudden clash of metal on metal, then silence again. Tom said, 'Look, I've told you before, keep away from that place. There's something in there.'

He talked about his father opening the windows before laying out the dead, 'so the soul can go'. His father swore he had heard a light whoosh one night. Tom talked more and more about his father.

⸺⸺✦✦⸺⸺

On the little road to the pub we came on two stoats playing in a patch of sunlight, dashing about on the road, back into the grass and out again, chasing each other, skipping and dancing, their long backs forming hoop shapes.

We must have watched them for about five minutes, the car engine running, and, even when we moved closer until we were only five yards away, they did not seem in the least bothered. In the end they disappeared into the grass verge. My wife said, 'We need to remember these days.'

We talked about it to Tom, who told us the following story. 'My father found a dead stoat in one of his rabbit traps, and thought he would bring it home to show us children. He was carrying it along when suddenly he noticed three stoats following him. He put the stoat down and hid in the ditch to see what would happen. One of the stoats bit off a fern, and laid it on the ground. They dragged the dead stoat onto the fern and then pulled it away. And that's Gospel truth.'

Tom was talking about the graveyard in his home village in Ireland, about how many people he had known were in there. He quoted a strange old poem, a sort of lament, then, briskly, 'But I'm not afraid of dying.'

'Nor am I,' said Joe Carr.

'Mind you, I wouldn't get up in the night to do it,' said Tom.

In those last few weeks, the clocks ticking away, his tales were increasingly about the past. He talked about his childhood in Ireland, of how he and his brothers had collected bits of broken coloured china to make tiny houses. 'My mother used to make rattles for the babies, weaving little boxes out of grass or rushes, and filling them with pebbles.' He remembered the Rat Man coming. 'It was just after the War. He had a sort of wand which he stuck down the rats' burrow, and said some Latin words, or words he told us were Latin. Then he had a ball of wool which he dipped in holy water. He pulled skeins of this off and draped it round the hole. "There," he said, "the rats will die inside the hole now." '

And of the London landlady who had appeared with the morning tea to her innocent young Irish lodger in fewer and fewer clothes until in the end, under an open dressing gown, she wore nothing at all. 'Ah, Tommy, they're that poor in England, my heart grieves for them.'

One night he was solemn, having heard of the death of someone who in his youth he had kissed in a haystack. 'I used to have daydreams about her, even now, that somehow the two of us would meet again. She rang me up once, she'd got this posh accent from somewhere and seemed be beyond haystacks, so I didn't mention it.' He shook his head. 'I also didn't mention that I always hoped that one day I'd have carnal knowledge of her.'

'In the haystack?'

'Where else? The haystack's still there, I checked last time I was home.'

The pub went on in this twilight state, with people talking in the old way. Grave goods, twenty-first-century style. Joe Carr buried his mother, she was a hundred years old and had long ago slipped into the twilight of Alzheimer's. He put a bottle of whisky into the coffin with her, and this made his brother very cross. George Humphreys said he had once worked in a crematorium, and they would always open the coffins and take out the bottles of whisky and such like, otherwise they would have exploded in the furnace. They then shared the whisky. Apparently a lot of people put bottles in coffins.

Sometimes we talked about the living, and about the hours some villagers now kept. A good-looking supermarket executive got up at 4.30 a.m. every morning to drive to head office in London, and did not get back until 8.30 p.m. the following night, so daylight in the village was something she saw only at weekends. We all thought this a terrible waste. 'She has powerful knees,' said Tom. 'A man should pay just for looking at them.'

Then the council found Tom a bungalow which his wife liked, so, meeting in someone's house, we started a collection which eventually realised close on £2,000, with which one of us, a man who got things done, bought Tom an electric buggy and one of those chairs with a motor that can alter its angle. We held a surprise party for him.

'Busy tonight,' said Tom, and then, as the pub filled, 'Something's up.' Trays of food were brought in, and a cake with whisky miniatures. 'Oh shit,' said Tom.

I made a speech in which I told them that, with the exception of church-goers and drug-dealers, we all lived in our own worlds, worlds of work and education, of home and background. We did not move outside these, but in Tom's pub we could and had. So the Old Red Lion had done what the University of Oxford had failed to do: it educated me.

The last night was very quiet. Tom sat in his chair, and there were only six people in the pub. Steve, obliged to stay at home for his dog's birthday party, wasn't one of them. I thought it a bit flat, but my daughter said it reminded her of the last episode of the TV series *Cheers* when all that happens is that someone switches off the light.

Miles away, men who had never been inside the Old Red Lion, men in suits who sat in offices with lists in front of them, took the decision and boards were nailed across its windows, so the morning after its closure it had the sad, sightless look all buildings have when this gets done to them. The process had been as abrupt as an execution. One day the lights were on, but after that those who had spent at least two hours of each night there found it hard to remember that such a place had ever existed, so you came on them in other pubs in nearby villages, like White Russian refugees in the Paris cafés of the 1920s. Some nodded distantly.

Now there would have been some who would not appreciate the enormity of what had happened, those who once or twice a month had come in out of the night, agonised over what drink to have, then talked loudly about sales figures or orchestral concerts. And of course there were those from the village who had not come in at all. But even they will eventually notice that something is missing in Litchborough, just as it is missing all over England, where it is now said that half the villages are without pubs for the first time since the Norman Conquest. How anyone came by this fact I don't know, or even how true it is, but it has become something deeper than truth: it is now a public perception as thirty pubs a week close.

For the loneliness is coming.

* * *

The Old Red Lion did not reopen as a gastropub. It did not reopen as anything. It stands shuttered and silent, only to me it isn't silent. I don't drive by very often for when I do I still hear voices and they are deafening.

George Humphreys, retired gritter, train driver and crematorium attendant, said quietly, which was unusual, 'What are we going to do now?'

I began to write books.

11

We Authors, Ma'am

I CAME TO authorship, like fatherhood, late in life, being almost sixty when my first was published. I had made various attempts at books, one of which was even commissioned. *A Guide to Great British Shits* was the result of reading through the entire *Dictionary of National Biography*, 30,000 memoirs of the great and good, when I was in bed for a fortnight with 'flu, at the end of which time I had had it up to here with the great and good. Shits, I came to the conclusion, were the neglected element of British life.

For when it came to their own great men the respectable Victorian intellectuals who compiled the Dictionary had nothing but good to say, as in this bland Sovietspeak description of the marriage of the poets Robert Browning and Elizabeth Barrett: 'Very soon after their first acquaintance they became engaged and were married in the autumn of the same year, 1846.' No father Barratt going apeshit in Wimpole Street, no middle-aged elopement. But ancestors were another matter. In the DNB it was open season on the eighteenth century, so people like the card-sharp and usurer Colonel Francis Charteris, ancestor of the Earl of Wemyss (whose family politely changed their name to inherit his ill-gotten gains), and a man who on his deathbed offered £20,000 to anyone who disprove the existence of Hell (as to that of Heaven, he went on, he was indifferent to that), such people included themselves by their sheer awfulness.

Sadly, they were also such fun, and the research into them so fascinating, I disappeared into this the way the explorer Colonel Fawcett disappeared into the Amazon rainforest in the 1920s. *Shits* never got written (but the late Willie Donaldson more than made up for that in his *A–Z Guide* to the species).

Then there was a historical novel set in the year 1403, when Owain Glyndwr, with an army of 8,240 men, more than most of his contemporaries had seen in one place, materialised in the Towy Valley. I actually started writing this, describing in the first chapter the unhurried hullabaloo and terror of a peasant army on the move, which must have intrigued the novelist J.L. Carr, who read it, for he kept making pointed inquiries about a second chapter. But I wasn't sure about where to take my army, and there they still are, ambling towards Carmarthen on a July morning: there was no second chapter and, eventually, no more pointed inquiries.

But even I couldn't abandon *An Audience with an Elephant*, for this was a compilation of things I had already written. The title came from a con I had perpetrated on the *Sunday Telegraph*, which at the time was running a profile on some celebrity or other every week. I suggested to them that I do one on the most successful teenager in showbusiness, who had been in more ads and films, and opened more supermarkets than the whole cast of *EastEnders*: the teenager was a circus elephant. I thought myself no end of a wag until I found myself having to write 2,500 words on a creature which all the time I was in its company did nothing except amble and eat apples.

The rest of the book was about people I had met, none of them, with the exception of the elephant, celebrities, which I suppose is very odd in modern journalism, also about places and events that had interested me, which again no one else seemed to have written about. Many were set in and around the area where I live, so a week before the book came out I called on Waterstone's, the biggest book shop in Northampton and now the only one in the centre of a town with 200,000 inhabitants. I did this because, as my frustrated mentor Jim Carr had told me, every man should at some point in his life try to sell something. I introduced myself as a local author.

'What's your book about?' The buyer was a very young man with a cropped head.

'Well, a lot of it's about this area.'

'Pity.' He looked at me. 'What I mean is, pity you're not a criminal.'

'I'm sorry?'

'See that table?'

Beside us was a table covered with books: books about the Kray Twins, about the Richardson Gang, even a guidebook called *Mad Frank's London*. The last, written by Mr 'Mad' Frankie Fraser, was, like mine, about people and places he had known, though, unlike mine, it contained such sentences as, 'She never really got over the time she was at home in bed, and her boyfriend brought a (man's) head on a tray into her room.' That one word 'really', I noted distractedly, showed the hand of a master.

'Anything about the East End or crime, we could have taken fifty. They're very keen on crime in Northampton.' He shook his head sadly, for he was quite a nice young man. 'You'll be lucky if we take two of yours.'

And that was my introduction to bookselling.

❖

I had been making a living from freelance journalism for almost thirty years, and had assumed that with books, once you were past the hurdles of acceptance and publication, the things more or less sold themselves. Discerning booksellers ordered them and sold them; discerning readers bought them. Oh dear.

'Basically you stock what people are going to buy.' Robert Webb had by then owned and run the Kingsthorpe Bookshop in the Northampton suburbs for twenty-eight years (it has now closed). 'If you stock what *you* want to read you'll find the books staring back at you for six months. It has been my perception that 5 per cent of titles generate over half my business, and 30 per cent some 99 per cent. These are books that accompany TV series, or have been reviewed, or been publicised in some way. It's with the remaining 70 per cent that the risk lies.'

Of the 100,000 books published each year in Britain, most do not get beyond a first printing, selling fewer than 500 copies. And it didn't help when I read the bleak statistics arrived at by the *Sunday Times* in its analysis of the 100 most reviewed books in one year. One out of three authors in that list, the paper found, was also among the reviewers of the hundred, and the message was clear: 'If you want to get ahead, find a literary Mafia prepared to mention your name at the right parties and review your books in the right papers.' To do that you had, of course, to live in London.

I drove gloomily home through the Northamptonshire countryside, for, like all authors, I was convinced that I had a reading public. It was just a matter of getting to them.

I was brooding on this when I called with my weekly order on Mr Julian Hunt, village butcher and philosopher, and the latest in eight generations of village butchers and philosophers, as he likes to inform his customers. I told him what had happened, and it was the first time in ten years that we had discussed books, though I had once mentioned Jeffrey Archer (to my great joy, Mr Hunt said he had never heard of him).

He heard me out, then said, 'You bring your books in here, I'll shift 'em.'

'But where would you put them?' It is not a big shop.

'Over there, I'll move the Paxo.' He pointed to a white-tiled shelf, above which there was in large capitals, SUPPORT YOUR LOCAL BUTCHER. 'And perhaps the mustards.'

'Well, perhaps we could try five books. Just to see what happens. But, hang on, there has to be something in it for you.'

'Thass all right.'

'No, come on. Tell you what, anyone who buys a book I'll stand him a pound of sausages.'

And that was my introduction to marketing.

--------◆--◆--------

A straight discount would have been easier. *An Audience with an Elephant* was priced at £12.99. Three quid for Julian, say, ten for me. But Fate had intervened in the affairs of men. Sell a book in a butcher's shop, and it is a good joke. But throw in a pound of sausages with each one, and it not only becomes a better joke, it is marketing.

I delivered the books. Half an hour later the phone rang.

'Told you, first one's gone.'

'And the sausages?'

'Gluten-free. She's with Weight Watchers.'

Within two days three more had gone, and at this point the local paper, the *Northampton Chronicle and Echo*, picked up the story. Only they picked up the story because I had picked up the phone and told them. 'Author Organises Sizzling Book Deal.' 'The 59-

year-old said, "I now see a future for a literature combined with sausages."'

And that was my introduction to publicity.

* * *

There was a photograph of Mr Hunt and me in the *Chron*, he in his white overall, me in a black coat looking like an undertaker's clerk, the two of us surrounded by books and sausages. Later that afternoon I put ten books on the shelf where the Paxo had been. White china tiles where late the stuffing sat.

The following night, in the pub, Steve Fielding asked me where I'd spent the day. I said I'd been away. 'That explains it. I've had to do some driving, and each time I put the radio on there was this butcher talking about you. He did mention your book, he didn't seem to know much about that, but he knew a hell of a lot about sausages. When I went to the gym earlier on, they had the radio on, *and there he was again.*'

Eight books went that day. On Sunday the story was on Teletext, and that week, after a features agency put out the story, I was being rung by the nationals. The story appeared in the *Independent*, the *Daily Telegraph* and *The Bookseller*, the last of which ruminated knowledgeably, 'Dame Barbara Cartland once struck a deal for the sale of her books with Dewhurst the butchers. Byron Rogers may not be aware that he is following in the Dame's footsteps.' That week Hunts the butchers sold thirty books, which, for a hardback by a first-time author, would be thought motoring by a large city bookseller. And then we made our big mistake.

'I'm going to create a special sausage,' said Julian Hunt. I could tell from his use of the word create that he had been enjoying the shenanigans. 'It'll be called after you.'

'What had you in mind?'

'Venison and Guinness. I shall call it the Byron Banger.'

Only it was a wet December, and the gamekeepers were finding it impossible to drag the bodies of the bigger beasts off the estates, so Mr Hunt bought some muntjac, the small deer which, having escaped from Woburn, had spread across the Midlands and even into the suburbs of North London.

The *Chronicle and Echo* had the headline 'Sausages are a Little Deer today', but that wasn't the problem, it was the photograph which accompanied it. A winsome face peered out of the leaves. Shit – Bambi. We sold just three books that week, and I ate a lot of sausages.

Still, feeling like Mr Toad that I knew all there was to be knowed about marketing, I put five books into the Old Red Lion at

Litchborough, adding airily that with each one there came a glass of whisky. But for some reason sausages are funny; whisky is not. It took four weeks to shift the five. After ten days Hunts had sold forty-five.

◆━━◆

Meanwhile there was the odd radio interview. I was again down with 'flu.

'Our guest this morning is Mr Byron Jones.'

'Rogers, actually.'

'Mr Byron Rogers.' He had not missed a beat. 'How's the flu, Byron?'

'Bloody awful.' Sitting in my armchair, the interview being done on the telephone, I had forgotten that the programme was going out live. Ah well, there went the Methodists.

The reviews were coming in. The *New Statesman* sounded enthusiastic: 'Rogers is a radically weird writer.' There went the Women's Institute as well. 'Never sentimental, despite a potentially dangerous taste for marginal railway lines, churches, Wales, Midlands villages, the countryside, ghosts and the past in general . . .' which must have seen off the upwardly mobile. *The Spectator* sniffed at 'a light-hearted romp', but found 'the early emphasis on Wales . . . a little heavy going'. Not something a reviewer would have dared say of the Jews. Or the Scots. Or anyone really, apart from the Welsh.

I rang my editor. 'Why don't we report this bugger to the Race Relations Board? That'd be a great marketing scam.'

'No.'

Then came something I had overlooked: suddenly there were no books. The first print run of 2500 copies had sold out, and reprinting started. At this point Waterstone's changed their minds.

My editor rang. 'They're stocking your book in their stores, so for God's sake stop talking about them and "Mad" Frankie Fraser, right?'

But I had hardly put the phone down when the first TV company rang. 'We see this as a Christmas story. First scene, Waterstone's. You are walking out of the store, the book in your hand. Close-up of you looking sadly at the book. Cut to Hunts the butchers: Mr Hunt is cranking out the sausages ...'

I rang my editor to share this piece of good news.

'Listen, you leave Waterstone's alone, do you hear?'

'But don't you see, this could be the perfect reconciliation. Last scene, I come into the shop carrying this pile of books, and the chap I first talked to is moving the "Mad" Frankie Frasers off the table. A male-voice choir is singing in the background as, very carefully, the two of us start putting copies of my book in their place. We shake hands. Dissolve to sounds of *Jingle Bells*. Perfect.'

Click.

⸻ ◆ ⸻

'You may not realise it, but as far as they're concerned you're becoming a bit of a monster,' said Henry Jones-Davies, publisher of *Cambria* magazine. 'Publishers have nightmares about authors getting stuck into the marketing.'

But all this time, looming up like the Lost World, was the vast escarpment of the supermarkets. Supermarkets sell books. You know the sort of thing – *The Waffen SS book of Christmas Carols*, or *The Posh Spice Guide to Church Interiors*, canyons of the things. But when you try to sell them books it is like trying to hitch a lift in mid ocean from a 200,000-ton oil tanker with a bow the height of St Paul's. Who do you approach?

You meet, after some negotiation, the store manager, usually a polite, harassed man who tells you he will see what he can do. But the first thing that strikes you is how little authority such a man has, even though he presides over an airship hangar of commerce. For however good your pitch, behind each manager is the demonic shadow of the head-office buyer.

And my pitch, though I say it myself, was good, if a bit wacky. 'A supermarket appears in a community like a space probe.' Actually I had intended saying 'an army of occupation', but thought better of it. You can just imagine the reaction of a man who after a long day of harassment from his masters, of complaint from his customers, has a loony with a book try that one out on him. But some points went home. 'A supermarket has no connection with a community or its economy except the cash till.'

The then manager of Sainsbury's at Northampton heard me out. 'Well, I suppose there's one thing to be said for books,' he said when I paused for breath. 'Unlike cauliflowers, they don't go off.' Exactly. No sell-by dates. I sometimes wonder what became of him, for the chain soon after embarked on a cull of its managers.

I learned certain things about supermarkets. The managers at Sainsbury's and Waitrose deferred to their buyers; those at Safeway, before the take-over, were allowed some independence, with those at Towcester and Carmarthen, to each of whom I had described myself as a local author, dealing directly with me. 'Four dozen, that all right with you?' Four dozen? Just like that. All for some reason paid in cash, Tesco taking the longest to settle.

<hr />

I have now published seven books in nine years. The last of them, *The Man Who Went Into The West*, a biography of the poet R.S. Thomas, won the James Tait Black prize, something which allowed me to start my acceptance speech in Welsh to the University of

Edinburgh, and to tell them I felt I had come home, turning up in the fine old Welsh city of Edinburgh. Unlike the bed salesman in the Old Red Lion, the University of Edinburgh heard me out politely.

I had known Thomas, just as I had known Jim Carr, the subject of my other biography *The Last Englishman*. This made me even more aware of just how much of an intrusion biography represents. I became a secret sharer, rummaging in things which until then only one other had read, until I knew more about a family than its members. A ghostly uninvited guest out of the future, I opened door after door which in their lifetimes neither man had opened for me, and I was nervous of what I might find; but the house was empty, its occupants gone. And even now I feel guilty, for the Thomas book has become Neil Mackay's ninety-minute play on Radio 3, *Alone Together*, and there is talk of a TV and even a stage production. I have invited the neighbours in.

Still, another man's life is neat. You look at it through the wrong end of a telescope and its outline is precise. It is when you attempt your own that you encounter muddle, for there you have always had the keys to every door, only each opens on a lumber room crammed with the past. But there is one thing about autobiography: it gives a man the excuse to meet women he would otherwise never meet again.

12

Research: An Epilogue

TWO OLD-AGE PENSIONERS, a man and a woman, are drinking Australian Chardonnay in a pub alcove under a shelf of books of the sort now only sold, unread, by interior decorators to pub chains. Above them is a ten-volume run of the late 1940s reprint of *The New Universal Encyclopaedia*, a set once given away free to its readers by the *Daily Mail*. The man, having had this bought for him sixty years ago by his grandfather, is the only one in the pub, and quite possibly in the whole world, who knows that the entry on 'Castration' contains the most snobbish sentence ever written: 'The only self-castrate of note was Origen.' He does not mention this.

Instead he says, 'Do you remember that New Year's Eve when you and I climbed Dryslwyn Castle at midnight?'

She, a bit distracted, having just come from her weekly art class, says, 'Remember it? You talked about it on the radio, and told everyone the two of us stood there holding hands.'

'With the river beneath us, in all that moonlight and frost, and everything so still we could hear the church bells and the singing, we could hear the singing all the way down the valley. When I can't sleep I re-run that scene.'

'You've got a good memory.'

'We'd been out for supper, four of us, and as we drove back I found myself staring out of the window. We were all about to go away, everything was coming to an end behind us. The town we'd grown up in, school, university, everything. And, just one month before that, my father'd had a heart attack. And at midnight, the end of the Old Year, you stopped the car. Right out in the country, no lights anywhere. Only you stopped it in the middle of Dryslwyn Bridge, and when we got out it was as though we'd stepped into some sort of metaphor. The darkness started on each bank, and above us, against the stars, was the castle.'

'Which you insisted we climbed.'

'I felt I had to do something, anything. The other two wouldn't come, they stood on the bridge beneath us. And of course you and I, we had to go and pick the steepest side where it's almost sheer.'

'That's why I got you to hold my hand, I suddenly realised how dangerous it was. You were hanging on to a bush, not that it seemed to worry you, you'd had a few.'

He says, 'It was just like that moment in *North by Northwest* when Eva Marie Saint is about to fall off Mount Rushmore, and suddenly out of the night sky comes Cary Grant's hand. The only thing is, you were Cary Grant.'

'And then a car came and in its lights the two on the bridge, Geraint and Eleri, could see us.'

'Weren't you going out with Geraint at the time?'

'No, he wanted to, but I'd just met the man I was to marry.'

'Well, whatever. Geraint was cross afterwards, I remember that. Eleri was just pissed off because it was so cold on that bridge.'

'One thing, you know I said you had a good memory? Well, you didn't remember everything. On the radio you said you stood on Dryslwyn Castle on New Year's Eve holding hands with the champion javelin thrower of Carmarthen Girls' Grammar School.'

'And?'

'I was the champion javelin thrower of Wales.'

'Christ, the gods walked on Dryslwyn that night.'

'Keep your voice down.'

'I never forgot it. What I found so wonderful was that nothing had led up to it, and nothing came of it, it was just a moment. Mind you, you didn't let go even when we got to the top.'

'I'd forgotten my gloves.'

The two burst out laughing, and they have another Chardonnay when they find that that week it is on special offer.

He says, 'You know, in all that time at school I had just one girlfriend, and I'd only met her because we were baptised at the same time. She worked in Woolworth's, and when we went to the pictures she paid. I still owe her two shillings and sevenpence, or whatever that is now, twelve pence.'

'Of course, you didn't go to the church dances. Did you come to that beach party Eleri and I had?'

'You didn't ask me.'

'You were never around, I was a bit nervous of you.'

'*You* were nervous? How d'you think I felt watching you from afar, the pleats in those short skirts flying as you played hockey and tennis? Watching you in coffee bars. Watching you throw that bloody javelin into the next county. You were never on your own. Then you went out with that rugby player and your parents disapproved.'

'People were so snobbish then. My aunt and I, we called on one of our old neighbours the other day, and she was asking about my grandchildren. Yes, there was a boy called Taliesin, I said. And the old lady's eyes opened in horror at this Welsh name. "Oh, poor little thing." I couldn't resist it, I said, "And he's doing very well at the Ysgol Iolo Morgannwg." There was this pause, and then my aunt took pity on her. "No blacks," she said.'

'Do you see him now, the boy you went out with?'

'Oh yes, he lives in Carmarthen.'

'When you meet in the street, what do you say?'

'Hello.'

'And what does he say?'

'He says hello too.'

The man says, 'Did you ever feel sorry for me?'

'Good God, no, we just thought you were aloof. Someone said you'd read every book in the library.'

'*Everywoman's Medical Encyclopaedia,* spent two weeks on that in the reference section. Pity you didn't know me then, I could have advised you on all kinds of things. *A Gazeteer of 20th-Century Murder. The Story of the Folies Bergere,* every photograph from the book torn out after just six weeks on the shelves. They didn't mess about in Carmarthen. But d'you think I wanted to be aloof? I longed to go out with someone.'

'Well you didn't miss out on much. It was so innocent, all of it, all those films, all that walking in the country, round the Mental Hospital, up past Trinity College, up Penlan. All those lanes.'

'Yes, but I missed out on it.'

'You haven't got the time, have you? Oh, it's not too bad, I've got an appointment with my chiropodist.' A pause. 'When you were saying you'd wanted to go out with someone, was there anyone in particular?'

'Yes.'

'Who?'

'You.'

But, Lizbie Browne,
I let you slip,
Shaped not a sign;
Touched never your lip
With lip of mine,
Lost Lizbie Browne.

There is one early twenty-first-century experience Thomas Hardy, who wrote those lines, would have loved. This is that facility whereby the old can make contact with those who shared their youth, something made possible by longevity, and the Internet. Hardy loved irony, so just think what it would have meant for him, forever rummaging in his past, to have been able to summon up Lizbie Browne, not in his imagination, but on Friends Reunited. And then to find himself squeezed in between the art class and the chiropodist.

It was a great mistake to go home, wrote the ageing Dr Johnson after a visit to his birthplace Lichfield. For there a man, meeting men he remembered as boys, would see they were now old, and it would occur to him, perhaps for the first time, that he too was old. Even the bullies are a disappointment.

'It's not Bobby?' I say.

I remember him as an eighteen-stone rugby forward. Now as he straightens up from the bar he is a neat, small man, and it is yet another example of the infinite physical manifestations of which some men are capable.

'I'm an accountant,' he says. 'I play squash. Also my marriage has broken up, that really takes the weight off.'

The last time I had seen him was a Guy Fawkes night in Oxford, when he was lurching down the Broad, trailing three feet of crepe bandage and trying to pick fights with policemen. He had been strapped up after a rugby injury, and the strapping had come undone.

'Let's see what you're made of,' said Bobby to a policeman who ignored him, being too busy staring at the ground where it was only too clear what Bobby was made of. Like Boris Karloff in *The Mummy* Bobby appeared to be made of disintegrating bandages.

But now he is tugging at a man's arm. 'You two must know each other. Byron Rogers, David Evans. You would have been in Carmarthen at the same time.'

A man neat in knitwear has turned. A golf-club, lawn-cutting man, except his forearms, the cashmere rolled up to the elbow, are as furry as those of an orangutan. 'They called me Dog then,' he says, and smiles.

It could have been worse. I might have found myself being introduced to Beria or Reynard Heydrich ('Only they called me Fluffy then'), but not much worse. Across fifty years I remembered the terror this man prompted. He and his sidekick, a fat boy called Aubrey, had only to appear in Carmarthen Park for the whisper to start among the roundabouts, 'Dog Evans is in the Park', and we little ones would scatter. I stare into that smiling face to see traces of the face I remembered, the spoilt, pretty face that did not smile, but there are none.

I was more frightened of him than of anyone I had ever met, or would meet, for with him it wasn't a matter of having your football stolen or your cap thrown into the vicar's garden. He and his sidekick tied your hands together, pulling you after them like slavers, stopping only when they had thought up some new torture.

'Do you go back? I'm afraid I don't, I think the planners have spoiled our town,' he says.

It is as though Jim Hawkins of *Treasure Island* has found Blind Pew not dead, and fifty years on is politely listening to him discuss welfare payments to the partially sighted.

I remember the summer evening when he and Aubrey tied me to a tree, face to the bark, and were taking turns hitting me with a bamboo. I was six years old, they would have been about eleven or twelve.

But then I saw something they were too busy to see. My mother had come looking for me, and was crossing the park like the US Cavalry. And she could run then. The two looked up just in time, and scattered like chickens in a farmyard, or, as I thought about it in later, bookish, times, like the Turks at the siege of Vienna before the charge of Jan Sobieski's Winged Lancers. For I have thought about it. Often.

'You know, I'm terribly sorry, but I can't quite place you,' says Dog Evans.

'I can place you all right...'

And of course he can't remember a thing, bullies never can. He stares, he winces, he explains how his father had died when he was small, and that Dog isn't a nickname, but merely his initials: D.O.G. Evans. He talks about his years in the Royal Navy.

'Been perfect for you that, 200 years ago that is. They'd have let you use the cat o' nine tails.'

He gives a strained New Labour type of chuckle, and looks suitably modest at 'You weren't just the school bully, you were the town bully.'

'Look, I can't remember any of this, but if I did the things you say I did, then I must make it up to you. Can I get you a drink?'

I sneer. 'Good timing, the bar's been closed for ten minutes.'

But when he comes back he has a double port and brandy in his hand. 'Not to bullies, it isn't,' says Dog Evans.

But nobody wants to summon up a bully. It is when in the silences of a long marriage the kettle-drums of old love's domain start up, faint and precise and persistent, that the temptation, and the trouble, come. Out of *Friends Reunited* have come divorces, and at least one killing.

> Dear Lizbie Browne,
> Where are you now?
> In sun, in rain?
> Or is your brow
> Past joy, past pain,
> Dear Lizbie Browne?

'You've kept your hair,' she says.

'So have you.'

'Women do.'

It is the most peculiar situation when old lovers meet. First there are the quiet, so quiet, sidelong glances as each checks on how well, or how badly, the other has weathered. Sometimes one catches the other doing this, and for a moment eyes meet, startled, then amused. Not that either says anything, not even about the way that hair, once coiled so carefully, seems now to have been chopped with a bill-hook. For there is a delicacy about such reunions. The moment has to be gauged of when to slip into familiarity: too soon, and it would be disastrous; too late, and it would be even more disastrous.

So there is a puzzlement. How can it have meant so much once,

that sudden upward movement of the head which then could stop the heart and now reminds one of a startled horse? And there are the memories that should be shared memories, but aren't. It is as though two members of a reading circle very slowly become aware they have been reading different books.

⸻ ◆ ◆ ◆ ⸻

'That was your room.' They are standing in an Oxford street outside a women's college. I wrote a poem about it,

> A silver birch you picked and kept,
> Cold in a blue-grey room;
> Black knickers kicked
> Under an unmade bed;

Curlers and the Bible
And some knitting wool
Were the regalia of being you.

'I never had black knickers.'

'Oh yes you did, I was forever trying to get them off.'

'And then I think you did.'

'Hmm...'

'How you managed it I don't know. I remember thinking, has he taken up conjuring? For I can remember the two of us, not long after we met, going to see the Roman ruins at Chester and you suddenly turned to me and said, "Do you know about erections?" And I stood there in that bloody amphitheatre, wondering, "Does he?"'

And that is the oddest thing of all. Love objects with not too much humour in their youth (or at least thought of by me as not having too much humour), have in their sixties become comedians. Lizbie Browne, twice widowed, has, she tells me, recently acquired what she describes as a pal ('So I'm getting stuck into the HRT, I'm back in business'). This from someone with whom I used to discuss on long autumn walks whether we should do what we called 'it', discussing this as earnestly as a war cabinet.

'You were never the romantic villain,' she says. 'When my cousin came back from her honeymoon you asked me, "Was she glowing?" You could have been you asking after the central heating.'

'I can remember you too, the first time we took our clothes off, and you looked at me and said, "Aren't you afraid you'll get that thing caught in a door?" I can even remember what you said when we ... finally ...'

She says, 'What did I say, the earth's moving?'

'No, you didn't, you said, "Hang on, you're not digging the road."'

'And what did you say?'

'Nothing. I'd waited so long, it was like being given a gold watch for long service to the company.'

I traced her through the Internet. Elizabeth Browne is a professor emeritus of social and economic history, her works listed: *Mill Rents and Ownership on the Welsh March, 1415 to 1536*, an early one, also the monograph that endeared her to feminists: *Droit de Seigneur: a modern mediaeval myth*. When I phoned, she said, 'Crumbs.'

'I suppose you could say we served our apprenticeship on each other,' she says. 'It was the oddest relationship, you never did anything that was conventional, and I wanted to be. Desperately. We didn't have much in common.'

'I tried. I went to the Church of England for you. Mind you, that was a time when I'd have turned Aztec if you'd asked me.'

'You didn't try for long.'

'I did until the night I heard myself praying for the Duke of Gloucester. I didn't mind praying for the rest of the royal family, but for some reason I drew the line at the Duke of Gloucester, I thought he could look after himself.'

'What did you see in me?'

'I had a shopping list. I'd always wanted to meet someone who was blonde and Welsh and at Oxford.'

'And you got me. Shucks.'

Apart from Walter Brennan and Gabby Hayes, old actors who provided the comic relief in Westerns, she was, and is, the only human being I have ever heard say 'shucks'.

————◆—————

An ancestor of hers was that President of the Board of Trade who, at the opening ceremony of the first railway, had been run over by the train. Public transport continued to cast a shadow over the family, and her grandfather was also run over when he got his bicycle wheel stuck in a tramline. His orphaned daughter (her mother being already dead) then brought up her four siblings herself, afterwards marrying into what the professor of social history called the respectable shop-keeper class in a small North Wales town. Her own father, she said once, would have worn a blazer inscribed 'Daughter at Oxford', had he been able to find one; nobody from her school ever went to Oxford. He was an industrial chemist, which had one unfortunate repercussion.

The first time I went to stay with her family I was shown a line of homemade wines in the larder: elderflower, elderberry, cowslip, the lot. But as the week wore on not one of these was opened, and one night, announcing I was going to stay up to read, I tiptoed to the larder when the house was quiet. In my cunning I did not put on the light, but reached up to the shelf where I had seen the wines, got one open and took a swallow, all this in the dark. What followed was out of a *Carry On* film.

The bottle contained soap solution, but not in a washing-up dilution: it was industrial strength. The next thing I knew I was on the ground, conscious only of the burning in my mouth. But in falling I had knocked some pans over, and became distantly aware of figures standing over me. 'Are you all right?' Only I couldn't speak, all I could do was froth, the bubbles exploding out of me, and faraway I could hear her mother's very clear English voice. 'But darling, didn't he pour it out first?'

The absurd always did have a walk-on part in our relationship.

Not long after we met I asked her round to tea in my rooms in college, which is what respectable young men did in the 1960s. Never having done this before, I was unsure what tea involved. When my mother had her friends round they would consume fairy cakes and discuss whoever didn't happen to be there; I didn't think it would be this. So at Oxford market I bought two cartons of buttermilk, and a pound of pecan nuts, then just being imported from the States; both these I considered the last word in sophistication.

But then it occurred to me that my sitting room looked bare. I thought I would buy some flowers, only these turned out to be expensive, and, besides, flowers die. I bought some plastic lilies, and then, having arranged them, it struck me they had no smell, so I dowsed them in aftershave. Imperial Leather aftershave. Of course the room then smelt like a ladies' hairdresser: it required some masculine corrective. So I popped out again, I was in and out of more shops that afternoon than I had ever been, and bought some thin Burmese cheroots. I had seen the Mexican star Gilbert Roland smoke these in a film, and smoulder, so I sat down and began to chain-smoke them. I had done, I think, about five, when there was a knock on the door. I got up and almost fell over.

Put yourself in her place for a moment. You are coming into a room so full of smoke (the windows are closed) you can barely see your host, only from what you can see he seems to be having some difficulty standing, and is holding on to an armchair. Then the terrible smell hits you. *And the truly wonderful, and poignant, thing is that you do not have the self-confidence to comment on any of this.*

'Of course I didn't say anything, I was too puzzled.'

So on an autumn afternoon in 1960, two lunatics, in what the *Daily Mail* a few weeks later would describe as an Oxford 'which selects the cream, produces the elite' (this under a photograph of me), sat down to a mound of pecan nuts and two opened cartons of buttermilk. And in something approaching an industrial fug, the two of them made small-talk.

> what we talked of
> Matters not much, nor to what it led. –
> Something that life will not be balked of
> Without rude reason till hope is dead,
> And feeling fled.

Standing in my door, the smoke swirling about me, I watched her walk away across the quadrangle, the sinking sun making the wisps of fair hair on her neck blaze. It took me a month to finish the pecan nuts. The buttermilk I threw away after a week.

Towards the end of our last year we decided there was no future to our relationship. We had too little in common: she was ambitious and had a job lined up even before she took Finals; I was hopeless, except that, according to her, I had vague, if alarming, plans ('I was going to be the boring one who worked, you were the talented one. I thought, "Sod that"'). So we parted.

Only, instead of just parting as any sensible couple would have done, we decided to invest our parting with ceremonial. We decided it would happen after a Commemoration Ball at my college, one of those grand affairs with champagne and straw-berries and punts in the dawn: this would be our last dance, though we hadn't been to any others, and anyway neither of us could dance.

I had borrowed evening dress from a well-off friend (who, because he was going out that night, had fixed my bow tie for me early in the afternoon). The evening dress included a waistcoat made out of cloth of gold which his parents had brought back from India, and which his father's tailor had run up for him. It looked amazing, and, when the spotlights caught it at a certain angle, I glittered.

The dancers, athletic and smiling, were already turning under the coloured bulbs, when El Dorado and his partner walked out onto the scaffold of their love. The dancers roared with laughter, they chased each other in and out of the bushes, white breasts bobbing, while, stiff and stately, we moved amongst them.

And, yes, there was a dawn, a livid dawn. And long empty pavements. And curious milkmen crashing by. Outside her college we stood, briefly held hands, then walked away with determination into our respective mornings. Ten years later we were still going out with each other.

⋯⋯◆▸◆⋯⋯

'You just kept turning up out of the blue like a troublesome brother,' she says. 'I suppose I was as much to blame as you, I'd be going out with somebody else and there you'd be again. I didn't know how to end it, for you'd virtually become one of the family ... and of course it got tiresome, you would keep opening drawers.'

In one I came on a packet of Polaroid photographs, on one of which she was lying on a bed, stark naked except for a black velvet choker around her neck, the photograph taken from an angle that made her bush seem enormous. She did not look particularly happy.

On another was a man, also naked, except for black ankle socks.

He looked very happy indeed, with, photographed from a similar angle, his happiness only too apparent.

'He was so proud of that bloody thing.'

'It was a shock for me.'

'You fool, what did you expect, rooting in other people's belongings?'

We slept in many single beds, met each other at many stations, saw each other off at others. 'See you.' It was always 'see you' with her. We walked through many ornamental parks, the most desolate places, apart from gaols, that mankind has ever designed for itself, hitched along many roads (once, without her contact lenses, she tried to hitch a lift from a hearse). There were many weekends.

The Friday nights, long looked forward to, were tremulous, the Sunday afternoons, usually in a flat in some huge Edwardian barn in the suburbs of a Northern city, bleak. The bathrooms were cold and shared (one with the typed instruction, 'Please do not blow nose in the bath'). We ate badly. She burnt toast, omelettes, steaks. Cakes failed to rise, flans collapsed, bread achieved the consistency of brick, and she stared defiantly at me over their ruin.

Many letters were exchanged, and hers were matter of fact. Mine were gloomy. I still have two, having stolen them back, and in one there is, oh dear, this little moment of joy. 'I went and stood on the platform where your train came in three years ago. There are weeds there now, and the line is closed.' The other ends on a practical note, 'Come in your camel-hair coat. Sheffield is colder than Oxford or London. We will have a heater in the bedroom. Love, Byron.'

'Were you ever in love with me?'

'Yes,' she says. 'It was the thing to be.'

Ignoring this, I say, 'For me it was that summer evening after we'd been to see the Sutherland window in Coventry Cathedral, and we were standing, waiting for a lift, by a bridge just below the village of Geddington. Light brown building stone, a tractor somewhere in the fields, and you with your thumb in the air. I stood there watching you, I had never been so happy in my life. I passed it the other day, at least I think it was that bridge.'

'Where's Geddington?'

'It doesn't matter.'

'I can remember an evening in Flint. There were some ponies there, on the marsh by the castle, and one had a willy that almost reached the ground. You said, "They're not all that size, you know." Only you said it in this awful reassuring way, like a vicar talking to someone about to go to war.'

'God, we were a curious couple.'

––––––•••••––––––

Two survivors, friendly, familiar, distant, puzzled. Four adjectives. Friendly. Familiar. Distant. Puzzled. Each one a fat brass screw into the lid over whatever was once between them.

'My mother thought you had a lovely smile,' she said.